Praise for Intuition at work

A timely and engaging read, packed with useful examples and tools. If you're going to buy one book about leadership and decision-making, make it this one.

Tanya Byron, Professor of Public Understanding of Science, author, broadcaster, and journalist

Those who understand their intuition and where it comes from can increase the quality of their decision-making and leadership.

Feike Sijbesma, former CEO DSM, Chair Philips

"Go with your gut" is what many of us like to say. In her book Intuition at Work, Jessica Pryce-Jones delves into what intuition is and isn't because it has a grounding in reality and what is possible. Intuition at Work provides insights into what you can intuit and learn in navigating life's challenges.

John Baldoni, Thinkers 360 Top 10 thought-leader and author

Jessica Pryce-Jones offers decision-makers this superb guide to sharpening and expanding their intuitive capacities. Read Intuition at Work and learn to rely on the rapid response team within you and amplify your feeling of knowing. That's particularly important at a time when decision-makers at all levels are increasingly depending on AI even as it spills out misinformation. Check out what seems obvious but wrong, or incorrect but right by using your intuition – and corroborate it with rationality when you need to.

Bernard Beitman, MD, founder and president of the Coincidence Project

Intuition helps us make decisions in complex contexts when limited data is available or when we feel an inconsistency in that data. We need intuition to see certainty through the mist of uncertainty.

How to grow this superpower? Intuition at Work offers practical and easy-to-use guidance for anyone who would like to build their intuition at work

Dr. Oleg Konovalov, author, speaker, and consultant

Intuition at Work

Intuition at Work

Using Your Gut Feelings To Get Ahead

By Jessica Pryce-Jones

SEQUOIA
B O O K S

First published in 2024 by Sequoia Books

ISBN
Print: 9781914110320
EPUB: 9781914110337

A CIP record for this book is available from the British Library

Library of Congress Cataloguing-In-Publication Data

Name: Jessica Pryce-Jones
Title: Intuition at Work/PryceJones
Description: 1st Edition, Sequoia Books UK 2024
Print: 9781914110320
EPUB: 9781914110337

Library of Congress Control Number: 2024903290

Print and Electronic production managed by Deanta Global

*"Le véritable voyage de découverte ne consiste pas à chercher de
nouveaux paysages, mais à avoir de nouveaux yeux."*
"The real voyage of discovery consists not in seeking new landscapes,
but in having new eyes."
Marcel Proust

For my friends Jane, Chris, and Diane. With love.

Contents

Acknowledgments

Every book is based on the thoughts and writings of hundreds of people that preceded it. And I'm truly grateful for all of them. I'm especially indebted to my interviewees: thank you all for giving me your time and fantastic stories as you make the book what it is; I'm only sorry that I couldn't include more of your wisdom. I'm incredibly grateful to Paul Opwora for overseeing all the transcripts and to Gemma Felsted for helping me get organized.

For inspiration, information, ideas, and support, thanks to Candida Mostyn-Owen, Arabella Caccia, Michael Carson, Christina Leong, Julie Pilat, Donna Racik, Lisa Ryan, Victoria Starkey, and Francesca Tamagini: it might not have felt like much to you, but it did to me. Bobby Mostyn-Owen, it was great to bounce titles around together and finally land on something inspired by you.

Merci à mes voisines et amies Mme Jeanette Brune et Mme Laurence Doat; j'apprécie votre amitié, conseils, encouragements, les repas, et les petits cafés. Bridget Temple taeverso for suggestions, Bergson, links, and check-ins. Kate and Henry de Montjoye, thank you for all the diversion and fun.

For feedback, friendship, and learning, enormous and heartfelt thanks to Claire Andrews, Jo Bishop, Stephan Chambers, Laura Day, Chris Gosden, Chris Mackey, Jummy Okoya, Gill Stevens, Anshul Taneja, Vicki Townsley, and, of course, my great friend and colleague Diane Lytollis. Andy Peart thank you for your trust – again.

More recently I've been honored and delighted to become a founding board member for The Coincidence Project. Thank you, Dr Bernard Beitman, for your knowledge, insights, and enthusiasm. Anyone reading this is welcome to join us at www.thecoincidenceproject.net.

If I hadn't had the joy and privilege of working with all the coachees, teams, and delegates I've met over 25 years, this book would never have been written. Enormous thanks to all of you. And for catalyzing much of that, I've been indebted for decades to Michael Hay, Patty O'Hayer, Jon Parker, Paula Dowdy, Mike Nowlis, JoEllyn Prouty-McLaren, and Lorraine Vaun-Davis. But further back, immense gratitude and love of a lifetime goes to my father and mother, David and Clarissa Pryce-Jones, who encouraged enquiry from an early age.

Over the past two years Simeon Collins has given me the space to get stronger and articulate ideas at the same time. A magic combo. And what would I have done without Olive for thoughtful walks, squirrel chasing, and general schnuffing?

Of course, the biggest thanks and most appreciation go to my family. Jack and Harry; your edits and questions helped a huge amount with clarity, and Kitty, your book suggestions were invaluable. Meanwhile thank you, Florentine and Hattie, for putting up with me while I did it. But biggest thanks of all to David for his patience, support, meals, and enthusiasm for this project. I'm so glad our eyes met across that kitchen all those years ago and that we both knew.

I also owe many apologies and much gratitude to Keble College, Oxford: while this book isn't on time or what I promised, I hope it does the job. And it goes without saying that any misinterpretations or mistakes are entirely my responsibility.

Finally, thank you for buying this book; I very much hope you enjoy reading it.

Introduction: Meet your superpower

When I was eight months pregnant with my daughter, I was working in a school running a psychology experiment with first-year children. During break, I went to the staff room to get a cup of coffee. I stood drinking it by a large glass window, watching the kids playing football in the playground. As I stood there, the idea came to me, "That boy is going to kick the football in this direction; and it's going to come through the window, I'll be hit by the ball, showered in glass, and my face will get cut." And having had that thought, I started to take a couple of steps back.

I'd moved about two paces when the football came crashing through the window to land near my feet; sure, a few glass shards were sprinkled on my bump, and I had a tiny scratch on one cheek. But that was all. As teachers rushed up to me to see if I was OK, they commented on how calm I was. I was totally unruffled because I'd known it was going to happen.

I've always had strong intuitions when I was in danger, when a car was going to come hurtling around a bend on the wrong side of the road, when an accident was about to happen, and when I needed to see a doctor to get checked out. It's saved my life at least three times.

Intuition really is a superpower, but it doesn't need to be that dramatic. You know about intuition if you have ever:

- Made the right choice even though it wasn't logical at the time.
- Looked at someone and just known that they would be a terrible or great hire.
- Gone against your gut only to regret it.
- Had a strong sense that something would happen without knowing why.

Ask any seasoned leader, and they'll tell you that they use it and that it's something that becomes more important the more senior they become.

> *Intuition is a very powerful thing, more powerful than intellect, in my opinion.* Steve Jobs, co-founder and CEO, Apple

> *Intuition has always played a big role.* Emma Tucker, editor in chief, The Wall Street Journal

> *I trust my intuition because that's where better decisions come from.* Dr Christian Busch, author and academic

> *Intuition allows you to be your own best counsel.* Lisa Buksbaum, founder and CEO, Soaringwords

> *For me, decisions are all about intuition.* Hal Reisiger, CEO, Cosworth

When you are a leader, you often need to make quick, accurate, and critical decisions based on incomplete information in a fast-moving context. These important tactical and strategic choices can't wait. Delay, and you miss the moment to launch a product, move into a new market, avoid a disaster or solve a crisis. Ignore your intuition, and you can do serious long-term damage to yourself, your team, and your organization's finances and reputation. Who loses? You, your stakeholders, and shareholders. Who gains? Your competitors.

Because if you're not using your intuition, others certainly are. Particularly when they're making critical decisions that involve several equally viable and credible options. You can program a spreadsheet with any number of variables and run any risk analysis you like, but a purely rational decision-making model won't work; there are always intangible pros and cons to weigh up. Ultimately, you're forced to use your intuitive abilities to help you with your choice.

In today's complex, ambiguous world of work, where everything is uncertain, your intuition is your superpower. Here's the big-ticket reason why: evidence shows that it results in better organizational performance in difficult times. When leaders use their intuition, they:

- Make better strategic decisions
- Problem-solve more effectively
- Assess and judge risks better
- Identify and hire the best talent

If you're a senior leader and part of an executive team, you'll use your intuition all the time and that's an important and often-replicated scientific fact. As Zak Brown, CEO of McLaren F1, says:

> *I think intuition cuts across everything that one does, whether it's in people management, or deal making, or whatever the case may be. Yes, decision-making is data driven, but then you need to add your personal experience and what your gut is telling you, because data doesn't give you all the answers. It gives you some of the answers to make decisions from. At the end of the day, you still need to make a call.*

Research among CEOs confirms that intuition specifically helps with both deriving meaning from numbers and models as well as enabling groups to reach important decisions. And these CEOs emphasize that a solid intuitive ability is one of the most noticeable differences between their best leaders and the also-rans. Here are some important data points backing that up.

- When questioned 69 out of 70 CEOs confirmed intuition was important in their decision-making. That's pretty much 99%.
- 75% of C-suite executives say they rely on it.
- 62% of leaders say they often use intuition when making decisions.
- Nearly 50% of managers consider their gut feel is very important.

Meaning the more senior you are, the more you use and value your intuition.

But it's not a unique skill available to the chosen few. One recent experiment showed that when executives were forced to use intuition to choose between two options, they were right 90% of the time. So, intuition works well, particularly in complex situations, and it improves with experience.

Best of all and contrary to received wisdom, you don't have to wait for intuition to turn up. Just as you'd use your laptop, you can access your intuitive process whenever you need it, so you know when to make that call, follow up on a seemingly random thought, choose a project, or decide where to invest your time.

If you stop to think for a minute, even in the most data-driven and research-based organizations, a hypothesis is simply an informed intuition about what the numbers are telling you. Dr Kate Macintyre, a senior public health social scientist, confirms this:

> *Looking at the big research questions means examining critical problems and pulling together a lot of data. Yes, you look at gaps, apply logic, and then you*

land on several potential questions. But in the end, it's often intuition which pulls you in a certain direction. I've come to recognize that an awful lot of decisions get made through intuition.

That intuition comes into play for many researchers is now itself a focus of empirical investigation.

But there it's still a reality that intuition remains very much in the broom closet. Last year I asked over 50 senior executives how they made their last difficult decision. All of them said that they had used their intuition, and all of them confirmed that they hadn't voiced that fact.

Keeping quiet about intuitively made decisions happens for three reasons. First, it's a difficult process to accurately describe; second, it seems flaky, so leaders justify their decisions by retrofitting analysis into them; and third, many people believe it's their secret sauce and want to keep that to themselves. It doesn't help that intuition isn't taken seriously by educational institutions. I'm not aware of any business school that will teach you how to use it. If something's not OK to talk about or teach, how on earth can you learn to listen to or leverage it?

And that matters because intuition is a key part of your human capital, that is your personal knowledge, talents, attributes, skills, capabilities, and experience that make you valuable. While the term was coined by Adam Smith back in 1776, in today's world your human capital needs constant upgrading so that you remain relevant. And your career options depend on it.

According to a recent McKinsey study published in 2022, the value of your human capital represents about two-thirds of your total wealth. So whatever boosts it or gives you a unique competitive advantage is worth investing in and developing. Using hunches, gut, or judgment well will propel you to greater and faster success, while enabling you to recognize when you might be ignoring what your intuition is telling you.

I'm sure you've rationalized and intellectualized some of your intuitions away or got into loops of neither noticing them nor trusting yourself. You may have hired the wrong person, accepted the wrong job, or got involved in the wrong project, by discounting prompts that your inner or outer world were giving you.

I know, I've done that; my first job was working in investment management. I didn't take to the dour South African who interviewed me; I thought the office atmosphere felt awful and the work sounded dull; and even as I walked up the marble steps on the first day, I felt a sense of foreboding and thought, "What am I doing here?" I spent an incredibly unhappy 10 months working for an alcoholic chain-smoking boss when I could have avoided the whole horrible experience if I'd paid attention to the many cues I was receiving.

You're going to use your intuition because everyone does. So, you might as well do a brilliant job by understanding what to do, when, and how to do it even better. And to recognize that when anyone around you talks about their opinions, feelings, senses, insights, heart, gut, and judgments, expresses doubt or danger, or uses "maybe," "should," and "would" to describe outcomes, that's their intuition speaking.

This book is about understanding when your intuition is at work, being aware of the forms it takes, and becoming more attentive to the cues you're picking up. It's a rich source of data and information and, like a muscle, intuition works better when you train it. Then you'll find it so much easier to navigate large and small life choices, saving time, effort, and energy as you do it.

Save time and make good choices

Right now, we are either overloaded with facts and data that take hours to sift through, or we simply don't know. The information required doesn't exist. Both situations lead to greater uncertainty, anxiety, and loss of a sense of control. In managing our professional lives, we want to know that we are making the best possible choices at the right time; intuition can help give us that information, providing encouragement and hope when answers seem elusive and times difficult.

But sometimes it's easy to trip up. It's easy to confuse intuition with creative thought, idle speculation, wishful thinking, logic, experience, needs, wants, and general internal brain chatter. This book will help you discern the differences so you can access useful, on-demand, consistent, and reliable intuitions that you trust.

Work best with new tools

With artificial intelligence (AI) rapidly becoming indispensable at work, it might be tempting to think that it could someday replace human intuition. After all, AI helps to provide insight and increase productivity on an unprecedented scale. But relying on it alone can create a false sense of security. There are plenty of instances where AI has been responsible for fake data, bias, and even malevolent outcomes. Its output is not infallible, particularly in uncertain and novel situations, which is when human intuition comes to the fore. Apply your intuition when reviewing AI results and you'll generate a dimension that's much richer and unique to you.

Who is this book for?

This book is for anyone who'd like a practical, easy-to-use approach to build their intuition at work. It's for you if you've ever wondered:

- What is intuition all about?
- How do I better use it?
- How do I trust it?
- How do I explain it?

Or on a more granular level, you might have also asked yourself:

- What does this person really want?
- How do I know if I can believe them?
- How can I be more effective right now?
- What is the most likely outcome here?

In short, you're asking questions that everyone asks themselves.

It's for senior executives because this is what got you to the top and why people ask for your opinions and advice. You know how to pick up on early warning signs or recognize opportunities without reviewing a ton of data. And when you have that ton of data, you know what to zone in on. Plus, you can defend your observations or choices under pressure. Your job is to mentor others to enhance this valuable skill and benefit your organization.

It's for middle managers because this is what will set you apart from your peers. The accuracy of your intuitions in seizing the moment and sizing up what's at play will propel you to the top. You're the layer that's most likely to be squeezed by above and from below, so it will also help you save time and effort.

It's for first-level managers, new hires, and anyone ambitious because you need intuitions to get up to speed and then to confidently accelerate your career. You are expected to be high performing faster than ever, based on an education that generally provided you with "the answer." That, coupled with metrics, dashboards, hardly any coaching, remote work, reliance on process and procedure, means it's tough to learn to trust yourself.

This book will help you do that and understand how and why other people operate because so many decisions are based on gut, intuition, and hunch.

What this book isn't

This isn't a book about avoiding facts, data, or analysis. Making good choices entails assessing evidence and using common sense. If you wanted to take a plane from Dallas to Dubai, I'd suggest looking online rather than intuiting which airline and route to take.

Nor is this book an encouragement to abandon rigorous scientific inquiry and known results. Both have brought us amazing advances; we know that the Earth isn't flat, that conspiracy theories are dangerous, and that consistently presented peer-reviewed results are meaningful.

And it's not about using intuition as an excuse. For example, you're in a meeting discussing an idea and someone says, "I just don't feel good about this." That's feeble. Your intuition should be able to guide you into where the problem lies and what to do, especially in a work context. Intuitions should lead you to precise and accurate information just like data does.

Finally, it's not about using anything other than your natural gifts and intelligence. You don't need to go to an ashram, call in angels, or cleanse your toxins, though you can if you want to. All that matters is that you can risk being wrong and try again.

The most responsible approach is to combine data, evidence, *and* intuition so that you arrive at the best possible ideas, decisions, and outcomes. Which means that it's much more about rebalancing than reorienting.

An overview of the book

Of course, you can read this book from start to finish. But it's also written for you if you prefer a dip-and-flip approach. That means dipping into what you're interested in then flipping through what you'd rather skip: the headings will help you do that.

Here's an overview of each chapter so you can choose your direction.

Chapter 1 covers what intuition is all about. You'll discover that it involves physical sensations, energy, and feelings. Then you'll explore how to distinguish it from other thought forms and investigate all the different ways it can be experienced.

Chapter 2 explains how to use your intuition, so you can start to access it on-demand. You don't need to wait for it to show up; intuition is your servant, and you can master it. That means understanding your personal process and prompting it for more.

Chapter 3 helps you build your intuitive skill set. Starting with a self-evaluation, you'll investigate the eight behaviors that boost your intuition. And you'll get tips for how to build what you intuitively think will add most value.

Chapter 4 examines meaningful coincidences, synchronicities, and serendipities. You'll read about the role of intuition as well as exploring what these coincidences are, how to think about them, and how to experience more should you want to.

Chapter 5 offers different techniques to develop your intuitive toolkit. When you read it, see what you're drawn to most, and try that technique first – and recognize that not everything works for everyone.

Chapter 6 reveals how to apply your intuition when you're in a leadership role facing ongoing situations as opposed to simple one-offs. It covers the main areas of focus for any leader and offers lots of tips for you to explore.

Chapter 7 takes a quick spin into intuition and the role that consciousness plays. It examines the different ways that it shows up as well as the various positions and possibilities that are out there.

After a brief conclusion, you'll find a toolkit to help you deal with intuitive blocks. If you get stuck, flip to this section, and look up what you are struggling with. I don't recommend reading it from end-to-end as that's likely to jam you up even more. Finally, you'll find a couple of pages of intuitive exercises for you to try.

In summary, intuition can make your life easier. It can guide you to answers, and help you identify pitfalls while saving you time and effort. Above all, it's a superpower to build your unique competitive advantage. What you need is to understand how it shows up, recognize what you get, and act on it.

Chapter 1 will start you on that journey.

1 Understanding what it's all about

This chapter gets to grips with the fundamentals of intuition. Why read it? Because it will help you start to recognize and then distinguish your intuitive thoughts. The biggest hurdle is learning to trust your intuition, and you do that when you know what you're looking for and how it shows up for you.

So, you'll read about what intuition is, where you can expect it to show up, what it's often mistaken for, and when you'll find it at work.

Here goes.

What is intuition?

The fact is we all use intuition at work but frequently call it something else. Your gut or, sixth sense, an inkling, hunch, perception, conviction, belief, expertise, judgment, doubt, or niggle are just a few of the socially acceptable terms used to describe it.

And you'll know it in the form of feelings of anxiety, hesitation, apprehension, suspicion; or positivity, certainty, joy, excitement, inspiration, and motivation to name a few. Often, you'll get physical cues like a tightness in your throat, a lurch in your stomach, or tingling skin. It might also feel like an internal itch or a sharp need to find out more.

These cues seem to simply swim into your consciousness, often appearing as a thought, a metaphor, or as images in the mind's eye. Or you might almost hear words as if they were being told to you. Or it might seem as if you've had a realization but can't rationalize how that thought came to be. Occasionally it's an external confirmation of an internal thought; you catch sight of a confirming billboard or hear a seemingly random but highly relevant song.

You might also find that you get combinations; for example, you "see" something happening and at the same time notice that your heart beats faster. Or you'll know an outcome and "hear" applause at the same time. It's also at play when your attention is drawn to objects in your environment.

Lisa Buksbaum, CEO and founder of not-for-profit Soaringwords, describes it like this:

> *Intuition is like a ticker tape going through my head. Sometimes I see a word and see a feeling that flashes across the mental screen on my forehead. Then other times it's a body-mind thing where I feel the hair on the back of my neck, tingling or something in my gut. But sometimes I ask myself, "Why am I looking at that sticky note? The framed print on the wall? What's the message?" When you're receptive it's as if there's a whole internal advisory board inside of you.*

Lisa's description shows that while intuitions appear in several different ways, most often you'll notice some kind of feeling and experience a sense of knowing too. Which is why I define intuition simply as a feeling of knowing. The knowing emerges into your consciousness, accompanied by one of three fundamental responses: "yes this is good, no, or no this is bad, or hang on, I'm not sure." Here's Alice Moore, General Manager in a global consumer goods organization:

> *I'm always looking for connections, looking for the spark because I work in multiple streams all at the same time. That means ideas have to keep coming. I've learned to make intuition a process and to describe it. There's a matrix or mesh in my mind of what we're trying to do, and I feel everything, information, data, and ideas positively or negatively in my chest. There's an energy there which I pay attention to and means I know when I'm drawn to something and need to follow it up or I'm not and I can move on.*

Intuitions tend to have attributes which you'll recognize. For starters, they're speedy. Because they are so quick and easy, you don't need to rack your brains or schedule them in to your day. You'll get an effortless answer the moment that you need it because at its heart, intuition is a pre-historic survival skill.

As early humans lived their lives, they collected food, made tools, and shared those resources. To do this they engaged bodily with the world, and that engagement is the oldest and most ancient element of being human. It contributed toward countless decisions about what was safe moment-to-moment because there were life-threatening hazards everywhere. Early humans would have integrated what they were encountering externally with their internal body references. And this was vital: paying attention to their guts or recognizing a hunch would have meant the difference between life and death.

They'd also have used emotions. And we know that because they cared for their young, sick, and old. You don't do that unless you feel love and affection for members of your close social group. They'd also have felt fear as they ran away from predators and anxiety as they anticipated them. The brain you have today has in fact been under construction for at least 200 million years.

What this all means is that our bodies and emotions are the oldest means of understanding and responding to our experiences; humans who had the best instincts and intuitions for avoiding danger and staying safe would have survived better, therefore having this skill would have guaranteed evolutionary superiority. And it may have been much easier for them to access.

Early humans didn't have language as we know it; that's thought to have arrived with Homo heidelbergensis some 400,000 years ago. Language provides a constant internal barrage which often drowns out more subtle signals, meaning we easily misinterpret, misunderstand, ignore, second-guess, and rationalize this quieter but important information. And that's made worse by a culture of being constantly on and responsive to external input like email, social media, TV, and music.

But when you shut down the noise and tune into your intuition through physical sensations, energy, and feelings, you'll be much more likely to be aware of it.

Notice physical sensations, energy, and feelings

Evidently the brain is important when it comes to intuition. Brain scans to discover the underlying neurobiology reveal several important areas such as the ventromedial prefrontal cortex, which sits behind your eyes and acts like an integrative hub for emotional, social, sensory, social processing; it's where you store information about past rewards and previous mistakes. The basal ganglia plays a role in learning, habits, and automatic behavior while the insula acts like a hub connecting different processes and taking care of body awareness. It also alerts you when your unconscious and conscious aren't aligned by drawing attention to your physical responses.

Then there's the precuneus which sits right on the line between the left and right brain hemispheres and plays a role in memory, your sense of self, and, perhaps most importantly, consciousness. But what goes on in your brain is hidden to your conscious self, while what happens physically and emotionally is absolutely available.

A knot in your stomach, feeling heavy or queasy, a thumping heart, raised blood pressure, tightness in your jaw, a sinking feeling, or headaches: all these tell you that things aren't ok.

Here's Jinny Blom, international landscape designer and author.

> *I'm very sensitive and in situations where people aren't functioning properly, I'll get a migraine within about a minute and a half – it happened yesterday when this person came into the room, a hate-filled rage machine who was like an attack dog every time someone opened their mouths. My team were texting me under the table, but the headache quickly went because I realized this was someone who laid himself open to being by-passed.*

But a relaxed belly, expansion in the heart area, a sensation of lightness, increased energy, feelings of alignment, or joy give you the opposite messages and tell you that your choices are right. Paying attention to your body, energy, and feelings helps you interpret what's happening.

There's nothing new about the mind-body connection; most of us intrinsically know that what we think and how we feel are tightly entwined. If you've ever had a headache as a result of mental effort or noticed your heart hammering before an important presentation you know what I mean. Back in the 1990s, neuroscientist Candace Pert coined the term "bodymind" to describe this unity. And many people, when they have an intuitive hit, experience a thought and feeling simultaneously.

Yet sometimes your body knows before your mind. That's been clear since the 1990s and Antonio Damasio's famous Iowa gambling task experiments. Subjects were presented with four decks of cards and told that each deck contained cards that would reward or penalize them, but they should win as much money as they could. Those decks had been pre-arranged to contain either good cards which would give slow but steady returns, or bad ones which would provide huge wins but, in the end catastrophic losses. Players' nervous systems were monitored through skin responses as they did the task.

Amazingly, results showed that after just 10 trials and long before their conscious minds had registered which decks were worse, subjects showed unconscious signs of physical stress as they pondered riskier choices. Damasio and his team explained this with what's called the somatic marker hypothesis. Somatic markers are body reactions associated with emotions, so your heart beats faster and you feel anxious, or your muscles tense and you feel irritated. Your body is leading your experience, giving you valuable information by working through your gut or heart responses.

Your gut, more formally known as the Enteric Nervous System, is a massive network of 500 million neurons and neurotransmitters wrapped in and around your stomach. There are so many of these neurons that they've earned the nickname "the second brain." And the highway that joins everything via your heart to your brain, is the vagus nerve. Your gut communicates with the brain, using your microbiome; that's the name given to hundreds of trillions of mostly beneficial microbes that live there. They send signals via the vagus nerve along what's called the microbiome-gut-brain axis supporting your positive moods and sharp thinking.

Your gut can give you some really clear messages if you start to pay attention to it. Here's Dame Louise Makin, ex-CEO, chair, and non-executive director.

I went on The Accelerated Development Program at London Business School in 1995. We had some really good coaches and I remember in a one-to-one session this woman said, "If you trusted your stomach, what would be different?" Because I was saying, "Well my head is saying this, and my stomach is saying that." It was such an alien concept, and it had this amazing impact on me. I thought, "Well, I didn't even realize that was a question. I didn't know I could trust my stomach." I've got so much more comfortable with it the more experience I have.

Your brain can also have a profound impact on your gut, which you'll know if you've ever experienced stress. But it mostly works the other way around, with an amazing 80–90% of vagal fibers communicating back to the brain. We all know that at some level when we talk about our gut feelings, butterflies, going with our gut, or saying that something was gut wrenching.

Whenever you turn inward to check what you're really feeling, what you're doing is sensing these gut feelings or the state of your vagus nerve. The vagus nerve also helps you remain calm when you're stressed, and to know when you're no longer in danger. That's the gut part.

Then there's your heart, which is known as the third brain because it too contains neurons and therefore memory; a heart wouldn't start to beat immediately after being transplanted without an embedded memory. Moreover, research shows that the heart, like the gut, sends more messages to the brain than the other way around and it has a role in processing and decoding emotional information.

Recent research has found that if you make a high-risk choice, rapid yet subtle physiological changes send direct feedback on changes in your heart rate to the brain. If you're tuned in to those sensations, you'll be able to make important decisions in quick succession without necessarily being able to say why, because you're recognizing at some level what's happening for you internally.

That would seem obvious to most people because it's part of our experience and language. How often have you been told to "follow your heart"? Or you "spoke from the heart" and to do that, you "learned your presentation by heart"? Maybe you experienced "heartache" when a close colleague left your organization and were "heartbroken" after a failed relationship. We have an intrinsic appreciation that the heart plays an important role in life.

Science is just beginning to show how important that might be. One astonishing recent experiment on heart intuition showed that the heart "knew" to correctly anticipate emotionally positive or negative pictures before those pictures were shown to participants. When researchers wired up participants, they saw that the heart fired messages to the brain to prepare what it was about to see before that information was available. The heart may be a thinking, feeling, sensing, and intuiting organ.

In addition to this, research shows that the heart seems to receive and respond to intuitive information and is involved in decoding it. The implication of all of this is that intuition is contained within a distributed network comprised of the brain, guts, and heart. And all three have an impact on your energy.

Think about intuiting that something's wrong. You might find that as your stomach clenches, your heart beats faster, and your energy changes. Or when you get an exciting opportunity your heart leaps and you feel a surge of positive energy. Here's how Julie Pilat, media and entertainment executive, experiences that.

> *When I get an intuition to do something, I literally feel like I'm in a cartoon where a lightning bolt goes off over my head. I'll physically jump because there's an energy to it and excitement, I just can't help myself. And I'm experiencing it all in my gut at the same time.*

What you have energy for is a great intuitive indicator because energy is so fundamental to the human experience. Your body gives off heat, light, and electromagnetic waves, all of which are types of energy. And you've probably noticed that when you're tired you feel cold; when you haven't eaten you feel faint; when someone is angry it's hard sitting next to them because emotional contagion is a very real effect. But this isn't anything new. Traditional Chinese Medicine is based on the ancient energy system, Qi, and if you've ever had acupuncture, you'll know when a needle is a miss or a hit. A miss and you feel nothing; a hit and you get anything from a small buzz to a bee-sting. A bit like people you work with who can make you feel buzzed or not depending on whether they add to or subtract from your energy.

If you've ever hung on to a job for too long, you know what this does to your energy. Here's Katie Demain, management consultant.

> *I've typically got a lot of energy, and I respond to and am uplifted by the energies of others. When it's positive I become more collaborative, more creative, more energetic and it's mutually reinforcing. But I stayed too long in my last job and the balance of what I was putting in, to what I was getting back was wrong. The more I felt under-valued, the more my energy spiralled down. For me energy is also a reflection of a bigger system at play, and I think it's true what the Japanese say that you "read the air."*
>
> *When I resigned, I felt that it was like taking a weight belt off after a scuba dive in terms of relief and how much lighter I felt. I should have done it way before it got so heavy.*

This sensation of heaviness tells you to move away or avoid something. And it's often associated with fear, anger, or frustration. On the other side of the coin if you get sensations of lightness, you'll be drawn to something as you'll probably also experience upliftment, confidence, and positivity.

Research shows when you're in a positive mood, your intuitions are better. That's one way of setting yourself up for success. Second, there's interesting empirical evidence that if you consciously focus on feelings instead of details, you make better decisions when dealing with complex information. This totally flies in the face of traditional thinking, which tells us to keep emotions away from decision-making and to keep it objective and detail-oriented. On the contrary: feelings first. There's discomfort in making a difficult decision but gauging your feelings matters and will help you choose; a strong sense of mismatch is important information. By the way, this research also found that when you start to overthink, you'll also make a worse decision.

Third, when you get an intuitive hit, and have correct information, you'll most likely experience feelings of "yes, that's it," which you might feel as a sense of relief, calm, or just a knowing. Psychologists call that a "feeling of rightness" and coupled with speed, they are both great indicators that you are using your intuition. If you get a nagging sense of unease, your intuition may be telling you've made the wrong decision. Either way, you generally get a recognizable sense of alignment or misalignment between you and your decision. If you think about it, it's as simple as knowing when you're doing a good job. You don't need to be told; you just *know*.

In summary, intuition is a whole organism process that you use to get to better answers quicker. And it has certain key characteristics that include fast, effortless, and judgment-free nudges. Just to be clear, this isn't about your brain. Your brain is a tangible, physical, neurochemical, and electromagnetic coordinating center which sits in your skull. This is about your mind. Your mind is intangible, and non-physical; in simplistic terms it determines how you think, feel, understand, and interact with the world. And it's your mind that experiences intuition along with your body. If a decision makes you feel aligned, light, expansive, and generally positive, you'll be more likely to go ahead; if you feel misaligned, contracted, heavy, or mainly negative, you won't. That's important intuitive information arising from body and mind.

Having understood more about the experience of intuition, now it's time to think about where it shows up.

Intuitions arise around your work, worries, and well-being

Your intuition works best around work, worries, and well-being because they are what matters most.

Your work

Most people spend an average of 45 hours a week at work. Over a lifetime that's some 80,000 hours give or take vacation and weekends if you spend some 8–10 hours a day focusing on your job. In short, you create a field that's ripe for intuitions because you'll probably have expertise and desire to be good at what you do.

Here's an example of what I mean. I was recently coaching a senior executive who had put in for a much-wanted CEO role. It was looking like he was a shoo-in for the job and that's what he was hearing around the business too. No one was sure when the announcement would come through but one Saturday morning, I woke up and my first thought was that Nick hadn't landed the role; someone else had been appointed. I just knew this in my bones. So, I sent him a text to check in; he texted straight back saying that an external candidate had been appointed the day before.

You could of course argue that it was 50/50 that he would or wouldn't be given the role and intuition had nothing to do with it. Perhaps. But the fact is intuition prompted me to get in touch and be more effective in a job I've been doing for 20 years.

What about intuitions with more heft? Here's an example of a negative but more important intuition that academic and author Dr Christian Busch experienced.

> *I grew up in a very head-led society where I was trained to make rational decisions, to have a strategy and a plan. Then real life happened, and I realized I should trust my intuition more because that's where better decisions come from.*
>
> *I found that out by having a company and being close to financial distress. I was in a state of "Oh my God! Bankruptcy! Terror! Distress!" I was in a fight-or-flight state when I took an investment which my colleagues were absolutely against, and I did it even though my gut told me that it wasn't the perfect thing to do. I didn't listen; it was a disaster.*
>
> *Afterwards I thought a lot about how to never get into that situation again and how to trust myself. Today I would stop and say, "Let me learn more about this, let me get more information and understand what it might be." It would have saved me a lot of heartache.*
>
> *Since then, I've found it helpful to have people around me who can support me to make sense of my intuition especially if it's something I don't have a lot of knowledge about.*

Marc Fox, musician, pop star, and talent manager, experiences it similarly.

> *I can spot the real deal and whether they've got it when I walk into a room. It's the handshake, the eyes, the energy that clearly manifests in everything they do, the way they talk, and have that inner confidence. I've only ever met two or three of them in my career that's spanned 40 years in the music business.*
>
> *Yes, there are workers, grafters, lucky people, and those who want it. But there's very, very few where when you meet it's almost like falling in love. If they are the real thing, you don't want them to leave because they grace a room, they make it come alive and you want to be part of that energy. For someone like me whose antennae have been finely honed, it's glaringly obvious.*

Notice the feelings in both Christian's account and the energy in Marc's. Often when there's high stakes or energy, you'll find strong intuitions. But that's not always the case. Intuitions can also show up as a nudge to do something you've never done before, like volunteer, go somewhere new, contact someone you don't know, send a seemingly random request, follow up on an article, or act on a whim. You do something small which has a much larger impact or significance than the initial act would suggest.

Your worries

Because you're generally so aware of your worries, your intuition is likely to be on red alert for any changes around them. The first part is around people, for example your colleagues, friends, and family. It's why for example, parents often know when their children are unwell or something's not right with a colleague even if nothing's been said.

It's not just about people, it's about the stuff that concerns the people you care about. Here's one I had about a house.

In the early days of the internet, we were living in Belgium. The three-year lease on the house we were renting had been terminated and we had two months to find somewhere new. I'd an image in my mind's eye of what I was looking for; a white house in what was known as "fermette" style; after scouring the agencies and papers, for a month, I started to worry that we wouldn't find anything, let alone what I was looking for. I decided to drive once more to the area I wanted to live in; at that time landlords would put notices saying, "*Te Huur*" with their phone number in the windows of their available properties.

After an hour of fruitless searching, feeling dejected and with the sun setting, I decided to go home. But then I suddenly knew that I should turn around, swing left, and I'd find the house I was looking for 200 yards on. I did exactly that and there was the white fermette of my imagination. I can still remember how my heart leaped when I saw it. Two weeks later, we'd moved in.

I had that intuition because it was about a home for my family. Dr Bernard Beitman, leader of The Coincidence Project, and someone whose work I recommend, talks about this as our human GPS. That GPS guides us to the people, places, and spaces we need when we need them, meaning that our worries get sorted out.

Your well-being

Your body is telling you all the time what it needs whether that's food, sleep, or exercise. So, in relation to your physical self, you'll often know when something doesn't feel right. But when it comes to intuition, there's a little bit more to it; I call it your internal health and safety inspector, which prompts you to pay attention, change course, get a check-up, or simply to drive more slowly.

For example, a couple of years ago, I was driving home down a four-lane highway in heavy traffic on a winter's evening; it was pelting with rain, and I was tired after a busy day's work. I had the idle thought as I headed down a long hill that if a traffic cone was in the road, I should just steer straight over it. There weren't any roadworks underway that might have triggered that idea.

Quarter of a mile later, there was a single cone, bouncing in a crazy way that I'd never seen before or since, leapfrogging across the lanes of traffic. Ricocheting off one vehicle and then another, it sprung 10 feet off the ground and headed straight at me. I tensed as I held the steering wheel straight, expecting the mother of a disaster as the cone suddenly disappeared under my car. Unbelievably, it popped out behind me then jumped over central reservation. If I'd swerved, I'd have caused a pile-up because it would have got trapped in my tires; I dread to think what would have happened. My adrenaline hit was enormous.

But this book isn't about developing your skill around your worries or your well-being; the focus is on work. But you'll find as you develop your skill that intuitions turn up in other parts of your life too. That's because as you build expertise and notice your successes, you start to find intuitions turning up elsewhere.

Intuition versus other kinds of thinking

Having investigated what intuitive thought is and when it tends to show up, it's important to compare and contrast it to other kinds of thinking. You'll be totally clear when you're using your intuition and when you aren't because intuitive thought isn't logical thinking, Eureka thinking, wishful thinking, biased thinking, following your instincts, or being in flow.

Here's how you recognize the differences.

Logical or analytical thinking

Logical thinking is the cornerstone to success when you start work because it's what gets you noticed. And deductive reasoning is one of the most regularly used logical tools. For example, your line manager said the person with the most sales would get a promotion; you generated the most sales in the past year, so you expect to be promoted. Let's say that this is really you for a moment; you'd probably be tracking your sales on a detailed spreadsheet.

It's that spreadsheet with symbols and formulas which are governed by strict rules, that are so important to logical thinking. You build scenarios, add assumptions, and work through possible outcomes from your base to your best case. There's a process as well as time, effort, and energy involved.

Of course, you might look at the output of your logical thought and then get a flash of intuition from it. For example, that even though you have the best sales, you won't get that promotion.

When you contrast logical and intuitive thinking, you'll see that it's slower, it's easier to explain because there's a methodology and shared language. Intuitions are the opposite: tougher to explain because of the way they arrive; moreover everyone's process is unique. Here's how investor and managing director Dr Owen Lozman puts it:

> *Afterwards when you validate your intuition and put it into a logical framework to try to explain it, the logic you come up with never describes the intuition you had.*

He's right. You probably wouldn't walk into a meeting and say, "My entire body feels electrified, so this is the right thing to do." You find data and information to justify your decision but it never captures the power of your intuitive moment.

Eureka thinking

Eureka thinking, those moments when you suddenly have an insight and get the answer, like intuitions, are fast and instantly move you from not knowing to total knowing. In a flash, you've got a totally clear answer to a tricky and unsolved problem. If you want to try for yourself, the famous Nine Dot Problem, while perhaps culturally skewed, is designed to study insight. It consists of nine dots organized in three layers of three dots. The task is to connect all nine dots using only four lines; in lab conditions with time limits of a couple of minutes, the expected solution rate is nil. That's right – no one will solve the problem. Time pressure doesn't help with Eureka thinking.

In fact, taking time away or sleeping on it helps because insights often arrive when you're exercising, relaxing, in the shower, cooking, visiting a gallery, or walking. You're not actually focusing on solving the problem itself but on something completely different while you incubate an answer. That's why Archimedes was in his bath, trying to figure out how to prove that the king's crown wasn't pure gold. And Newton had, so the story has it, taken a break under his apple tree in the garden when he discovered gravity.

Insights also require expertise and deep knowledge because you're looking for a solution. Archimedes was a physicist, astronomer, inventor, and engineer; Newton was a man of science and one of England's greatest mathematicians. That doesn't mean you need a lifetime of achievements and awards, but you need a certain level of ability in your field.

What are the main differences between insights and intuitions other than incubation and deep expertise? First, they appear to happen in some shared and some different areas of the brain; that's probably because intuition is a precursor to insight. Second, insights are clear, easy to talk about, and objective: it's obvious when you have the answer. Intuitions are often fuzzier, may not need deep expertise, are harder to explain, and subjective.

Wishful thinking

My brother has been a fan of the London-based soccer club Tottenham Hotspur for about 40 years. For him it's been a lifetime of misery as Spurs so rarely pull off serious wins and so often crumble under pressure. With a current taste for sacking their coaches, winning a prestigious trophy any time soon is just wishful thinking.

Wishful thinking or daydreaming is when you are attached to or invested in a specific unrealistic outcome. As in, "Wouldn't it be great if my true talents were recognized, and I got a call from a head-hunter who'd offer me a job with a big promotion. Then everyone could see how hard I work, appreciate my brilliance, and I'd earn what I'm really worth." There's a bunch of vanity and ego in these thoughts. Ironically the more time you spend in wishful thinking the less you'll be able to really sense your intuition.

Let's take the same situation and look at it from an intuitive perspective. You'll know it's an intuitive thought if you are motivated to talk to a head-hunter, are energized about a possible new role, and feel uplifted by your next career move.

Intuitions feel true and have a certain vitality to them, moreover they don't change; you'll continue to get the same nudges about a person or situation even if you ignore them.

Using your instinct

Although instinct and intuition often get muddled up, it's easy to recognize the difference. Instincts refer to your hard-wired therefore innate biological responses. It's why birds migrate, spiders spin webs, you are probably afraid of snakes and disgusted by feces. These last two would have been important to helping your ancestors survive and survival is our greatest instinct.

Like insight, we experience instinct in flashes. For example, if you step unthinkingly into oncoming traffic, your internal alarm system will kick in and you'll hurriedly step back out of harm's way.

To be successful at work it's critical you use your survival instinct, recognizing it for what it is. The trap that I've seen a lot of people fall into is to revert to survival when it's unnecessary and cause a lot of personal and professional damage on the way.

Biased thinking can similarly limit options and choices if you never question what you're doing.

Biased thinking

First off, biases aren't always all bad even though they have a bad rap; that's because the word bias is often linked to prejudice and propaganda. In fact, biases are just heuristics or rules of thumb that we develop to be as efficient and effective as we can be. Useful rules of thumb might include "checklists prevent mistakes"; "a call is better than no call"; "don't put up with jerks"; "get feedback"; and "trust your intuition." The problem arises when biases or heuristics get in the way and prevent us from seeing or using information. These unintentional biases, which are shaped by our experiences, aren't helpful when we slot new information in with our pre-baked and preconceived attitudes or stereotypes.

There are hundreds of biases but here are the ones that particularly can be mistaken for intuitions:

- Confirmation bias: is what it says on the tin. It involves looking for, valuing, and remembering information that supports your beliefs.
- Anchoring bias: causes you to rely heavily on the first information you might have been given on a topic.
- Availability bias: means you assume what you remember matters and that more recent information is most important.

- Hindsight bias: results in you overestimating your ability to see an outcome. The "I always knew that would happen" phenomenon, which can feel like intuition.
- Action bias: is the mother of all biases as it means we jump to doing, rather than feeling, reflecting, and intuiting.

There's also intuition bias, which speaks to a preference of following intuitions because doing that feels good. As an aside, there's no such thing as analysis bias, which would be a similar tendency to analyze a situation that would be better suited to intuition. Part of the problem with bias is the word itself which is laden with judgment: who wants to be told they're biased? It would be easier to conceive of them as thinking patterns or thinking habits.

Unfortunately, even if we know about our thinking patterns, we don't always recognize when we default to them. That means tumbling into misperceptions, misjudgment, and mistakes particularly when we're tired, emotional, short of time, and feeling overloaded, which are big clues in how to catch yourself thinking, "Is this bias or intuition?"

Biases generally reflect decisions you've made before. Simply asking yourself if that's what you're doing is a great way to check. Second, a bias should dissipate when you challenge it and see that if there are other possible answers; an intuition will keep popping back, nudging you in a certain direction. There's a lot more about recognizing and dealing with bias in the toolkit at the end of the book if you'd like to skip ahead.

Flow

If you've ever been completely absorbed in an activity, you might have been experiencing what psychologists know as "flow." It's an immersive experience when time falls away, you're using your skills to their utmost and your whole being is involved with what you're doing. Flow for me is writing or coaching when I can get so engrossed in what I'm doing that I'm not that aware of anything else. When writing is going super well, I'm not sure if I'm writing a document, or if in a sense it's writing me because I feel so wrapped up in what I'm doing.

According to Mihaly Csikszentmihalyi, the psychologist who identified flow, there are various factors that are associated with it, including:

- An activity that's intrinsically rewarding
- Clear, manageable, and achievable goals
- A complete focus on what you're doing
- A lack of awareness of physical needs
- Loss of a sense of time
- Feedback from the task itself

Being in flow or in an intuitive state feels similar because both are centered, open, and in the moment. And in both there's no conscious wrestling with what you're doing. But they are different because flow can last over hours; intuition is fast, and then it's done. And their purpose isn't the same. Intuitions help with decision-making and problem-solving while flow is about task immersion and completion.

The great news is that you can use flow as a gateway to intuition and as an incubating process. If you find it hard to have intuitions, set an intention to find an intuitive answer. Then get into a flow state using sport, work, music, or whatever activity you can fully immerse yourself in. When you're done, reflect again on your question and see what bubbles up. This is a great way of distracting yourself into intuitions.

Let's now turn to the different kinds of intuitions, because once you start recognizing them, you then notice them more. And the more self-aware you are, the more you'll observe your intuition at work and learn to trust it.

Types of intuition at work

I'm sure you've experienced this situation. You work through the data, listen to everyone around you, and in the end, you go against the analysis but with your gut. And you're mostly proved right. Sometimes you might even go through that process without really recognizing what you're doing, which is a blessing and a curse: if you paid attention to everything going through your mind, you'd be overwhelmed. On the other hand, self-awareness and understanding how you work effectively are important parts of leadership.

While in the wider sense, intuition is mostly about decision-making, in the narrower sense it turns up in various arenas. These include what you're an expert in, what lies outside your expertise, people, crisis management, timing, creative problem-solving, and working as a team. If you want to harness intuition, ideally, you'll recognize which of these contexts work best for you because often people are skilled in a couple but not all of them. I recommend leveraging what you do well rather than working on weakness: it's more fun, you'll do it better, and that's how you'll accelerate your career.

Expert intuition

There's a heap of research showing expertise is the proving ground for intuition. You easily find answers and can swing into action because you've done something tons of times before, got feedback that you did the right thing, and know what success looks and feels like. The great advantage of expert intuition is that you can make decisions super speedily. That's because you've got a deep understanding of the underlying patterns and principles of what you do, meaning you can quickly identify what is and isn't relevant to any decision.

Here's Paula Dowdy, board member and consultant, describing that:

Experience gives you a feel for missing data, incorrect data, and the spin that other people put on data. It's the expertise you develop and that sits at where the subjective and objective meet. You listen to scenarios and intuitively know that something is or isn't right because it does or doesn't add up.

And Willie Walsh, director general of the International Air Transport Association, describes a time that illustrates expert intuition in action.

When I was CEO of Aer Lingus, my COO came to me and said, "What about launching a new route from Dublin to Malaga?" I said, "Perfect. Sounds great. Do it." Now, that was the 14th of November, and we launched that new route on the 14th of December. Within five months it had become the most profitable route we were operating.

In about April this guy came into my office with a big report, you know, maybe a couple of 100 pages. He presented it to me, and he said, "This is the route analysis, Dublin to Malaga." And I said, "Oh, thank you." I don't read big reports, but I started glancing through the executive summary. And basically, the executive summary was we shouldn't do it.

I asked him, "Who worked on the report? Why don't you bring them in to meet with me?" So, I had this team of people in front of me and what they'd done was a general assessment of the economic conditions, all the macro issues, the micro issues and travel patterns. And they concluded there wasn't enough business to support it, but they never looked at what was actually happening.

We'd launched the route because this was one of these things where the gut said do it. And that's exactly what I called when my COO came to me. If I'd waited for the report, it would have been months later, and it would have told me not to do it.

I was there as CEO for over three years. During the three years that I was there, we launched 42 new destinations, new routes, and we didn't commission a single piece of analysis to justify that. We kept operating on the basis that we knew what was right to do.

Yes, it takes time to develop this level of expertise, but you start to build it more quickly than you might imagine. Executive coach Diane Scott explains:

As a clinician, physician, doctor, or nurse, you can very quickly walk in to see a patient, and know that something is wrong without empirical evidence, lab results, or objective data.

It happened to me hundreds of times when I was on the front-line in intensive care units. For example, early in my career, when I'd been a nurse for less than a year, I walked into a liver transplant patient's room and knew something wasn't right. I called the doctor and I said, "I have no reason to tell you this, but something's up." Sure enough, the patient had a cardiac arrest in the following 45 minutes. She was a young woman in her early 30s and there were no observations to suspect it would happen.

I think learning intuitive skills quickly and early shows you're in the right job as your talent for it shines through. Pretty much everyone delivering patient care develops a nose for doing this through experience, expertise, and a level of trust in themselves.

Once you have that level of expertise, it saves you so much time, effort, and energy as Paul Parsons, senior principal auditor at a global pharma company, says:

I just walk into a facility and after the first impressions, I know. There are lots of subtle cues that make me feel comfortable and that everything is under control – or it isn't. And it's all gut feel. I use it as an auditing strategy and evidence my gut to see if it's correct; 90 percent of the time it is, which is why I trust it.

This kind of intuitive expertise, which is fast, accurate, and actionable, takes time to develop, which is why it's often so tough to swap employers or move industries. Rebuilding it takes time and effort. I coached one senior leader who'd moved from financial services to a social enterprise, which was she'd always wanted to do. She'd totally lost her mojo because she felt she had no intuitive feel and was frozen by every decision, second-guessing everything she did.

The way around this is to work with non-expert intuition.

Non-expert intuition

Non-expert intuition describes those times when you have an intuition that isn't based on solid evidence or experience. They happen when you're not constrained by too much knowledge, by previous thinking, or by "how things are done around here," and they are really helpful when you're new to a role. You can see things untainted by politics or prejudices because you are an outsider.

You also have non-expert intuitions once you start to manage managers or lead specialists whose jobs you've never done, meaning you're never the expert yet you have to sort out gnarly situations. Here's Claudia Rossler, customer experience officer in a financial services organization.

I lead a team of people for whom I have never done any of their individual jobs and I'm not a specialist in any of their single areas. The intuition that comes into play is about the business context for what we're doing or adding a different perspective. I think the skill is often how to introduce that non-expert intuition into conversation, so it's heard. If you have to use your seniority in order to put it on the table, it's not constructive. It's about framing what you say so that you're enabling people to see things differently. In a flat hierarchy when you hire people who are specialists it's important to respect their views.

You can have them about situations you aren't directly involved with, as Mark Dean, CEO of consultancy En Masse, has experienced:

I was working with a well-known academic who experienced an awful work-related potentially career-ending trauma. It seemed like he was being taken down by those who had the power to do it, but not for anything he'd either said or done. One day I told him, "I don't know how I can justify this to you, a scientist. But it's going to be okay even though everything logically right now is saying it won't be. And I've never felt it appropriate or warranted to say something like that because it would be irresponsible."

When it was all over, he said to me that our conversation had felt right to him too despite the bleak circumstances at the time.

Non-expert intuitions can also be around the small stuff. A few years ago, I was invited to give a lecture at Oxford University's business school. I built my 90-minute session around six video clips that illustrated what I wanted to say and allowed for audience interaction. On the morning of the lecture, I had a nasty feeling that the clips, which I had embedded in a presentation, wouldn't play. I checked. Everything was in perfect working order. But the niggle was still there, so in the office I connected to a projector just to recheck; everything was fine. Still feeling uneasy, I asked Ian, my head of IT to come with me just in case. We got to the business school early, found the lecture theater where I fired up my laptop and checked all my videos twice; like before, everything was in perfect working order. I began my session, played the first clip, and watched Ian slip out.

My lecture was an absolute mess because none of the other videos worked. I'll never forget the business school's audio-visual technician turning to me and quietly whispering, "They've all corrupted including on your USB drive," while the audience was distracted with a task I'd given them to buy me some time. I had a non-expert intuition in the form of a precognition, tried to work around it, and was so frustrated when it played out for real. I'm not alone in having experiences like this. In fact, there's solid empirical evidence which shows that people who practice precognitions are better at them. What a shock.

But it explains why most people are pretty good at social intuitions because you probably use that ability all the time inside and outside work.

Social intuition

This is all about sensing people's vibes or where they're coming from. It's particularly important when you develop new relationships at work. Take this situation. You walk into a new project or team meeting: immediately you sense that the man to your right is warm and friendly. But the woman leading the meeting? There's something you just don't trust about her; you have an inkling she's hiding something. Your intuition is leading you to thoughts about her, her intentions, personality, attributes, and beliefs. Then there's also your awareness of how to behave in this room; that's because each organization has unwritten rules that you'll learn to pick up on without even being aware that you're doing it.

Here's biotech general manager Mark Robinson.

I think carefully about other people in the room, and their perspective; I try to put myself in their shoes to get a sense of where they're coming from and how they'll react to what I'll say. I'm aware of how things might resonate with them, and I think about that quite a lot. I can pick up relatively easily on how others are feeling and reacting to a message.

In my last company we used to talk about "walking the square" before a big or important meeting. When that wasn't done what would happen is people would sit and go, "Yes, yes, yes," then afterwards would go, "No, no, no," and there'd be lots of sidebar conversations. I attuned myself to make sure that I was aware whether a meeting would trigger conversations that would need circling back to bring people on board afterwards. My preference is to recognize it, acknowledge it, and put it on the table: it makes it so much easier to get alignment.

You're hard-wired to do this because again, back on the savanna, your ancestors needed to quickly and accurately tell friend from foe – which is why first impressions are so important. That's when your antennae are up and looking for verbal and non-verbal cues like smiling, eye contact, tone, or voice modulation and what might lie behind them. Here's Efrain Ayala, Marketing Diversity Equity and Inclusion director:

Early in my career I worked for an ad agency on a large consumer goods account. We'd go to meetings in the middle of the mid-West twice a week – not the most progressive of places. I realized then at the time, "They think I'm a caricature," even as they appreciated the flair and ideas I brought. And I thought I need to not dial it back, which I'd done to then, but lean into this as I saw their response to me and my queerness. I used that to strengthen the relationship and our partnership; I started to dress the part too.

Othered people and minorities have to navigate corporate spaces in a distinct way. I know immediately and intuitively by the tone and the non-verbals, even on a Zoom or Teams call who's an ally and who isn't.

It's social intuition that tells you your presentation isn't landing and how to redirect it. Or when to bring more energy to a meeting, who's on-side, and to engage more or differently with your colleagues. In short, it's a key to your success as it guides your frequent daily interactions. Moral intuition, on the other hand, hopefully crops up more rarely.

Moral or ethical intuition

When you hear about companies that dump toxic waste in rivers, employ child labor, or fail to provide basic safety kit, you'll probably think, "That's just wrong!" Those are moral judgments. But when organizational crises arise, moral intuitions often guide a situation because decisions aren't that black or white. Moreover, it's not clear who's responsible and there just isn't the time to investigate because of an intense pressure to respond. The trap that so many fall into is opting for the easier, less costly choice because moral or ethical intuition is about accountability and responsibility. And that's driven to a large degree by empathy and emotion, but it's also supported by beliefs and values about what's right or wrong. Here's Patty O'Hayer, seasoned communications exec:

> People in a crisis respond with denial and think, "It can't be us." They seek reassurance that "we can't be wrong. We can't be at fault." Yet when you act as if it is us, it changes the dynamic and the decision making completely – but that's a very counter-intuitive approach. Then there's another important layer to add to that, which is "If this was happening to me, what would I want us as an organization to do?" And that gives you the right way forward.

> We once lost a part of a shipment when a container went overboard, and all these pink bottles washed up on the beaches of Cornwall. Our head of supply was trying to prove it wasn't us and didn't want to do anything until he knew definitively that it was our product – which justified not doing anything. But what if it was us? If you lived by that beach, what would you then want us to do? We involved local rangers, the Ministry of Defence and the National Trust. They were all incredible and afterwards spoke up on our behalf because we did the right thing and didn't wait. Nothing gets better while you wait for data, you just get paralysis by analysis; big problems simply don't disappear by themselves.

Doing the right thing right is at the core of moral intuition and my experience is that most people use it most of the time. The key to getting a situation right is to think through all the possible consequences of every option you have, then feel what you would most want associated with you and your organization. You're always going to face struggles about uncertain choices, and there are plenty of dubious ethical boundaries where top leaders turn a blind eye. When people cut corners or fail to consider all the stakeholders, they 100% know what they're doing, and at that point their motivation has nothing to do with morality.

Temporal intuition

Timing is everything when it comes to work. At a personal level, think about pitching a new idea, flagging a concern, giving feedback, or switching up your career. At an organizational level, there's developing a new product, launching in a new market, finding new partners, or acquiring a business. Whatever your focus, temporal intuition involves a sense that the window of opportunity is there right now. Yes, there's no such thing as perfect timing: wait too long and you miss the boat; jump right in, you stretch people and resources too far, demotivating and burning out employees in the process. That means there's tension to balance between what's going on both inside and outside your organization.

So how do you know that your timing is right? You think through the trade-offs you're making, which if it's a significant decision will be around cash and people. Cash is easier than people because it's always a tough call to decide if your best employees work on a new project or product or whether they keep the wheels on current business.

Here's Neil Ward, biotech senior executive who describes being part of a team that developed a new test to track SARS-CoV-2 variants at the start of the pandemic.

During the very early days of the pandemic, there were already small-scale histories from SARS, tuberculosis, and Ebola that we felt we could leverage to understand the family trees of how the virus would evolve. The academic community responded very quickly to sequence the genome of small sample sizes, but we thought if this thing is going to explode, the world would need to quickly test hundreds of thousands of samples. This, remember, was before the world really understood the need for surveillance.

There were quite a few internal arguments, but I and others felt we had an obligation to genuinely help the world in a time of need and that working on this was the right thing to do.

We had a lot of conversations particularly with the Sanger Institute as they had a great deal of expertise at automation and scaling samples. Their know-how allowed us to iterate quickly, and we accelerated something that would have taken two years to develop to two months.

Initially it was almost a skunkworks project but once politicians and others in the US realized we needed to understand new variants, we pivoted and deployed a huge amount of resourcing. We were fortunate that in the end, the hunch turned out to be true and useful.

This is a fantastic example of how different kinds of intuitions, expert, temporal, and moral, come together at the same time. The more that happens, the stronger your intuition is likely to be.

Finally, when it comes to timing, remember that whatever you do, you'll always have critics who tell you that you're moving too fast, too slow, or that you shouldn't be doing this at all. The point is that *you* sense that the timing is right.

Creative intuition

Creative intuition is slightly different to what I've already described because it isn't about a decision. Creative intuition produces new, unexpected, and innovative outcomes in response to a fresh need or recent change. It helps you come up with an answer or the embryo of an answer often in a fragile and fleeting way. But for people who use it a lot, working like this feels natural and easy.

Creative intuition often arises when you're alone and in an environment that's comfortable to you and when you have a relaxed and gentle focus on what you're doing. Struggle and it's unlikely to happen. People use language like "bob up" or "drop in" to describe the experience of their new ideas emerging.

Here's what footwear designer Kitty Shukman says:

> *I work better at night when it's quieter, and there are fewer distractions. I have a bit of a technique now where I always listen to the same genre of music, which is energizing and upbeat. I meditate before and do some cross-channel body movements; then I imagine my energy flowing and a fire inside.*
>
> *When everything's syncing, I do other small tasks to get my brain flowing too, so I work on shoes that don't matter. What's important for me is to try to play with ideas and to take the stress off, so I give myself some space. I don't remember and I'm not very aware of how a good design happens because it's so fast, effortless, and easy. It just falls out and it feels like I'm a vessel for this thing to come through my hands.*
>
> *I know I've made something I really like and that it's good because I feel happy, and I don't want to look at it too much. It appeared so quickly, I'm almost scared it's going to vanish; it's as if it's shy – so I slowly peek at it and think, "I'm just going to let you be in the world."*

Yet lots of leaders think that they don't use creative intuition because they aren't involved in creative industries. That's plain wrong and is backed up by recent research which investigated different types of intuition by interviewing seven CEOs. Findings showed that creative intuition was used the most often by all seven because it's so vital for finding innovative answers. When you're being creative, you envisage what doesn't yet exist and you bring it into being; leaders do that all the time.

If you find yourself stuck and can't come up with any ideas, like Aristotle did, go for a walk. Landmark analysis at Stanford showed that creative thinking improves when you walk and it's the act of walking not the environment that truly matters. Walking relaxes you, releases feel-good endorphins, and helps creativity because it stops any hyperfocus. That allows free-flow of information from your subconscious mind which most often results in an answer.

Team intuition

This type of intuition is different from all the others because it takes place in a group. And there's clear data showing that teams who use it are more successful than those who don't. Moreover, it's particularly important for senior leadership teams because their decisions have the greatest impact.

Briefly it works like this. Effective teams bounce ideas, information, expertise, hunches, and scenarios off each other as everyone compares information, discussing what data or situations might mean. At its best, new ideas arise out of the discussion itself and that's something that won't happen unless the team comes together. One of the mechanisms that seems to be driving this is brain synchronization among the group.

This was first explored by Professor Uri Hasson at Princeton, who put participants in fMRI scanners as they were listening to stories and showed how their brains started to synchronize. That also happens when groups share stories and experiences or brainstorm ideas. The greater this shared interbrain synchrony, the greater everyone's ability to learn, communicate, and understand their environment.

There's a lot more about this in Chapter 6 but team intuition arises most when individuals know and trust each other. That promotes oxytocin, also known as the love or tend-and-befriend hormone which results in empathy, bonding, and cooperation. And if you've ever worked in a dysfunctional group, you'll have felt its absence. When that's the case you're less likely to voice your intuitions and more likely to make mistakes.

Here's Jinny Blom again:

For group intuition to work well, you can't have people who use the group as an energy source, or dominant personalities. If you have someone incredibly dominant, it shifts the dynamic and everyone shrinks away from them. That means you have to keep paying attention to the group and psychologically cleaning things; I'm a trained psychotherapist and my experience is that you have to keep working at it.

Just to be clear, intuition isn't about abandoning all analysis. It's about using data and applying intuition too as Emma Tucker, editor-in-chief at *The Wall Street Journal*, points out:

Intuition has always played a big role in journalism. Apart from the crude metrics of newsstand sales and letters to the editor it was pretty much the sole mechanism to decide which stories would resonate with readers. It still matters but these days we have data to inform it and an editor is no longer "always right" if she can't point to the data that backs up her intuition.

But intuition is probably more important when it comes to deciding which stories to pursue, which leads to follow, which data sets to dig into. Having an intuition as to where the good stories are buried is still an important attribute.

Ideally, you'll be applying intuition to your analyses and investigating your intuitions, and it doesn't matter which comes first because both are just as effective.

When you think about all these types of intuition, you can see that they cluster into three theoretical buckets. There's what happens internally, which is personal to you, like expert or creative intuition. That's the result of synchronization within our bodies. Then there's interpersonal intuition which includes social or team intuition. Again, that happens when people are synchronized in a specific way. Finally, there's extra-personal intuition, which includes non-expert intuitions and amazing coincidences. Maybe, as others have suggested, there's an as yet unknown but synchronizing mechanism at work: I'll explore this more in Chapter 7.

You can also see from reading about all these types of intuition that first, they interact with each other. You might use temporal and team intuition as you decide to part ways with a supplier, followed by expert and social intuition as you select another, and finally creative intuition as you start to work together in new and different ways. The more types you intersect with, the more likely you are to have powerful intuitions to use to your advantage. Second, you're probably using intuition a lot of the time whether you recognize it or not. But if you're deliberate about it, you'll reap much greater rewards.

As surgeon, beauty researcher, and key opinion leader Dr Jonquil Chantrey says:

> *There's the 10,000-hour rule that it takes to become an expert, but I've now worked on almost 60,000 cases and of course the more I do the better I get. I move between all these types of intuition, which for me act like a wheel with different spokes that come into a center and I intentionally use that interplay all the time.*

Conclusion

Intuition is like noticing without noticing that you've noticed. It's there to help you in multiple situations when you're working alone and with others. All the evidence says that you'll make better decisions if you use it alongside any analysis that's available. Will it always be correct? No, but neither is data, which only gives you a snapshot of what has happened. Projections are just about as good as intuitions for the similar reasons: unexpected external factors and life get in the way. Bill Gates, when asked about his intuition on CNN, said, "I'm often wrong but my batting record is good enough that I keep swinging every time the ball is thrown."

When you use your intuition, understand what you're good at, and know how to develop it, you can access it more intentionally. And then you can begin to share that with others. The more you share, the more you bring this subject to light while getting to know yourself and others in a profound, interesting, and meaningful way.

Summary and next steps

Top takeaways

- Intuition is a feeling of knowing, so it's a body-mind experience that involves feelings, physical sensations, and thought.
- Most intuitions arise around our work, our worries, and our well-being.
- Intuitions are fast, accurate, and additive; they benefit you in some way.

- There are clear differences between intuition and other kinds of thinking processes.
- To leverage your intuitive ability, focus intentionally on what you're already good at.

Read

- Chou Locke, C. (2015) When it's safe to rely on intuition (and when it's not), *Harvard Business Review*
- Kutch, L. (2019) Can we rely on our intuition? *Scientific American*
- Sadler-Smith, E. (2023) *Intuition in Business*. Oxford University Press

Try

Jot down any intuitions you've had at work and think through:

- When did these intuitions arise? Where were you and what were you doing?
- What physical sensations, energy, or feelings can you recall?
- What kinds of intuitions have you had?
- How have they helped you?
- What do you want to pay more attention to?

2 Developing your intuitive process

Although it might seem paradoxical to think about a process for something that originates in the subconscious, you can make intuitions much more likely if you create a personal procedure. That's because repetition creates expectation, which your brain and body already are aware of. For example, perhaps you get going at work by grabbing a cup of coffee and opening your emails. Or switch off in the evening by checking your agenda and to-do list for the next day before turning off your laptop. These rituals signal start or stop in your mind and result in a flow of actions.

Similarly, a process for intuition helps because the intuitive mind is a fast worker but often slower learner, while the rational mind is the opposite; it's a slower worker, but fast learner. That's one of the reasons that doing a new job is so hard and tiring even when you have a ton of experience. But putting a series of steps into place helps your intuition jump into action quicker as you teach it that's what you're looking for.

With that in mind, this chapter will cover what that process is and focus on:

- Setting an intention
- Relaxing
- Asking useful questions
- Noticing what you get
- Challenging the information
- Trusting yourself
- Practicing

I know this looks laborious, but in a very short time you'll be able to do it in seconds. Here's how it works.

Set an intention

If you don't give your intuition a metaphorical prod, you can find that very little happens. Which is why intuition so often feels like a random occurrence over which you have no control. Setting an intention shifts this pattern as it does in other areas of your life that you are already familiar with. That's because intentions have energy; they are the engine that drives you from thought to action.

For example, you might want to do a workout before starting your day. So, you think, "I'll get up 45 minutes earlier to go to the gym." That's your intention. And you follow through by pulling out your gym kit, throwing work clothes in a bag, and turning on your alarm. The intention catalyzes your preparation; your preparation then ensures action so when your alarm goes off, you leap out of bed and head on out.

When it comes to intuition, intention setting works just the same, bringing focus and oomph to the information you want to intuit. Here's Diane Lytollis, intuitive life coach and mentor:

> *Intentionality catalyzes intuition because you put your weight of expectation and energy behind what you're aiming at. It's almost like being a runner on your own bobsleigh, giving yourself that mental push to get going and stay on track while navigating all the twists and bends.*

Intention is the action, but intuition is inaction – you've opened the door to see what comes in.

The key is to keep it simple; just say to yourself something like, "I intend to now intuit useful information about these circumstances." It doesn't need to be any more than that. In some ways you make it more real for you if you say it aloud and that can also distract your rational brain from filling in an answer.

When setting an intention, it's important to keep it positive, meaning for example, "I want to be less closed to intuitive information" is better expressed as "I'm choosing to be more open" for three reasons. First the words "I want" create a gulf between what you've got and what you're aiming at. Second, you solidify this negative position in your mind, so it's more likely to turn up as the anchoring effect shows. That's when you're influenced by whatever information or idea is immediately to hand. And third, our brains find a negative state tough to move away from, as Dan Wegner's white bear experiments clearly demonstrated. He did decades of research asking people not to think about a white bear. The major problem is the only way to be certain you're completing the task correctly is to – yes, you've got it – think about a white bear.

Instead, words like "I'm choosing" imply direction and ownership of what you're targeting.

If you expect your intuition to guide you and cue it with an intention, then you'll be more likely to notice what shows up for you, particularly once you've calmed your mind and body.

Relax

Tight deadlines? Too many meetings? A massive to-do list? Constant mails and messages? Stress, pressure, and being always on mean you're often less present to your intuitions, as your mind frenetically bounces around. To be more aware of intuitions means some space and place for headspace. That means time in your diary and a setting where you'll be free from interruptions or a ton of distracting internal or external clutter.

If you're an adrenaline junkie who always crams in just one more thing, you might need a quick burst of exercise to help empty your mind. Of course, a walk in nature is always good if you have time, but skipping, high knees, star jumps, or push-ups are great physical releases that can help downshift your energy to increase your intuitive focus.

Another way to become calmer and more present is to breathe deeply and regularly. When you're stressed it's easy to hold your breath without even realizing that's what you're doing; deep breaths force you to relax your shoulders. To do that, as you sit in a chair, put your hands on your stomach, or one on your heart and the other on your stomach; feel your sitting bones and feet on the floor as you extend your spine. Then focus on your breath and feeling centered. Make sure you're comfortable and breathe deeply in and out a few times. Try to lengthen your inward and outward breaths and the gaps in-between them while keeping it a relaxing experience. Soften your face, jaw, shoulders, arms, hands, torso, and feet. Spend a few moments noticing your body, sending breath to anywhere that feels tight or tense, observing a calm baseline. The aim is to let go of any mental froth so that you can check in with your guts, heart, and feelings.

If you want to go one stage further, try meditation. Not only will it reduce stress, but regular practice also builds internal peace and calm. And it's simple: the easiest way to meditate is just to count 10 breaths and to start again, bringing yourself back to one if you get distracted. Or try the 4–6–8 technique, where you breathe in through your nose for a count of hold for four, hold for six, and breathe out for count of eight either through your nose or mouth. Breathing in and out will also do just fine. Don't worry if you get distracted; at some point you'll notice, then just let any thought go and start again with your breath. Do this for a period of five or 10 minutes. If you prefer, there are plenty of apps like The Way, HeadSpace, or InsightTimer to help you.

But most people don't mediate despite all the evidence on how positive the short and long-term effects are. That's probably because it gets to feel like another chore rather than a way of simmering down and being present to yourself. And people quit because it's frustrating to deal with a monkey mind which bounces about. If meditation isn't for you, try playing an instrument, peeling vegetables, gardening, yoga, or whatever you do to still a buzzing brain.

The point is that stepping back from the maelstrom allows you to notice your mental and physical state and to listen to what your intuition is telling you. The irony is if you take some time out from the stress and pressure, you'll more than make it back because you'll access a faster and less labored way of working. It's all too easy to keep pushing on through a to-do list when a break to allow for intuition would add much more value.

And coming from a calm perspective means you're less likely to pressurize yourself to deliver immediate intuitive hits. That's because when you tell yourself you "must" now find solutions, you just get in your own way and increase your chances of coming up with nothing or duff information. If you find this happening to you, try imaging yourself with your foot off your own accelerator and return to relaxed breathing. Wait a minute or so until you intuitively feel the moment is right, then try.

Slowing down the mental whizz greatly helps with on-demand and anywhere intuition. When your brain and body are calm, it's easier to pay attention to your physical sensations, feelings and mental images that float up. You'll notice recurring thoughts and be able to pay attention to any feeling of knowing that you have. And the more you practice getting to and being in a relaxed state, the easier it is to hear yourself and the more you listen, the better you'll trust yourself.

Tip: Here's a quick tension buster which you can do sitting at your desk. Massage your jaw, then extend your arms so you form a T, with your body being the vertical and arms the horizontal parts respectively. Point your little fingers to the ceiling and thumbs to the floor. Now swivel your hands so your palms are skyward and feel your shoulders drop as you do this. Breathe out at the same time and notice your guts and heart. This is a great mini physical technique to get back to noticing your body.

When your mind is still, you're ready to open the gateway to intuition by asking a question.

Ask good questions

First, good questions to ask your intuition are ones that don't contain judgments like, "Why is he so stupid?" or "How come she's getting so much attention?" Your aim is to be neutral because ultimately intuitions are too. Your circumstances, feelings, physical responses, energy, and values are what drives their interpretation.

Second, open questions work best if you want intuitive information. These are ones that can't be answered with a yes or no answer, so start with "what," "how," "who," or "where," or "when." Closed questions just give you a yes or no answer and your analytical mind may jump in. But when you have a quick answer to an open question, it's more likely to be your intuitive brain; the rational brain at this point goes out trawling for information and therefore takes a bit longer to get back to you. The quicker answer to an open question is therefore more likely to be intuitive.

Of course, you can ask a closed question and if you want a simple yes or no answer, they are useful. But you tend to get more helpful information if you try questions like these:

- What will the outcome be if I choose this option?
- How might my boss react if I do this?
- Who can help me be successful right now?
- Where should I look for support?
- When might this be resolved?

If you find it hard to come up with questions, "What would be best right now?" is always helpful.

A large percentage of what we do at work is around people and how they show up, so if you want to build your social intuition you can try these instead:

- What's going on for this person?
- What do they need in this situation?
- What's possible for them here and now?

These are what I call primary questions because they give your intuition something to play back to you.

Then there are secondary questions which relate to the information you receive. If you get something that you don't understand, just as you would for a friend who was unclear, you ask, "Why" or "What does that mean?" Or if you're curious, you'd say, "Tell me more." Doing that usually takes you to another set of images, feelings, sensations, or body experiences. The key is to keep asking questions until you feel that you have what you need.

Tip: Don't worry about the perfect question because that doesn't exist, and you can always edit what you've asked. It's always better to ask something than nothing. And don't worry if you don't get much or it feels hazy to start with: you'll get better with practice.

Notice what you get

Once I've asked my question, I notice whatever my attention is drawn to. Sometimes that might be a yellow pencil on my desk, my screen saver, laughter from the nearby school, a jackhammer in the street, or a pain in my wrist. I'll then follow the initial trigger, then to whatever my attention is next drawn to, and I just keep following that thread of attention. That often moves from external stimuli to internal images which I see in my mind's eye; to internal sounds which I hear in my mind's ear; or heart and stomach sensations and feelings which I simply follow. I'll use all these bits and pieces to help with an answer.

At other times I might first notice what I'm feeling once I've asked my question. When it's positive, I feel any of the following: confident, calm, energized, satisfied, assured, reassured, pleased, hopeful, excited, trusting, understanding, curious, relaxed, sure, willing, eager, keen, and energized. Either way I feel aligned. If it's negative, I'll feel anxious, uncomfortable, concerned, frustrated, pressured, worried, unsettled, suspicious, tense, blocked, that something's missing or wrong. And I definitely feel misaligned. When I'm not sure, there's uncertainty, hesitation, doubt, or indecision associated with the question.

Sometimes things come in dribs and drabs. At other times I quickly have a feeling of knowing and sense that I'm done.

I also pay great attention to the symbols my intuition throws up. These are often a big part of your intuitive lexicon and give you a shorthand for understanding a situation. For example, when I'm coaching someone, in my mind's eye I often see a gateway and beyond it, between two to five paths. That's when I know a coachee is struggling with choices. Generally, I then see one or maximum two paths that are broader and easier to follow than the others. Quite often one has a brick wall across it, so I know that won't work. But I always get the same gateway, paths, and wall which give me confidence when they turn up. By the way, I don't generally share this; it just helps me understand what someone is experiencing.

Here's another example. When someone or something's stuck, or I am for that matter, I often perceive a massive smooth, gray concrete block in my mind's eye. It's so big that it stops me from moving forward. But I always find a way past by imagining I'm walking around it, and that then leads me to the next image.

Symbols aren't only visual; you can hear and feel them too. For example, you might be wondering about working with someone. If you see an image of a storm cloud in your mind's eye, chances are it might be a difficult relationship. If your mind's ear works for you, you might get the sound of rain or thunder; if both are loud and noisy that too is part of the answer. If you feel your symbols, you might sense the wind whistling, then feel cold, wet skin. The main point is that it's unlikely if your symbology is a storm, that it's going to be a fabulous relationship.

Carrying on with the question about working with someone, you might get a symbol of a spreadsheet with a negative number, suggesting that there's a cost to working with this person, or in the same vein, feel that your wallet is skinnier than usual, or perhaps you'll hear breaking glass meaning a lot of trouble and clearing up. What you get is what you get; what it means depends on you, your culture, and your experiences. If you don't know what a symbol means, just ask your intuition and invite it to clarify. In most cases it will throw up a secondary helpful symbol.

When you start noticing your symbols, you'll probably use one approach over others; for example, I always visualized everything. But as I became more experienced, I started to notice sounds and feelings more; last of all, I started to pick up body cues because I'm the kind of person who used to find bruises on my shins and wonder how they got there; I just didn't notice when I bumped into the furniture. Now, I can connect all modes of information as they arrive in a stream of intuitive information.

For example, if I'm thinking about an upcoming meeting and my attention is drawn to a pair of sneakers on the floor with one lying on its side, I might intuit, "Oh, someone who was supposed to be making the running perhaps hasn't got anywhere." If I then notice the local school bell ringing at the same time, I might get the thought, "Oops perhaps they ran out of time." And then if my palms also get sweaty, I might then intuit that there'll be general discomfort around this lack of progress. I would then mentally visualize who would be at the meeting until I noticed my head, heart, and guts were in alignment around certain people. At that point I'd know to check in with how they were doing.

Noticing your symbols is one way of accelerating your intuitive practice, so I recommend recording what you get. That way you build your own dictionary of what consistently turns up. Here's a starter list for you if this is all entirely new. Simply take a moment to think about the items on the left-hand side and notice what pops into your mind. You can triangulate your symbols by then thinking about a specific event; does or did the same symbol arise? Now think about a future event. Is it the same? If it isn't, just replace the symbol with whatever feels most evocative to you.

Meaning	Symbol
Do it	
Don't do it	
Hire this person	
Meet with someone	
Leave	
Invest	
Call	
Start	
End	
New client or customer	
Wait	
Good relationship	
Bad relationship	
Be careful	
Drama	

Intuition doesn't just show up as symbols. It also turns up as:

- Persistent and recurring thoughts; they just keep coming back to you over the short, medium, or long-term. They come back to you so you can act on them.
- Body cues: does your heart sink or rise? Stomach lurch, skin tingle, feet itch? What part of you feels like it gets lighter and is more expansive for a "yes" or heavier, contracted, and sinking for a no?
- Things making sense; sometimes when you intuit information you just get more muddled. But when you give up, do something else, then it comes to you. That means knowing your best ways of relaxing without using a screen.
- A sense of confidence, unease, or calm which you can't explain but it gives you a powerful and steadfast feeling of knowing. Recognizing when this has happened in the past will help you build belief in your skill.
- Synchronicities that confirm your intuitions. You meet someone else who answers your question; you listen to a podcast which confirms your thought or experience. You'll get more on this in Chapter 4.

When you get any of the above combined with your symbology, you'll have a powerful feeling of rightness.

But suppose you try all this, and you get nothing. You've done the process and drawn a blank. Try imagination instead. George Bernard Shaw, the playwright, said, "Imagination is the beginning of creation. You imagine what you desire, you will what you imagine, and at last you create what you will."

If you find yourself blocked, let your mind freely focus on your current situation without wanting any particular outcome. Try to expand what you see in your mind's eye, what you feel, hear, or might know. Ask yourself, "What might be lying just out of reach?" This is a really effective way to jump-start your intuition as you wonder. Then pay attention to your interoceptive signals. What are they telling you? Of what you've been imagining, what feels more right?

If you're now thinking, "This is way out woo-woo," remember that the chair you're on, the light you see, the window you're looking out, the car you drive, the picture on your wall, the coffee you just drank, all of these were all at some point something in someone's imagination. This isn't about fantasy but powering up possibilities when you're stuck.

Tip: If you want to get better at noticing, go for a walk and focus on the detail. What colors and shades do you see? Who do you notice? What sounds do you hear? What sensations do you feel? You can't see what's in front of you if you are operating at 100 miles an hour all the time.

So, you have some intuited information, but is it right?

Test your intuitions

Probing or testing information that you get is an important part of the intuitive process. First, you'd never make any big decision based on one data point on your spreadsheet; it's the same with intuited information. Second, a big problem with intuitions is that they come in two main types: the powerful and accurate; the powerful and inaccurate. But these invalid intuitions are hard to ignore because strong gut feelings linger. That means it's important to check what you get so you don't act on the inaccurate or ignore what's accurate.

Asking other people what they think and getting them to critique your intuitions is a great first step. Sleeping on what you've got then rechecking when you're fresh is a must for anything important. When you awake, reimmerse yourself in the previous day's intuition. What does that do? Inspect this intuition briefly from your perspective, from the perspective of other involved actors, and finally, from the perspective of any bystanders. What changes and what feels the same? Are they all aligned? It doesn't matter whether they are, or they aren't, you're just getting more information, so you don't perceive something that isn't there. Then stop. If you overthink this part of the process, you won't be using your intuition.

You can also test your intuition by asking yourself how this would be different if some of the information was missing. And when you've done that then ask yourself, "In this situation what would make me change my mind?" I really love this question as a double-checking mechanism. Testing your information and ensuring you get feedback are really important; empirical evidence shows that both help you get faster and more accurate results.

If you want to push yourself, you can deliberately pause your decision to allow for more time and possible synchronicities to turn up, or override your intuition if the consequences are insignificant. That's different from ignoring it – it's a strategy to see how things turn out. Pay attention to any feelings of confusion or unease, internal signals, red flags, and any related but unexpected conversations you have at the time because it's confirming or disconfirming data.

But please do remember that if you have what seems to you to be an intuition about public health policy or macroeconomics when you have zero experience of either, you might want to be more self-questioning. That's particularly the case if you tend to get your information from Facebook or any other social media platform.

Tip: Remember that intuition is a feeling of knowing. It's easy to go wrong if the feeling and the knowing aren't both in place. Second, test your intuition by projecting back from the future. Imagining that the decision or choice has been made in alignment with your intuition, and you're looking back, assessing what you did and what's now true. Do that again but this time imagine that you went against your intuition and reflect on what is now true. Which option feels better?

So now you have your intuition, you've tested it to your satisfaction. Are you going to act on it?

Trust yourself

I'm sure that if we met, you'd be able to tell me about several occasions when you've ignored your intuition and gone against what it was telling you. You took a risk despite whatever your intuition was whispering to you, then then you kicked yourself hard afterward. Don't worry; you're normal and everyone's had that experience. Here are three anonymous examples for you:

> *"We did one acquisition which wasn't good. I knew that but overrode my judgment because I felt we needed to do it for momentum."*

> *"I've hired the wrong person. There was a remark that I decided to overlook at interview, but I took them on and at a certain point in time it came to real blows. Bringing in the wrong person is one of the most painful, hard to unravel, messy, and time-wasting decisions – particularly when I knew all along it wasn't the right thing to do."*

> *"I went into a toxic business deal where my judgment around a partner was clouded by the excitement of the vision. I wound up not sleeping or eating and got sick before it all went sideways. I hadn't listened to my instincts or intuition."*

When you don't listen to your intuition, you cause yourself double stress by first not listening to what you know, and then having to unwind a bad situation. The net result is that accuracy and trust are often harder to come by because you've been blocking yourself. In effect, you fail to have faith in your own judgment.

How do you get past this?

The easiest way to start to build trust and belief in your intuitive capacity is to record all your intuitions in one place: your phone or a small notebook is perfect for the job. Then every time you use your intuition, add the date, the subject matter, your feelings, any physical sensations, symbols, energy around your thoughts, or information you feel relevant. Try to pay no attention to the squealing, objections, or judgments of your rational brain. Self-editing isn't helpful and if you write as you intuit, you'll capture the little details that you may otherwise think irrelevant. It doesn't need to be long-hand or elegantly phrased: key words are fine.

If you don't do this when you start, you tend to lose pieces of information. The fact is that intuitions often feel quite smoky or misty, and if you don't write them down at once they quite literally evaporate. In fact, for me, that sense of smokiness is an indicator that I'm intuiting not using my rational brain.

Making notes means you can then go back and check your hits, the times you are successful, and the misses, or times when you weren't. Plus, it allows you to notice other things that help or hinder. For example, I find intuition easier when I'm fresh but mostly dire when I'm tired, stressed, or emotional. Your journal will give you useful feedback and insights into what works for you. And a track record means you can validate what you get. If you can't validate your intuitions, they aren't useful because they won't teach you anything.

Closing this loop on what you intuit and what then happens, is hugely important because it really accelerates your ability and your confidence. And by the way, it's been known since the 1990s that poor intuitive performance at work is highly correlated with lack of feedback. But for that feedback to work, as in any context, it must be immediate, appropriate, and clear. Moreover, research shows that when you get positive or negative feedback on your intuitions you get faster and better and that's what your journal will give you. And at the same time, you'll be signaling to your subconscious mind that this is the kind of information you're looking for.

If you like, you can gamify what you do by keeping a running total of your percentages for your hits and misses. You can download a programmed spreadsheet that will do just that if you want to at www.webpsyched.com/resources.

Tip: If there's only one action you take from reading this book, keeping a record of your intuitions and reviewing them is the one to choose. That's because it has the greatest impact on your learning.

All you need to grow your confidence is evidence of a few small hits, which is what a journal will give you. And it will stop any negative self-talk. It's incredibly easy to tell yourself, "I'm no good at hunches," or "Intuition is beyond me"; these are limiting beliefs or ideas that restrict you in some way. And what that does is prevent you from learning or growing.

When you lift the covers on limiting beliefs, what you're really saying to yourself is, "I don't want to make myself vulnerable or frustrated and I'm afraid of failing in some way." You can change that thought by telling yourself, "I'm learning a new, exciting skill and it's OK to make some mistakes." That's also why a record is so important: it's hard to deny positive evidence.

But suppose that belief was true? And you have very little intuitive ability. Do you really think that people can't develop? And if that's not true, why are you holding yourself to a much tougher standard than others? If you're still not convinced, think of the personal cost if you never trusted your intuitions. And now turn 180 degrees and ask yourself what would happen if you absolutely believed that you were naturally highly intuitive? If you lived this new belief, what would you do differently? I know you'd have a go, write up your intuitions and own your successes.

Tip: Tune into your body when you're confused as it just won't lie to you.

You've got the process; now it's about your practice.

Practice

Yes, the old saw is true, and practice makes perfect. But it doesn't need to take you long; you really don't need 40 minutes of chanting to use your intuition. A few breaths, a good question, and an ability to observe is enough. And what you'll notice is that even after a few sessions, it gets quicker, meaning you get to the fun part faster. Which is all about getting information that helps you do better at work. Here are some questions to help you strengthen your practice.

If you want to start with the small stuff, before you go into any meeting intuit some of the following:

- What's the energy going to be like in this room?
- What surprises might I find?
- How might I feel about the outcomes?
- What would make this a better meeting?

When would be the best moment to raise my concerns? Or if you want something meatier, have a go at these:

- How can I better learn to leverage my intuitive skills?
- What should I do to ensure my team's success?
- What might the outcome of this be?
- What is the next role for me to work toward?
- How will this person handle that project?

You'll be amazed by how accurate you can swiftly become. Particularly if you build your supporting skillset, which is what the next chapter is all about.

Conclusion

If you read this it might sound like a long-winded process with lots of bits and pieces to commit to memory. In fact, it's the opposite and, because it feels natural, will happen super speedily. There's a quick caveat here: this is a process that works for me, so you'll need to adapt it to make it your own. If that means lighting a candle, or doing 10 push-ups, go for it. The most important thing is to develop a practice that works for you, and you'll know that because it will give you valuable information.

Of course, the toughest part is learning to trust yourself and that's why a journal is so important. Once you start to see that for example, that your intuitions are 85% correct, you'll build confidence in what you do, and you'll create a wonderful virtuous circle.

Summary and next steps

Top takeaways

- Intuition is a process and a practice both of which you can sharpen and improve. Intention setting is the gateway for both.
- Intuition is tougher when you're in full focus. You need to downshift your energy and turn attention inward to notice your intuitive cues.
- Testing your intuitions is key and makes you quicker, more accurate, and more trusting of what you get.
- Keeping a journal builds your understanding and gives you feedback on your hits and misses.
- The point is not to have a perfect process but to get information that's useful.

Read

- Briggs, H. (2014) Truth or lie – Trust your instinct says research, BBC
- Hayashi, A.M. (2001) When to trust your gut, *Harvard Business Review*
- Santas, D. (2022) Your intuition is real. Here's how to strengthen in, CNN Health

Watch

- Green, M. (2019) Know thyself; The value and limits of self-knowledge: The unconscious, Coursera
- Saint John, B. (2021) The creative power of your intuition, TED
- Shukman, H. (2021) Original love and the path of awakening: Meditation with Henry Shukman, YouTube

Listen

- Cultivating your own intuition with Laura Day, Amazon music
- Tavakoli-Far, N. (2019) Intuition: Why should we trust it? BBC
- Winfrey, O. (2023) Intention: Oprah's Super Soul

3   Boosting your intuition with behaviors

If you want to have faster and more accurate intuitions, then this chapter is for you. Because it outlines the behaviors of an intuitive leader. Yes, intuition is a lightning-fast process, but that process is rooted in a set of behaviors that are not only grounded in robust research but that are also all learnable. And that's the good news: you can quickly develop all of them if you're motivated and willing. In fact, you'll rapidly start to recognize your personal patterns and body responses once you look for them, which is how you set yourself up for success.

How intuitive a leader are you?

Before you get stuck in, grab a pen and rate yourself on how often or how much you do each of the following using a scale of 1–10 (1 being low and 10 being high). Then read this chapter to check your choice and get tips for what to work on.

To intuit well, you:

1. Recognize and work with your internal cues.
2. Are open to experience.
3. Notice the physical cues you get.
4. Use emotional intelligence as a gateway.
5. Are observant of external intuitive cues.
6. Focus on relevant information.
7. Identify what's missing or wrong.
8. Trust the information you get.

Now you'll read about what exactly these behaviors involve so you can develop them for yourself.

Recognize and work with your internal cues

If you're working well with your intuition, you'll notice what your heart and gut say, and their alignment with your mind and energy. You'll recognize that sometimes it's the heart that leads, sometimes the gut, and sometimes it's the whole body. You'll have found that occasionally your intuition is just a gentle push in a certain direction. You'll also be aware of what pops into your head when pondering a problem, and finally, if you aren't sure of the information you've got, you'll be able to wait or question until you are.

If this isn't quite you, all you need is a little more practice. Use the exercises at the end of the book to help you. What you'll find is that when you've honed your intuitive abilities, you'll start to develop your own techniques, like Matt Pycroft, polar explorer and film-maker. This is what he does when he needs to make a quick decision:

> *I work in extreme and hostile environments on a regular basis where intuition is a huge part of what we do. Do we go left or right? Do we abseil down there or not? Does this system look safe? Of course, I'm going to check things, but really, I tend to know. And if I have a big decision to make, I do is this thing I call the coin flip, where I don't actually carry a coin, but I think to myself, "Okay, I've got to decide right now. Is it x or y?" Then I flip the coin in my head, thinking, "What do I want it to land on? Is it heads or tails?" I know that while the coin is flipping in slow motion in the air, what I hope it lands on. And that tells me what my intuition says. I use that all the time to make decisions.*

That mental coin toss is a fantastic way of pushing yourself to feel your intuitive answer. But if you do that and still aren't sure, just allow your discomfort to be and name it for what it is. I know that in most organizations, that's counter-cultural, but if you put it on the table, then you show others that it's ok to put their stuff on the table too. I recommend instead of saying, "I am uncomfortable," or "I'm worried," because then you internalize and create more of that for yourself, is instead to say, "I am experiencing or noticing feelings of discomfort." Where are they? What are they telling you? Mainly the answer is fear, but fear of what?

Quite often that fear is of making the wrong choice. Don't worry about that; you can self-correct. As Theodore Roosevelt said, "At the moment of decision the best thing you can do is the right thing, the next best thing is the wrong thing, and the worst thing you can do is nothing." Making no decision never improves any situation and fighting an internal battle with the unknown is much tougher than facing it.

Tip: Think through what happens to you when you encounter uncertainty. What pops into your head? Try giving this internal feeling a symbol, for example a question mark, an alarm, a shivery feeling, or whatever works for you. If you associate that with uncertainty it will start to alert you in similar circumstances.

Now dial up openness to help you find good answers.

Openness

Openness, which helps you pay attention to new ideas, is one of the more important traits within what's called the Big Five, the most scientifically valid and reliable models of personality. If you're high in openness you'll enjoy exploring ideas, observing patterns, and your mental images. You'll want to find out more both about your inner and outer world, folding this information into new approaches and different ways of doing things.

High openness means you'll know about complex feelings that always help with intuition. For example, you'll recognize that bittersweet sensation, when someone you've been mentoring or that you're close to gets a job elsewhere; or times that make you angry-scared, like when your boss shouts at you; you'll know the nervous excitement of doing a presentation to a large audience. If you're sensitive to complex emotions, you'll grasp everything that might be at play faster than other people. That's also a competitive advantage.

Here's a smidgeon of the brain science that lies behind that. Your ability to be aware of information that other people filter out is because your default mode network (DMN) operates more efficiently when you are high in openness. It's your DMN that lies behind mind-wandering, future thinking, and imagining others' point of view. The importance of this network is reflected in the fact that it uses up some 20% of the body's energy while at rest and only 5% more when active. It's no great surprise to find that openness is therefore significantly linked to intuition.

And openness brings other attributes with it as Dame Sally Dicketts, education specialist, retired CEO, and chair, reflects:

> For me openness is being alert to the world around me changing, being open to people changing, and being open to all things that come your way and not immediately sitting in judgment. When something challenges you, hold on to it, ruminate, and explore it with curiosity of the mind and curiosity of the heart. As a leader that changes your emotional response, so you and people around you will react very differently. That's how you get a different quality in everyone's thinking.

That curiosity means it's easier for you to examine new ideas and different ways of doing things. You'll question and encourage information sharing, thereby creating literal and figurative connections.

Here's Vas Blackman, actor and screenwriter.

> *I was doing this film recently in Edinburgh and I went to costume to get fitted and the head of costume said that she wasn't going to be around the next day, she was flying to New York to fit Whoopi Goldberg. But she said, "You'll get sorted out when you come in."*

> *The next day I go to my trailer and this Black girl walked in with an Afro, these Afro earrings, and swanky 1960s trousers. She gave me my stuff, and as she was leaving, I said to her, "Where are you from? Where your parents from?" She said, "Oh, my parents are from Jamaica." I said, "Where?" She said, "St. Mary's." And I went, "Oh, my mum's from St. Mary's; ask your dad if he knows Mr. Hudson." She said, "I'm going to – he loves things like that."*

> *She came back an hour later, and it turns out we're related and she's a cousin. So, I'm thinking, "Well, there you go again!" I didn't have to ask, "Where are you from?" and "Who were your parents?" But all through the shoot, we just went, "All right, cousin!" It was great bonding and really did touch me.*

> *I get this kind of thing all the time. I'm not inquisitive or asking because I'm rude, it's being open, connecting and using my voice to be in and make community.*

Openness is also connected to imagination. Imagination generally refers to the mind's eye pictures of non-existent scenes. That's the DMN again, which works to project different scenarios, providing you with options and choices. It does that in three interconnected ways: simulation, mental time travel, and perspective taking. Simulation gives you options; time travel shows you how things might work out down the line; and perspective taking how others might react.

As you do this, it's your intuition that kicks in to let you know the right choice or solution. For example, your image might be brighter and more detailed and may keep coming back to you; your feelings or body response might be more positive. Or someone will say something that confirms your hunch.

Here's Lisa Buksbaum, founder and CEO of not-for-profit Soaringwords:

> *Be open to being open, then you can let yourself fly. If you're trying to please people, look the part, or say the right thing, then there's no room for your inner voice to come through because you're guarding yourself and closing down.*

When I intentionally want to be more intuitive or I'm looking for answers, I say to myself, "Hey more, I'll have more." Then the next day something will happen. It's like flexing a muscle: the more you work out, the stronger you get. The more you are open to being open, the more you trust yourself and can be your own best counsel.

When you're open, you'll also notice synchronicities and serendipities turn up. If you're too wrapped up in your thoughts, you simply don't see or you discount these meaningful coincidences that can help you move forward in life.

The good news is that openness can be increased, and it doesn't take a huge effort if you're consistent about it. Have a conversation with someone unlike you; instead of trying to prove your point listen to their ideas. Talk to someone in a team or business you generally don't interact with. Or get out of your routine; go to an exhibition, doodle, draw, or paint; read or watch something you usually wouldn't. Then think about what that experience gave you. If it didn't give you anything, try something else.

Tip: Decide to put your skepticism in a mental draw while you're developing your intuition because research shows that this kind of mentality simply gets in your way. Another tactic is to revisit your past; there's evidence that going through old photos and meeting with old friends increases openness and adds to your self-esteem at the same time.

Openness leads to greater tolerance for ambiguity, better ideas, more connections, and improved intuitions, so, it's a career-booting attitude and practice. And you will be even better informed if you pay attention to your body signals as you do this because they work together beautifully.

Minding your body

You are about to give an important presentation; there's a lot at stake. Your heart starts racing, your muscles tense, your breathing speeds up and your stomach lurches as you open your laptop. These body sensations are letting you know you're nervous. That's because of interoception, the name given to your awareness of sensations from your guts, heart, skin, muscles, and bones all of which are central to well-being – and decision-making.

The study of interoception is one of the fastest-moving areas in neuropsychology, psychology, and physiology; so many researchers are interested in understanding how these signals and subtle nudges work because of the impact they have. See someone you admire smile at you, your muscles relax, and your heart softens as you experience connection; but meet an angry customer or client, your muscles tense, and your heart pounds as you feel fear.

To measure interoceptive ability, scientists use the heartbeat awareness test. Participants in experiments are simply asked to identify their heartbeat without feeling their pulse. Or to judge how close a recorded heartbeat is to their own. While everyone experiences interoception, like most skills and abilities some people are better at it than others. But research shows that the more you can track your heartbeat, the better you'll be at intuitive decision-making. That's been replicated many times over in experiments getting people to intuit which deck of cards a single card belonged to.

The good news is that even if you're disconnected from your body or can't sense your heartbeat, you can improve your interoceptive awareness.

One way to do this is the body scan technique. Sit or lie down, either with your eyes closed or semi-focused. You can start at either end of the body, so your head or your toes. If you start from the head, slowly paying attention to your crown, moving to your ears, then your forehead. Notice any tension and breathe into it to relax those muscles. Focus on your eyes, cheeks, and jaw and do the same. Move through the body and when you get to your heart, see if you can feel or hear it beating. Don't worry if you can't, imagine it instead. Continue to move through your body and if you become distracted simply reconnect to where you were. Doing this doesn't need to take more than a few minutes; it's a body scan not a forensic investigation. More and shorter is better than slow and longer so you get used to tuning in to your internal states.

A second way is to think of something stressful. Fully put yourself back in that memory and see what you saw, feel what you felt, and hear what you heard. Now connect to your body and check out what's going on for you. Is your stomach tighter? Jaw clenched? Breathing shallower? Skin prickling? You may feel none of these and have different stress indicators but noticing what happens for you is the key to understanding when your body saying, "I don't like this." And it will repeat the same signs whenever a negative or stressful situation appears. It's 100% worth noticing because this is a very accurate way of tuning into your intuition.

A third way of increasing interoception is through exercise and sport, particularly yoga, pilates, dance, or anything that involves different body stretches. Whatever you choose, when you've been pushing yourself physically, it's impossible to ignore your sweaty skin, pumping heart, and trembling muscles!

Tip: One of the ways to use interoception effectively at work, is to oscillate between inner and outer awareness. That way you're in touch with what's happening and your reaction to it. For example, if you're in a meeting you might switch your focus from the group and what's being said to how you are then reacting physically and mentally. And then you'd flip your focus back again.

Your body is a rich source of information; if you have higher interoceptive abilities, you'll be at an advantage as you'll make and interpret better choices and answers. Interoception is also closely connected with greater emotional intelligence which won't surprise you. That's because you'll be very unlikely to misinterpret a body "no" as "go."

Emotional Intelligence

If we're going to talk about emotions, let's first clarify the difference between emotions, feelings, and mood; they are often used interchangeably but they actually refer to different experiences. An emotion is a body state that arises out of a neurochemical response to external stimuli. Faced with danger, your heart will race; that's an instinctive reaction which kicks in unconsciously. In turn, this evokes a feeling of fear, which is conscious, highly individual, describable, and measurable. So, feelings are your conscious interpretation of an emotion. Meaning that "Emotional Intelligence" should really be called "Feelings Intelligence."

Then there's mood. You know the phrase "I just got out of the wrong side of bed"? That's a mood. Unlike emotions, they don't start with an event or a person; they're more nebulous, can last longer than a feeling, and impact what you think and do. Sometimes you might not even be able to identify the trigger for a mood. Mainly, a mood is less intense than a feeling and can be influenced by diet, physical health, exercise, your thoughts, and your environment.

When it comes to intuition, what you're mostly working with is feelings because they are one of the big drivers of your intuition. Empirical research suggests that the more you are aware of your feelings, the better you are at using your intuition. When you're being intuitive, you identify feelings around a person or subject and that results in a deeper understanding or knowledge that emerges out of these feelings. That's the bridge between them.

How do we know there's a real difference between intuition and feelings? First underlying neural mechanisms are different even if they are connected. Second, they often don't show up in the same way. For example, you might be managing someone new and feel pleased by their performance on their first high-stakes project. But you might at the same time have an intuition that they aren't happy in their role; perhaps this thought keeps bouncing back to you, so you'd decide as your next step to have a conversation. Or you might feel that a project team has great morale, but at the same time sense that they won't meet an important upcoming deadline.

If you want to increase awareness of your feelings, and research shows you can do this pretty quickly over just three weeks, spend time noticing what's going on for you internally. It doesn't need to take long, just occasionally ask yourself what you're feeling. What do you notice? What can you name? This isn't by the way about suppressing anger if that's a legitimate response. Nor is it about repressing feelings; surface acting, when you pretend one thing but feel another, is a fast-track to burnout. This is about perceiving, interpreting, expressing, and using feelings to achieve your goals.

Then you can try to think honestly about the last couple of stressful situations you were in; how did you react? What did you like about what you did? What could have been better? Remember that we all believe we are more capable of managing our internal states than we probably are – just as we overestimate our levels of self-awareness, our intellect, our leadership, and if we're honest, probably most of our abilities.

The reason you want to do this is because recognizing your own feelings helps you become more aware of the feelings of others. If you can understand how someone feels, you can tune into their intentions and make sense of their behaviors. That's the bridge between sensing feelings and using intuition.

Here's James Fearnley-Marr, communications and government affairs executive:

> *I've always put a premium on reading the room, thinking what people's perspectives are and thinking how others will interpret information. I'm a big fan of focus groups for that reason because you're getting impressions, intuitions, feelings, and perceptions about an issue at hand; right or wrong doesn't matter because it's those visceral reactions about a topic that drive everything else.*

Tip: To tell the difference between a feeling and intuition if you're unsure, ask yourself, "Where is this feeling coming from and what's it rooted in?" If you can explain it, it's then it's your awareness of feelings. If the answer is, "I just know," then it's more likely to be your intuition.

Being observant

Foresight is a lot cheaper than hindsight, but you can't have foresight if always in the thick of it. Standing back and observing allows you to sniff stuff out, read between the lines, and spot what's changed, whether that's around a feeling, a project, the business, or a market. No observation means no intuition: if you're oblivious to external or internal cues, you're going to miss the subtle hints and messages your intuition sends you. But of course, that's easier said than done in an attention economy where distractions ping and zing around you all the time. Even when you want to pay attention, you can fail to see what's right in front of you. I know that I've missed goals when I've been watching football matches on TV because I'm distracted by something else on the screen.

Leaders know observation skills are important to their success, but because observation is learning, it's exhausting, which is why most people do it so badly. But the upside is, every time you really observe, you add to your knowledge, so it's remarkable how little value is attached to this vital skill.

Think about most meetings you go to; I suspect you believe many of them are a waste of time. But if you were to be a little internally quieter and downshift your energy, you'd glean so much more by missing so much less. When you calm your mind, and stand back, you access another whole level of information about what's going on. It's those small but important nuances, signs, side glances, and gestures that help you understand who people are, what they want and think, and how they might then behave. That's part of building your intuitive ability.

The more you observe, the more you can interpret; the more you interpret, the better your information and intuition. If you're always involved in running a meeting or leading a conversation, you can't spot changes in patterns, energy levels, and performance. You're less likely to pick up on the casual remark that everything then turns on. Plus, you don't add real value by hogging all the air-space and your team members won't like it either.

Observation allows you to also notice what isn't there. The items that haven't been done, the conversations that were closed off, the distractions or unspoken comments. They'll tell you much more than words can.

To build your observation skills, read body language and expression. What do you notice? What's consistent and inconsistent? Sit in a meeting and ask yourself, "How does this person or subject make me feel?" If I'm feeling uncomfortable why is that? And then the question I love to ask myself is, "So what does this all mean?" Getting the information is one thing but it's worthless if you can't extract insights from it by interpreting what you see. And your intuition can then help you sense whether you're right in what you're concluding.

If you really want to understand what's going on, try mentally putting yourself in someone else's position, literally, when you're with them. Then consider if a trusted friend was in your seat, what would they see, think, hear, or feel? Or if you made a film of it, where would the camera focus? And why? What you're trying to do is get different viewpoints of the same event to see what new information it brings you.

Tip: A great way to test your powers of observation is to articulate what you sense is not being voiced in a conversation. You can do this by saying, "If I were you, I might be thinking or feeling…" and test if you are right. If you're wrong, it doesn't matter; you've just shown that you've been putting yourself in someone else's shoes.

When you observe what's going on, you're much more likely to be able to spot what's relevant to a situation – and what isn't.

Focusing on what's relevant

For some people sifting tons of information to make sense of it and arrive at a conclusion is an integral part of their working life. Here's Jinny Blom, international landscape designer and author, describing how she works:

> *I have tons of things to think about at lots of levels and at the design stage I pile them all into a big heap, scooping everything up like a whale sifting krill. During that process I see things finished and that happens fast. I know by the time I've drawn it, that it's fine, that I've reached the right conclusion. Because something inside goes, "Alright, I've done it." Things just settle. My job is about being intuitive and responding to things but scaffolding them with a good process.*

Jinny has developed a personal way of focusing, which is something everyone needs to do. Without it, it's easy to feel like you're either drowning or that your head is crammed with disconnected data. When that happens perhaps you become tetchy, lack focus, or sleep badly. You might make a decision just to get something – anything off your plate. Watch out. Research shows it's more likely that doing this leads to suboptimal outcomes.

It's far better to disconnect yourself, get organized, and knock items off your to-do list. Ironically humans often lean into the very thing that's causing the trouble, squandering yet more time and attention. Tell me you've never wasted half an hour on YouTube, TikTok, or Instagram when you've been under pressure to deliver. And if you find yourself stopping two or three tasks to start another, well that's not good for you either. Multi-tasking doesn't work except for the simplest of tasks. You might be on a Zoom call and send a text saying you'll be late for your next meeting, but that won't help you solve the toughest strategic problem you're working on.

To focus on relevant information or perform a task really well, you need time, space and, as Jinny says, a good process. That means not filling your days with stuff that adds little value or the crisis du jour. Giving yourself a chunk of time without phone or email interruptions is of course linked to better outcomes.

Tip: Here's how you can build a process for yourself so like Jinny, you can sift your krill.

Let's assume you've booked that time with yourself because you've got something to do which you've never done before. As you begin, think about what specifically you are trying to do. As Patty O'Hayer, seasoned communications exec, says:

> I'm always asking what problem are we trying to solve. It's no good jumping straight into action but it's tougher to figure out what we are trying to do. What are we solving for? And, when you are done, it's important to ask would we actually be improving matters by taking these actions.

Once you've articulated your problem, check that solving it will help you or others you work with meet your professional or personal objectives. It sounds daft, but there are plenty of projects that should have been put out of their misery well before they were. The sponsor doesn't really question their value, and then sunk costs get in the way. So, remind yourself of the problem you're solving and the benefits that will bring.

Then look at everything you know to assess what's salient and what isn't. Write down each data point, workstream, or activity on a separate sticky note. Which ones seem to draw your attention? What seems to be connected? Sort them rapidly into relevant and not relevant, or more important and less important, then sit back. Pay attention to your body cues and your feelings. What's the summary or conclusion? Take a photo of them then mix your sticky notes up, grab a drink or take a break, and do the same again. Sleep on it and take a third look. Doing this regularly takes very little time but will teach you how to intuit what's important.

When I do this, it's almost as if some sticky notes seem more vibrant, as if they were written in bold. And coachees have told me that they have "a sense of insight," "a feeling of these but not those," "signposts and direction," "it's coming together," or "the right pieces of a puzzle."

Once you have the main points, you can then start to work out what to do. What you're doing is building your intuitive muscle so that it gets easier to focus on two or three key items and accepting that the rest that are merely a distraction. When that becomes easy, you've built your expert intuition, like Dr Izolda Heydenrych, dermatologist and key opinion leader.

Although I know there are 20 things I could do for my patients, there's something that tells me these three are right. I also know that today is the day and now is the time. Or it isn't. I'm very risk averse and attuned to not causing complications and I've published a lot on that. If it doesn't feel right to treat a patient, I'll ask and probe; maybe they've a bad tooth, an infection or don't feel quite right. I just listen to the metaphorical little voice on my shoulder which I'm attuned to. I've always honored that, and I believe the more you acknowledge that, the more you own it.

To get better at this skill, notice others who do this well. What is it that they focus on? What told them? What patterns did they recognize? Try to tease out their thought process. Practice and see if you land on the same information as they do.

Tip: Summarize what you know out loud, so you can hear if the individual elements add up. Or try turning them into a story. What is that story? Pay attention to your body as you speak. What do you notice?

There's a caveat here: it's super easy to focus on what you know, because that's safe and comfortable but may not result in the best outcome. In the same vein, it's easy to ignore what's missing and that can be a terrible tripwire.

Identifying missing or incorrect information

There's no such thing as perfect data because it's often noisy, incorrect, or incomplete. And it's true that the better the facts, the more you feel certain about what to do next. But in a complex situation you'll never have perfect information: if you've got 70% of what you need, you're probably doing fabulously well. But uncertainty or unpredictability, particularly in high-stakes situations, provoke a fear response and everyone's nervous systems get jammed on high alert for fight, flight, or freeze. That's when stuff gets stuck. Everyone's scared to decide, so nobody does, then you wind up with a decision vacuum and a dash for more data.

When you feel a niggle or sense that something just doesn't add up, it's time to sit up and pay attention so you can get to its root cause. Here's ex-CEO and now chair and board member Dame Louise Makin:

When I feel a sense of discomfort, I drill into that with rigor, because as CEO you rarely get the first-time data even if it's first-time conversations. It's a sense of non-alignment, just unease. I spend a lot of my time in my role as chair and before as CEO role, thinking, "What are the right questions that will help us move forward or will help us get to the nub of what's the real issue?"

If I've got something on my mind, I go into myself, I don't want to talk about it but the whole body is processing it. It's normally quite short-lived, a couple of days. Then it lands. I have a phrase, "I've got an itch about this" and sometimes you can't name the itch. But the itch is the intuition.

Here's ed tech entrepreneur and CEO JoEllyn Prouty-McLaren building on that perspective:

I'm the kind of person that needs to answer all the little questions, because when I'm solving something, I gather data from a lot of different sources, experiences to pull it together. I reassemble and give it meaning for myself. If something's missing it feels like it's nagging me; I can't explain it and it's not as if I've got a formula, but I can't let go of the thought. It probably makes me an irritation to people but at the same time, it results in some of my keenest ideas and insights.

Of course, we've all experienced bosses and colleagues who nit-pick; this isn't that. Nit-pickers focus on inconsequential details that don't add up to a hill of beans, damaging everyone's motivation and morale. Whereas someone with high expectations lets you know about what's nagging them as they search for better answers. Unlike nit-pickers, they are trying to find hidden gems.

If you sense that something is missing or not right but can't articulate what, try bringing it to the attention of your team. If you're right, someone else will most probably be experiencing the same thing, and quite often, talking it through helps you land on what's not quite right.

Tip: To truly put your finger on an issue, talk about it to several different people. Perspectives of people different from you often help in working out what's missing or wrong. Connect to your heart by putting your hand on it and asking it what it's trying to tell you. Do the same with your stomach and voice your thoughts aloud. If nothing comes to mind, imagine you know; you might be surprised by the insights you have.

Trusting your hits

Last summer I went to my niece's wedding. I chatted to one of her friends, a super bright strategy consultant, and told him about this book. He was intrigued because he said even if he had an intuition, he wouldn't know how to trust it. And we discussed the fact that education has a large role to play in this. Around the world, students are taught there are right and wrong answers. But to be successful at work, you learn to recognize that there are also many shades of gray and it's your job to learn to pick the best.

How do you do that when you're doing something you've never done before?

You learn to trust yourself because when you get an intuitive hit, it feels complete and right, even if the answer's negative. For example, suppose you ask yourself, "Should we ditch this?" And your intuition tells you, "Yes," if it's the right answer you'll feel a sense of alignment, peace, comfort, and rightness. That's your feeling of knowing. You certainly won't sense any deep anxiety.

Here's venture fund Managing Director Dr Owen Lozman:

> *The real things are never in the data. One of my colleagues brought me a deal and on paper it looked great, everything added up. I never went to the company or met anyone from there, but I said, "This deal is never going to work." Something didn't smell quite right, didn't fit. There are nuances when you're buying a business that you pick up.*
>
> *I make decisions with head, heart, and guts and if I have a sense of misalignment between them, an internal dissonance, something's up.*

Whether you've got an itch, a niggle, a nag, or a lack of alignment that's your intuition saying, "Watch out." A great way of double-checking with yourself is to remember what it feels like when your intuition is working really well.

Here's Owen again:

> *There was another deal – we were skeptical about whether it was going to be a fit for the business. We didn't know the team and it was an outlier: but we went to meet them and within 10 minutes I said, "We have to do this." I was so surprised at how quickly we managed to switch from uncertainty to complete certainty, based on just a short conversation. It wasn't only the founder it was the conversation about the technology and how we all saw the fit; he was excited about what he could do for us, and we were excited about we could do for him. That happens a lot, and it happens better in person.*

One warning: if you've ever worked in the wrong job or wrong culture, you'll find that you lose your sense of self-trust extraordinarily fast. That's because it's tough to believe in yourself if others around you don't value your skills, strengths, and achievements as Dame Sally Dicketts, ex-CEO and board member, explains:

I remember once being in this organization where thought and intellect were very important, and intuition was perceived to be abominable. That crushed it. I tried hard to give all the evidence needed and then intuition would creep in, and I had to give more evidence to evidence my intuition. It's easy to second-guess yourself as it is, but being in the wrong culture just puts a lid on and closes down your intuition.

You'll quickly recognize you're working in the wrong culture because it's like wearing uncomfortable clothes all the time. Nothing fits. You never truly feel you can be yourself or that you're part of the team. At best everything seems uneasy. At worst, it's isolating and lonely both personally and professionally. And in terms of work, you might have to do things you disagree with or that you feel are meaningless. In short, you'll know you're misaligned.

When you're in a job where you can be yourself and you can say what you think, you'll be able to develop a good working relationship with your intuition. You'll have confirmation of that through what other people say, you'll start to anticipate reactions and sense you are aligned and on track.

You can start trusting your intuition more by treating it like the friend it is. Chat to it, ask it questions, check its preferences and notice what turns up. Value that information. Anything you don't have a relationship with or don't value, you'll never trust. Recognize that it's there and invite it to turn up more by making time for it. Minutes will do, you don't need hours.

Then think about other areas of life where you do trust yourself. What makes that possible other than having knowledge or expertise? What can you transfer from that domain to your intuition, so you learn to trust it better? Then reflect on what else you need to trust your intuition more and see what turns up.

Finally, the best way to learn to trust what you get is to practice and get better.

Tip: Think about those intuitions which you discounted but that later turned out to be accurate. Try to put yourself back to the time when you knew. What did you know that you knew? And how did you know that you knew it? Try to identify the signs, feelings, and sensations that you landed on at the time.

Conclusion

Now that you've read this chapter you'll have more insight into what each attribute is all about. Go back to the start to re-evaluate your skills once more and check what you could work on to strengthen your intuitive ability. You don't need to pick your weaknesses, as it's great to improve what you're already good at as that will feel less effortful. Meanwhile, if you're struggling with a long list, use your intuition to pick just one item or action using the sticky note technique I've already described. You'll know you've got it right if it doesn't feel like hard work; intuition is always inspiration not perspiration.

And in the final event, if you struggle with intuition, think less, and feel more.

Summary and next steps

Top takeaways

- You can learn to better use your intuition, and there are practices that help you do that.
- Once you've understood your internal cues there are other focus areas that will help you build your ability.
- Pick only one item to work on at a time: it shouldn't feel effortful but easy and fun.

Read

- Hayden, J. (2022) How the smartest minds use intuition and emotional intelligence to make better decisions backed by science, *Inc*
- Robson, D. (2021) Interoception: The hidden sense that shapes wellbeing, *The Guardian*
- Smillie, L. (2017) Openness to experience: The gates of the mind, *Scientific American*
- Wilding, M. (2022) How to stop overthinking and start trusting your gut, *Harvard Business Review*

Watch

- Sarah Garfinkel's TED talk on interoception (2018), The science inside our hearts and minds
- Daniel Goleman Introduces Emotional Intelligence (2013), Big Think, YouTube

Listen

- Adam Grant on the Power of an Open Mind (2021) Well Said
- 4 Business Ideas That Changed the World: Emotional Intelligence: Harvard IdeaCast, October 27, 2022
- 3-minute body scan technique, https://www.headspace.com/meditation/body-scan

4 Working with coincidence, synchronicity, and serendipity

A few years ago, I quit the business I'd founded after fourteen years of hard work. Quite naturally I'd been worrying that it was the right thing to do. There were plenty of projects to work on, and people around me were trying to get me to change my mind. On my last day, the final event was our annual Christmas party which took place in a central London restaurant where we'd hired a large upstairs private room. Just after I'd said goodbye to everyone and started down the stairs to leave, the *Frozen* song "Let It Go" started playing and got turned up extra loud. What were the odds? In that moment I absolutely knew that I was doing the right thing particularly because the song, which I actively dislike, felt so appropriate.

Why do coincidences matter? Because for one thing they can help you with decision-making and change. They seem to confirm your choices, point you in new directions, lead to new discoveries, interpret, or inform a situation you might be facing, inspire, predict, challenge, or connect you with someone or something you need.

Intuition has a role to play in many meaningful coincidences before, during, or after them. Before, it might prompt you to be in the right place at the right time with the right tools, doing the right thing. During, it might nudge you to do or say something, and, afterward, it can help you interpret your experience.

Some, like mine, feel like important signifiers at pivotal times, and others range from interesting through weird to simply funny. Not all of them are helpful, and indeed they can be actively harmful. From time immemorial, wars were started because the omens looked right. More positively, coincidences often cement relationships because they are what we share with others and then think about; indeed, there's a Chinese saying: "for every coincidence there's always a story to learn." In other words, meaningful coincidences are there to teach us something.

You know it's a meaningful coincidence because the attributes are always the same. First you recognize that there's been an unlikely pairing of two or more elements, neither of which appear to cause each other. Then there's astonishment, curiosity, or wonder generated. Finally, you're left with the question "What does this mean for me?" Because the most salient of coincidences feel not only amazing but instructive. The easier part is recognizing a meaningful coincidence; the harder part can be working out what it means.

Using a high-level perspective, meaningful coincidences can be divided into synchronicities and serendipities. The former involves two or more seemingly unconnected events happening at the same time, for example, I just had three consecutive coaching clients wanting to talk about the same issue. The latter involves finding something you haven't been looking for; for me that's often reading a seemingly random academic paper or article which is then appropriate for the next coaching session.

These meaningful coincidences differ from intuitions. Intuitions are internal events which involve your feeling of knowing, while a meaningful coincidence is external and involves something happening out there in the world. For example, having a sudden strong sensation to call an ex-colleague might be an intuition. But it would be a meaningful coincidence, a synchronicity, if you have that thought and before you could call them, their number flashed up on your phone.

Here's how synchronicity and intuition came together for Jeremy Bowen, international editor for BBC News. The former was how he came to be there, the latter prompted him with what to say.

A big moment in my career as a BBC reporter was in the 1991 Gulf War. I was only there because John Simpson, the correspondent had been taken ill. The Americans had bombed a shelter in Baghdad, killing more than 400 civilians. We heard it happened first thing in the morning in the early hours and we went down there.

It wasn't like the other times when the Iraqis were trying to stage things. It was so genuine. There were dozens and dozens of bodies being carried out, and families grieving outside. It seemed to be an open and shut case, that the Americans had bombed the wrong place. What I didn't realize until I got on air, was that the Pentagon and the Ministry of Defence in London were saying this was a command center. I thought, "No, it wasn't. It couldn't have been."

I did a two-way with the studio, and the presenter was giving me quite a hard time, "Well, they're saying that it's a command center." And something made me come up with a formulation, just as I was live on air, I wasn't an experienced a journalist at that point, but I said, "Well, I can only go by what I've seen with my own eyes and heard myself, with my own ears. I have been all around that shelter and there are no signs of it being a command center." As I was grilled on the subject in the succeeding days, I used that formulation a lot.

It was a massive story because it was the first evidence of big civilian casualties, and I got a lot of criticism at the time. I had an opportunity, and I used those words almost like a shield. If I'd screwed up at that point in my career, this succeeding 30 years might have been rather different. But because of it, I got to be seen as a safe pair of hands.

Whether a situation is horrific, mundane, joyful, or bizarre, any meaningful coincidence takes seemingly random cogs to work together.

What's involved?

When you start to think about what's involved in a meaningful coincidence, you quickly see that they are complex physical and mental events involving opportunity, recognition, primary, and secondary analysis.

To flesh that out some more, first, you need to be in a setting where a coincidence might happen. Then you link an internal thought with an external event and recognize it as a coincidence; for example, you think of an old boss, then 10 minutes later, see them in the foyer of your building. For that to happen, you need to recognize you had the thought and now you see the person, so you've made a mental connection. Once your coincidence has occurred, you decide if it is or isn't meaningful to you. Then you have the trickier part of going deeper to assess its personal significance.

You can see from this process that coincidences rely on selective perception and retention, in other words, the human tendency to notice and remember some things and not others. That poses some challenges. You can't see the world as it is because the sheer amount of data would be overwhelming, so you only pay attention to what matters to you. So it's easy to make mistakes, to misremember, and of course bias is involved. You're looking at the world through your lenses and no one else's.

But because coincidence is such a key part of human experience, with so many relationships, opportunities, solutions, and discoveries due to it, I'd argue that perhaps we are hard-wired to have a coincidence bias, though that term doesn't exist. I think it should – I mean who remembers events that didn't happen?

Before your brain implodes, I'm talking about all the times you walked down a street in another country and didn't meet a friend? Or thought of a colleague and they didn't call? Or sat on a train next to a stranger who had nothing to do with you? These events don't stand out, so we never think about them.

Bias can carry big benefits if you consider it a thinking pattern. Any bias provides speedy understanding and less cognitive effort. And a coincidence bias alerts you to something that's worth your attention, categorizing it at the same time. Finally, it prompts you to explore something which you might otherwise fail to do. All of these suggest that a coincidence bias would be highly adaptive behavior because it offers personal competitive advantage. Since meaningful coincidences appear to be woven into the fabric and key turning points of our lives, it's highly likely we're attuned to them.

How do they arise?

Humans like patterns. We look for patterns everywhere because they help us understand and interpret our worlds. It's how we learn: all our educational systems are based on patterns, just think languages, math, or science, and it's how we make meaning in every culture. Moreover, we start young. A nine-month-old baby can infer that when they throw their spoon overboard at mealtimes or a toy out of their pushchair, a parent or caregiver will retrieve it for them. That teaches them about cause and effect as well as showing them that they have agency and impact in the world. And there's an evolutionary advantage to noticing patterns and coincidences: failing to notice a connection between two things might cost you your life while noticing them would bring you greater resources.

Other than quantum mechanics (which I cover in Chapter 7), there are essentially three very different views about how these coincidences arise: chance, connection, and fate. Here's something about all of them so you can draw your own conclusions.

Many scientists would say that coincidences are simply noisy random events that are misconstrued by the public who just don't understand basic statistics and rely instead on unfounded and irrational beliefs. Indeed, the law of Truly Large Numbers suggests we shouldn't be surprised by coincidences because given enough opportunities we should expect a specified event to happen no matter how unlikely it seems to be. For example, if I say my husband is one in a million, living in London with a population of some nine million people, I'm likely to find eight more just like him. In other words what may seem remarkable isn't, simply because we misunderstand probability, which plays an essential role in critical thinking.

It's certainly true that we get probabilities and odds colloquially confused. When talking about coincidences we often say, "What are the odds?" when we mean, "What's the probability?" Mathematically they are different even though they are both about the likelihood of something taking place. Odds are ratios of the likelihood of an outcome. So, the odds of choosing the queen of hearts from a deck of cards is 1:52 assuming you've removed the jokers. The odds of choosing a queen are 4:52 so 1:13. But a probability is most often expressed as a percentage. So, the probability of picking the queen of hearts is 1/52 × 100, which is about 2%.

Probability is most often used to express whether something has happened by chance. The main issue when applying probability to coincidence is trying to work out what numerical values to ascribe to any part of what happened. For example, my son and my niece passed each other one on an up escalator, the other on the down one in a museum in New York. The former was living and working there, while the latter visiting for a long weekend. They hadn't arranged to meet up: in fact, my son didn't know that my niece was going to be there. What numbers would you use to work out the chances of them both being in the museum at the same time and then passing at exactly the right moment to catch sight of each other?

Perhaps this meeting was simply a random event. It's always healthy to add a dose of skepticism when analyzing any coincidence because events which you think unlikely may in fact be probable. For example, the birthday paradox shows that if you have only 23 people in a room, there's a 50-50 chance two of them will share a birthday. Without knowing about the paradox, most people think that is remarkable or random.

But random wasn't a satisfactory answer for Swiss psychiatrist Carl Jung who in 1952 published his paper "Synchronicity – an acausal connecting principle," which offered an alternative explanation. Coincidences to him were meaningful events which happen far more frequently than chance allows. Because they can't be explained by cause and effect, he hypothesized another force which he called synchronicity. To Jung, synchronicity offered glimpses of the *unus mundus,* or the "one world," which he thought contained the potential for both mind, matter, and more.

This "one world" offered an underlying structure to reality in the shape of a network that connects everyone and everything. The network was there because for coincidences to happen, there had to be something connecting two disparate events when cause and effect are missing. He believed that meaningful coincidences reflect deep psychological processes, carrying messages the way dreams do while offering meaning and guidance depending on how much they reflect emotional states and inner experiences.

The seminal story that catalyzed his understanding of meaningful coincidences came about during one of Jung's therapy sessions. He'd been working with a young woman who was highly educated, very rational, and resistant to opening up, so their sessions weren't progressing. Jung hoped that something unexpected would turn up that would enable psychological change. The breakthrough came when she described a dream she had the night before, in which she'd been given a piece of jewelry in the form of a golden scarab. As she was talking, Jung heard a tapping at the window behind him, so he turned and opened it only to find the closest thing to a golden scarab, which was a scarabaeoid beetle. He caught the insect, handed it to the woman, and said, "Here is your scarab." The symbolism plays an important role here because a scarab is a classic sign of renewal and rebirth. This coincidence and its meaning were the keys to unlocking her treatment.

(As a curious coincidence, when I was writing this section, and considering whether to include it in this book, I got up to find two extremely large beetles behind my desk. If you've ever seen a stag beetle. you'll know what I mean.)

The Austrian biologist Paul Kammerer, a contemporary of Jung's, built on synchronicity with his theory of seriality, which says that coincidences are a basic force of the Universe, like gravity. Albert Einstein found seriality intriguing and is rumored to have called it "original and by no means absurd."

Dr Bernard Beitman, founder of The Coincidence Project, has a different take on a similar concept, using the term "psychosphere" to describe a mental atmosphere in which we are all immersed but experience separately. He writes that "each human mind interchanges ideas and feelings and behavior patterns with the psychosphere by expressing them and drawing them in." An internet for the mind if you like which is evidenced by meaningful coincidences.

Unless it's down to fate, destiny, god, kismet, predestiny, karma, the field, the universe, gods, source, or God, call it what you will. A fatalist would think that whatever happens was meant to be and there's no such thing as coincidence because there's orchestration of some grand plan going on in the background. This growing tendency to trust personal beliefs, delusions, and magical thinking much more than hard science, results in many people believing that there's a plan which is somehow yours, even if you aren't driving it.

This group of people is more likely to be dubious about random or chance events, and their belief systems tend to support superstition or divinity rather than personal agency in making things happen. If you want to go and explore, there's a huge group of people who call themselves Godwinkers led by SQuire Rushnell who believe that coincidences are divinely ordained.

In summary, we have probability or chance responsible for coincidences which may offer an explanation; visit a bookmaker and you can get odds and probabilities for pretty much anything. Then we have Jung's one world or the psychosphere as a mental connector, both of which are unproven. A third option is fate in whatever flavor you choose.

But maybe the mechanism doesn't matter. According to anthropologist Michael Harner, many cultures consider that meaningful coincidences are a kind of directional radio signal indicating you're doing the right thing whether it's large or small. And that's probably how most people experience them.

Here's how author Mohamed Mohamud describes that.

I'm doing my usual day-to-day grocery shopping at my local supermarket and this lady comes to me and says, "Hi, I'm sorry but could you help me out with picking an item from the top shelf?" Being tall I often get asked this and I said, "Of course I can help you." Once I picked up the item and gave it to her, she asks rather shyly, "Oh by the way where are you from?" When I get asked this question I don't know to say. Shall I say I'm British or Somali? I said to her that I'm born and raised in London but originally from Somalia. To my surprise she says, "Yes I would have thought you were Somali."

You think that would be the end of the conversation, but it then gets very interesting. She then tells me, "I saw this book online called, 'Somali Sideways' and I bought it and I'm currently reading it." I then whispered to her, "Oh, by the way the book you are reading, I'm the author."

Her facial expression was priceless, and she continues, "You are Mohamed Mohamud? I can't believe it!" She then tells me that her husband took a photo of her holding the book and she'd been hoping to meet the author one day.

Moral of the story: sometimes when you think something won't happen to you, life teaches you that anything is possible.

Perhaps this was a random event but even so, beyond the coincidence itself, it obviously provided both people with an enriching experiencing as a reflection of their lives. That's how we get the sense that we are somehow on or off track depending on the type of coincidence we have.

Types of meaningful coincidence

There are dozens of different types of coincidences once you start to categorize them. They come in important and unimportant circumstances and have tiny impacts or massive ones. But it's worth thinking about how and when they show up because you get insights into what you're noticing and paying attention to. And research confirms the more you notice them, the more you get.

The easiest way to map your coincidences is by using this matrix. The situation is whatever you perceive your context to be, while the outcomes speak for themselves.

	− Outcomes +	
+	Learning	Affirming
−	Limiting	Surprising

(Situation on vertical axis)

Here's how each quadrant works.

Affirming coincidences

These are coincidences in which the situation and outcomes feel great, just like coach Katrin Windsor experienced.

I'm heading home from visiting my favorite chemistry student, son Daniel, in Durango. I'm deeply happy, driving through gorgeous mountains with glorious vistas, listening to an audio book, "The Prosperous Coach," about getting more coaching clients.

Just as I'm climbing a mountain pass, the author asks, "Who would you love to work with? What kind of client would you be really excited by?" I didn't have to think. I immediately say out loud, "Doug," who is a cool, successful CEO of a global, publicly traded company that he built from scratch, doing really interesting work. I reach the top of the pass, and cruise down the other side. As I come back into having cell reception, the phone rings. "Hi, It's Doug, could I hire you as my coach." Jaw drop.

It's this type of coincidence that seems to affirm we are doing the right thing because when they happen, they often fill us with amazement, awe, and wonder. They stand out forever because they are such remarkable personal experiences. Now when you read Katrin's story you might think, "Well not so surprising – plenty of weird stuff happens." But the point of any coincidence is that it's meaningful for the person who experiences it.

Limiting coincidences

Turning to the exact opposite in the matrix, you have negative situations and outcomes. Here's one from someone who prefers to remain anonymous but who works for a large multinational organization. Like many people, they find being assertive and managing conflict hard.

I was walking down a corridor at work not wanting to see or engage with a peer who I'm finding hard going; we have different views about how a project should advance in every single respect. Plus, I've found that they withhold information – a pet hate of mine. My intuition told me that I was going to bump into them, so I ducked into an empty meeting room on my right and thought I'd check my emails for a few minutes.

After literally thirty seconds, in walks the person I'm trying to avoid who becomes even more agitated than usual because there's no one else to observe what's happening. We normally do our meetings with plenty of other team members. After a minute or two, I pretend that my phone's ringing and leave. But that whole interaction meant our relationship has taken a turn for the worse and I feel the conflict between us has escalated.

In this case it doesn't take a skilled coach to see that my coachee threw away an opportunity. Failing to manage so-called difficult people is something which will ultimately be career limiting unless they develop some useful personal strategies. In my experience, what you find hard to manage is presented to you again and again until you learn to overcome it. Then it magically goes away never to reoccur.

Surprising coincidences

The third box in the matrix concerns negative situations with positive outcomes. As a young woman early on in my second job and late for a meeting, I sped down a corridor with an armful of files. Stewart Wrightson, a London-based insurance broker where I was working, was located in a curiously shaped building. As I hurried around one of the triangular apexes, I ran smack into our CEO, the charming and urbane David Rowland who was walking in the opposite direction. To my intense embarrassment, I dropped my files, spewing papers everywhere. While I was flustered, apologetic, and red-faced, David asked me my name and what I did, helping me pick everything up. Then he said to tell my boss that he'd detained me if I was asked why I was late. That night I didn't sleep a wink, consumed by shame and mortification.

But from then on whenever I saw him, David would say hello. He chatted to me in the elevator, asked about my work, and introduced me to the senior leaders he was with. What I perceived as terrible at the time in fact got me some amazing connections around the business. Best of all, his recognition made me feel really motivated, so it was a meaningful coincidence for me early in my career despite its inauspicious beginnings.

Here's a much more dramatic but surprising coincidence, which demonstrates the fact that reciprocity is often present, so both people benefit from an encounter. This is part of an interview done in 1979 with Frank Prentice, the assistant purser on the Titanic. After all the lifeboats had been launched, he was left on the ship warning people as they jumped to keep clear of the propellers. Just before she sank, he and two colleagues climbed onto a railing and jumped into the sea.

> We had orders to get the lifeboats out and the same old order: "Women and children [first]" and we swung the lifeboats out and gradually filled them up. The first boats were on the port side and didn't have many passengers on board. They were afraid to go down; There was a 70 ft drop to the water and they didn't

think she was going to sink. A few of the lifeboats got away half filled. We had 16 lifeboats and they each carried 50. If they'd been filled, we could have saved 800 whereas we only saved 500.

Then I had orders to go down to the storeroom with a gang of men and get all the biscuits we could find. When we got back up onto the boat deck, we couldn't get near the lifeboats ... by that time she was listing very badly to port, and we couldn't get the starboard boats down. But before I got my life belt on, I met a young couple ... her name – it was a Mrs Clark and she was having trouble with her life belt. So I fixed that on to her and I said, "You'd better get into a life boat and there was one on the port side." So she said, "No I don't want to go, I don't want to leave my husband." I said, "It's just a precautionary measure, you get in, your husband will follow later on." I got her away and that was that ...

She was sinking fast now and all of a sudden, she lifted up quickly and you could hear everything crashing through her. Everything that was movable was going through her. Then she went down and seemed to come up again, so I thought, "Well now I'm going to leave." And I was hanging onto a board – we'd said keep clear of propeller blades and I was hanging onto one of these and I was getting higher and higher in the air, and I thought, "Well now I'll go" and I dropped in [to the sea]. I hit the water with a terrific crack. Luckily, I didn't hit anything – there were bodies all over the place. Then I looked up at the Titanic; the propellers were right out of the water; the rudder was right out, you could see the bottom. Gradually she glided away and that was that. That was the last of the Titanic.

I didn't want to die but I didn't see much chance of living; I was gradually getting frozen up and by the grace of God, I came across a lifeboat, and they pulled me in ... I sat on the seat next to Mrs Clark. The first thing she said to me was, "Have you seen my husband?" So, I said, "No I haven't but I expect he'll be alright." Anyway, I was in a pretty bad way then as you can imagine frozen solid almost. She wrapped me round with her cloak; she had some sort of blanket or a coat on. I think she probably saved my life: I saved hers...and she saved mine.

If you want, you can find the clip on YouTube and I recommend watching it as it's very moving. As a coincidence the situation was appalling; Frank Prentice lost his two colleagues and Mrs Clark her husband in the most terrible circumstances. But there's great beauty in the fact that they saved each other's lives. Because reciprocity is one of the fundamental drivers of human behavior, it's not surprising to find that mutual benefit is a big part of many coincidences.

Learning coincidences

The last category in our matrix are those seemingly positive situations that wind up with negative outcomes. These often appear to involve an opportunity that looks good to start with, then doesn't turn out as well as expected. For example, I was coaching a senior director, let's call him John, who'd been in his role in a multinational for only three months. At that point his boss told him that she needed him to increase his visibility around the organization. He'd been hired to lead and build a new team whose function not many people understood.

A few days after being given that feedback, John's boss had a customer visit and couldn't attend her own senior team meeting. She asked John to update everyone on her behalf. This seemed like a golden opportunity for him, and he worked hard to get his presentation right. But a full-scale row broke out over what he said, and he was chewed out in public by one of the senior executives. Obviously, John was mortified.

Now the technique for dealing with coincidences that have a negative outcome is to get away from personal value judgments like, "I should have done better," or "I failed," with a ton of self-blame and a rear-view mirror focus. It's more helpful to coach yourself by asking, "What's my insight?" and "So what am I going to do now?"

You know you need to do that because you'll be feeling unsettled at best or terrible at worst after the event: that's a nudge that there's something to learn. Paul realized that he's always preferred to build relationships and get feedback privately in one-to-one settings. This was particularly true at that moment because he'd joined a new industry and was working hard to get up to speed. He'd ignored his preferences because he'd been told to be more visible, an opportunity had presented itself and he was keen to please his new boss. The second and even more interesting part to this meaningful coincidence was that he told me he'd had a niggle that the meeting would go badly for him, so his intuition was spot-on. Coincidences with negative outcomes often have lessons in them around being true to yourself and paying attention to your feeling of knowing.

To conclude this section, whatever your coincidence, you'll be able to interpret it at two levels. The first is simply the story around what happened. The second concerns the more profound meaning you derive from it, for example that you're on the right track, that you need to do something different or perhaps even make a big shift in life.

Additional categories of coincidence

Coincidences often seem to happen around signs, symbols, animals, or numbers and seeing them unexpectedly repeat. The experience is usually comforting or affirming in some way, so in terms of type, they belong in the top right hand box of our matrix. Just to add a little more about numbers because life is full of them – think phones, times, dates, prices, calendars, and all travel, so it's hardly surprising that this is a routine experience.

Lots of people have favorite numbers or patterns which don't apparently seem random. For example, you notice the time is 11.11 then 12.12 followed by 13.13. Or that you've driven 11,111 miles or that a task takes you 2.22 hours when you're tuned into a series ending with repeating patterns of the same number. Of course, if numbers carry a personal meaning for you that's simple and easy to connect with. If they don't, it's easy to get distracted by questioning what it all means. Instead, I prefer to think about:

- What are you doing at that moment?
- What are you thinking?
- What are you feeling?
- What is the challenge you're managing?
- What does this coincidence represent for you?

Talking all that through may give you more insight than the numbers themselves or the fact that for example, you've seen a squirrel five days in a row.

Numbers are one type of coincidence and signs are another. They often show up externally and synchronistically to validate your intuition, thoughts, decisions, or choices when you are trying to process information. For example, you're considering promoting a woman on your team who you think has lots of talent but lacks confidence. As you're thinking this through on your way home, you notice an advert for Nike saying, "Just Do It." Later that evening you open your Kindle and the first book that's on your recommended reading is "She thinks like a boss." If you're attentive and observant, these prompts will give you pause for thought.

Other typical signs include picking up a book that opens on a page with a relevant message. Or trying to solve a problem and a coincidental meeting or Instagram post catalyzes new thinking. Or driving home having felt rushed and behind yourself all day, you almost speed through a red light when you notice a road sign that says, "Slow down." Or you come across an old childhood toy as you've been thinking you'd like to be more playful. Or you notice you've got a tickly rash as you're thinking, "I'm itching to get out of this work commitment." If you're not sure that a sign is significant, pay attention to any frisson you get; it's always gut before Google.

How do I know if it means something?

What happens if you're not sure whether a coincidence is meaningful or simply a random event? The day before I interviewed Zak Brown, the CEO of McLaren, I was doing research about the business and of course their driver Lando Norris came up; the next paper that I wanted to read and had already open on my screen was by T Lando. Was that a coincidence? Yes. But it wasn't a meaningful coincidence because neither of these people have a significant role to play in my world. What was more of a coincidence was that when I was looking for a non-meaningful coincidence or random event this one immediately appeared!

My father, writer David Pryce-Jones, had an astonishing coincidence which he's been wondering about for 40 years.

I was on a train from Charing Cross in London to Tunbridge. In my carriage there was a young couple with some very well-dressed children. I noticed because there was a difference between them and the untidiness of their parents. I was wondering why that was the case, when the train stopped at Orpington and out they got. As the train started to move, I saw the man, the father of the two little girls, very agitated on the platform. I realized that it could only mean he'd left something on the train. I crossed the carriage to where he'd been sitting, and sure enough, there was his briefcase. By that time the train had got up speed so I couldn't throw it out of the window, so I opened it up to see who it belonged to and how to return it.

Inside it said, "Property of Australia House." On the top was a passport, so I got his name, and that he was working at the Australian High Commission. There were some traveler's cheques, and then there were a lot of bills for enormous sums of money paid by the Australian Government. At the very bottom of the briefcase was copy number eight of ten copies of the defense plans of Australia. I then realized that this briefcase was extremely important.

I got to where I was going, rang the High Commission and the operator said, "We have nobody have the name of Dr Thompson on the register. Goodbye." I called again later and this time I asked, "Who's in charge of scientific affairs?" And she said, "You mean Dr Prescott?" So, I said, "Put me through to Dr Prescott." He answers the telephone saying, "We need to get that briefcase back." On my return to London, I was met by both men and a couple of heavies. Dr Prescott was there white-faced as I handed back the briefcase and was given a bottle of Australian champagne.

About a week or two later, I went out for dinner and told this story. I saw that one of the guests — we were about eight people — became agitated. When the dinner was over, I asked him why. He said, "I don't like hearing strangers recount circumstances about which I know nothing." I said, "Well no harm done," but it turned out he was the Australian High Commissioner who hadn't been introduced as such. I just think it's wild — it's not a thing you could have arranged. I haven't met anyone from The Australian High Commission before or since.

Academic, consultant and author Dr Christian Busch suggests that you examine coincidences from a point of view of agency, surprise, and value. If you played an active role, were highly surprised, and derived benefit, you'll find your coincidence very meaningful. In this case my father clearly experienced only one of these three elements which was astonishment; his role was more inactive than active, and he didn't derive great value from it. That may explain why it's been hard for him to find meaning in it.

I believe that sometimes when we're bystanders rather than actors in a coincidence, we're there to help others not ourselves. Perhaps this was a wake-up call for the commissioner about how he and his senior team worked together. Or maybe it was simply a series of curious random events.

How to make sense of your coincidence

Coincidences come in all shades from extraordinary, delightful, weird, and funny, both peculiar and haha. But when they seem to whack you in the face and generate amazement or other strong emotions, then it's worth working on what they might mean. One of the best ways of doing that is writing down what happened and then answering these questions either out loud with a friend or using your journal.

- What big thing is going on in your life; what problem are you solving or what decision do you need to make?
- In what way might this coincidence relate to what you're solving?
- What might the timing suggest?
- If you think about the coincidence as a metaphor, what's your insight?
- What is your intuition telling you about this?

For this last question remember you should have a quick answer without rational or creative thinking and that will be accompanied by your feeling of knowing. If you run through these questions more than once, you're more likely to arrive at fresh insights.

If, however, you really can't find actual, metaphorical, or intuitive meaning and someone else was involved in your coincidence, consider how this coincidence might have benefited them rather than you.

Have more positive coincidences and be more lucky

Most people enjoy the positive coincidences that they encounter in their lives and would like more of them. Interestingly, coincidence doesn't seem to favor any group of people. Large-scale surveys examining individual differences show that experiencing coincidence isn't predicted by age, gender, IQ, or education. But what research does show is that the more you notice them, the more they seem to happen.

Back in the 1990s Richard Wiseman researched what made people lucky or unlucky, in other words what lay behind good or bad coincidences. He found that there were four basic behaviors. First, lucky people were skilled at making and paying attention to chance opportunities. To do that, they build and maintain strong networks while being open to new experiences. Second, he found that they make good decisions by listening to their intuition, taking the time to actively boost those abilities by meditating and clearing their minds. Third, they use positive expectations to create self-fulfilling prophecies, and finally when it all goes wrong, they adopt a resilient approach to turn their situations around.

What makes these behaviors possible? Wiseman looked at personality and found that anxious people were unluckier because anxiety prevented them from noticing the unexpected. If you're relaxed and open, you literally have a broader vision, so you pay attention to chance and coincidence. If you're anxious, you see just what you're looking for and no more.

Wiseman demonstrated this with an experiment. He asked people to look through a newspaper and count the photos. The lucky people took seconds to do this task because on page two there was a message in type that was two inches high saying, "Stop counting – there are 43 photographs in this newspaper." Unlucky people missed that message, and they missed a follow-up second message half-way through which said, "Stop counting, tell the experimenter you have seen this and win £150." They were too busy looking for and trying to track the number of photographs.

Wiseman then did a further experiment to see if it was possible to teach unlucky people to behave like lucky ones by sending them to what he called Luck School. That involved understanding lucky behavior, breaking their daily routines to create more chance opportunities or meaningful coincidences, and dealing with bad luck by imagining how things could have been worse. After a month, an astonishing 80% of people reported more luck. You can enjoy more fortunate coincidences, whether synchronicities or serendipities by making small changes to the way you think and what you do.

Serendipity

Because serendipity means unexpectedly finding something useful when you weren't looking for it, it's a type of coincidence that isn't recognized until after the event. Like coincidence, there's often an element of surprise. At its most usual level, it involves opening a book, magazine, or newspaper or talking to someone unexpected and finding the answer you need. On a train from Reading to Oxford, just as I had my first book contract, I was struggling to work out how to write it. I sat opposite someone cheerful, and we got chatting. He turned out to be a well-published teen author who at that point had written 18 novels. He told me that the answer to my problem was simple; set a word count to do every day, write that number of words, and stop the minute you've arrived at it. He explained that the easiest way to get going again the following day was by editing the output of the day before. Simple and brilliant advice which serendipitously solved my problem.

The word serendipity was coined by Horace Walpole, the eighteenth-century writer and politician. He took the word from a fairy tale, "The Three Princes of Serendip," Serendip being the old Persian name for Sri Lanka. These princes had been sent out to travel and learn; while they did that, they made accidental discoveries of valuable information. Walpole used the word "serendipity" when writing to a friend explaining how he'd found an unexpected link between two families by glancing through an old book.

Serendipity has been associated with a host of organizational and scientific discoveries. For example, Alexander Fleming was researching flu when he came across penicillin; George de Mestral was walking in the countryside in Switzerland when he saw his coat and dog were covered in burrs, ultimately leading to Velcro; and Geoff Nicholson was trying to create super strong adhesives for the aerospace industry when he invented the Post-it or sticky note.

At a more everyday level, serendipity can help us help ourselves.

While writing this book, I started to get shoulder pain and repeated tennis elbow. That's because I was unconsciously twisting my body when sitting at my desk. I'm fairly fit because I lift weights three times a week and do yoga. But I kept having the thought that I should also try Pilates. After about the fourth time, on a summer Sunday morning my husband, David, wanted to fill up the car and run some errands. To keep him company I went along, too.

At the garage, he jumped out to wrestle with the petrol pump and I turned to my newsfeed. The first article that popped up was how Pilates had changed the author's life. All that was needed was a yoga mat, a Swiss ball, and a ring; I already had the first two but not the third. Three minutes later we were inside the small supermarket next to the garage. I wandered down an aisle past a bin of random stuff. There to my amazement, lying on the very top, was one and only one Pilates ring for sale. I grabbed it and went to pay.

Back in the car and then on the way to the local deli, I said to David, "I don't know how to use this thing. I need a teacher." Five minutes later we were at the till with a basket of goods, and I spotted a single stack of leaflets: there were no others on display. Of course, they were for Pilates lessons. Within 20 minutes I'd read the article, bought the ring, and found the teacher. The next day I met Monique, and six months later with effort and application, the pain had gone.

Have more serendipities

Despite its accidental nature, there are some factors that help. First, you've got to be looking for an answer, so you're actively engaged in a process. The difference with serendipity to usual research or development lies in the surprise or chance associated with it. That gives you a clue to the second factor.

When it comes to serendipity, answers arise out of unstructured or unplanned conversations. That's why fresh ideas and insights come from bumping into people in hallways, kitchens, and cafeterias. You and they take the time to chat through what you're doing, share a problem, and your colleague or friend knows someone else who has a solution.

When you bounce from meeting to meeting and topic to topic with zero downtime, you're less likely to make those crucial connections as your brain gets overstimulated, then tired. At that point you'll probably close off the chance encounters and unexpected conversations because they happen in the moments between, so are neither planned nor scheduled. It's one of the reasons that Zoom or Teams meetings can feel less effective; they don't allow for serendipity, which is what it often takes to solve something complex and nuanced.

Even if you make deliberate time for unscheduled video chat, spontaneous conversation flow is missing. And not all knowledge is the same or shared equally; you need to trust people before you'll open up to them. That takes more time when relationships are forged virtually.

And it's relationships that count the most.

Twenty years ago, Professor Ron Burt found that good ideas are generated by managers who have broad relationships across their organizations and could therefore connect very different groups of people. Because these leaders are exposed to more diverse ideas, they have a natural advantage in coming across potentially useful knowledge. This explains why cross-functional teams help, and bureaucratic structures hinder innovation; in siloed organizations or teams, information flows less freely. What that means is the more you are connected to multiple parts of your organization, the better your problem-solving is likely to be.

While you can't say, "OK, I'm going to find an answer by using serendipity," what you can do is create the space for unplanned encounters. For example, back in 1999 I had a coffee meeting with a previous boss of mine at a time when I was trying to decide whether to take a job or go fully freelance. After we'd chatted, my old boss invited me to stay on for 10 minutes to meet his next guest, Professor Michael Hay, who at that time was Dean of the Sloan Programme at London Business School. I thought, "Why not" as I had just about enough time between that and my next engagement.

Michael asked me what I did, and I went with the freelance line; he then told me that he was looking for someone like me and asked if I'd be willing to meet his program director. Very quickly that led to 10 days' work, and I ditched the job offer. From that one contact, within five years I was working with 10 other business schools and was building a consulting and leadership development business. Meeting Michael was a serendipitous turning point in my career for which I will be forever grateful; there was synchronicity in the meeting because he was looking for someone to fulfill his students' needs. There was reciprocity too as we solved each other's problems. But more importantly, there is a process to it.

Here's what that is.

I was looking for my next steps in career terms. I said yes to an unplanned encounter when asked to stay on for coffee. And it seems from research that lots of serendipity triggers are verbal. Then I made an immediate new and unexpected connection; this connection is either to someone or something. It takes place either instantly as in my case, or over time if there's reflection or discovery involved. After that, there's follow-up which involves grabbing the opportunity and taking practical action. My serendipity was easy to pursue, but in the Velcro example, it meant eight years' development work. Finally, there's a successful outcome for everyone involved; for significant serendipities like the discovery of penicillin, that could mean an impact at a global level and across generations.

You can help yourself with serendipitous encounters simply by being willing to experience them; obviously the larger and more diverse your network, the more dynamic the environment you'll find yourself in. And the more you'll increase the probability of finding useful ideas or information. Once you've found your answer, you need to notice that something useful has turned up; as Pasteur said, "Chance favors the prepared mind." When you're negative, tired, or feeling overwhelmed, you're more likely to be closed connections and patterns.

That makes me wonder about lost serendipitous opportunities due to the daily grind of non-value-adding tasks like weekly meetings used for updates, administrative tasks, or email management. A meeting with someone new might change the world but clearing your in-box won't. If you get a feeling of frustration about doing this kind of task, perhaps intuition is telling you to get out there instead and, as Professor Ron Burt says, "Put yourself at the risk of productive accidents." While obviously there's no guarantee, zilch is always the result of a missed opportunity.

In conclusion

If you've ever said, "I just happened to be in the right place at the right time" as you were searching for an answer, then you're someone who noticed and took advantage of the coincidence you experienced. And while some scientists would say that there's nothing to any coincidence, when an event is personally significant, others' opinions won't undermine its importance to you. And for me that's the point. Just as you are moved by a poem, a novel, or a movie, if an event is meaningful to you, who are we to deny it?

Summary and next steps

Top takeaways

- Meaningful coincidences are entirely subjective occurrences that have personal impact often way beyond the event itself.
- Synchronicities involve seemingly unconnected events taking place; serendipities involve finding something useful that you haven't been looking for.
- Many people believe that coincidences indicate you're on the right path, and making choices that are taking you in the right direction.
- Going to different places and meeting new acquaintances leads to a greater likelihood of experiencing meaningful coincidences.
- There are active behaviors and thinking patterns that increase the chances of positive coincidences taking place.

Read

- Beck, J. (2016) Coincidences and the meaning of life, *The Atlantic*
- Erard, M. (2004) Where to get a good idea: Steal it outside your group, *New York Times*
- Johanssen, F. (2012) When success is born out of serendipity, *Harvard Business Review*

Watch

- BBC interview with Frank Prentice on the sinking of the Titanic (1979)
- Bijl, A.-H. (2020) Remarkable coincidence, a valuable compass? TEDx
- Jeffery Mishlove (2022) Meaning and coincidence with Dr Bernard Beitman

Listen

- Busch, C. (2020) The science of serendipity, *Harvard Business Review podcast*
- Mackey, C. (2020) A series of related coincidences (synchronicity), Thinking Psychologist podcast
- Merchandi, R. (2016) What are the odds? BBC

If you have any coincidences that you'd like to share or explore, visit The Coincidence Project at www.thecoincidenceproject.net. You'll find events, blogs, research, and a group to connect with.

5 Extending your intuitive skills

That ordinary people have extraordinary intuitive experiences which are beyond current understanding is a truism. But the numbers reflecting this are astonishing. In one recent study, 94% of the general population said that they'd had such an experience, and when asked, 93% of scientists and engineers, people you'd expect to be highly skeptical, said the same.

To flesh that out, here are a couple of intriguing examples. in 2014, 10 non-expert students were asked to predict movements of the Dow Jones; they made $16,000. Another group who wanted to repeat the experiment in 2017 similarly forecast the German stock market. While this group only invested a small sum over four weeks, they were correct on 38 out of 48 trials: that's almost an 80% hit rate.

This kind of stuff gets psychologists falling into two distinctive camps. Those who spend their careers being super sniffy about extraordinary results and those who try to investigate and understand them. But here's the rub: research that's done in a lab tends to be divorced from what happens in real life because when it comes to intuition, it works best when there are real world consequences. For ethical reasons you'd never be able to replicate unexpected positive or negative occurrences that happen to close colleagues, friends, or family members. But that's when intuition kicks in most: when you're close or invested both person-ally and professionally. When you care, you share, in every sense of the word.

To try to understand what's really going on, in 2018 Professor Etzel Cardeña at the University of Lund in Sweden reviewed masses of evidence for all kinds of intuitive techniques. And he concluded that the results of these experiments can't be explained away by lousy design, fraudulent findings, or the cherry-pick-ing of data. And he also noted that some individuals produce spectacular find-ings. But as his paper reported, "Our knowledge of it is far from satisfactory."

What we do know from experimental data is that if you believe in intuition, it's more likely to show up for you. Ironically, if you are hugely skeptical, experi-ments show you do worse than chance. In other words, suspend disbelief and judgment while you try anything outlined in this chapter. I've tried to give you enough information, so that you know what each technique about and how to use it. In addition, I suggest you notice whatever you're most drawn to because that's your intuition nudging you, telling you which method to try first. But the key of course is practice; it's how you'll get better and trust yourself.

When you find yourself feeling like that and needing quick answers, the yes/no technique is often a great help.

Answering yes or no questions

Quite often we want a binary answer to questions like, Should I take this job? Hire this person? Start this business? Other than a list of pros and cons, you can also intuit your answer by working with your internal yes or no.

Like this.

Find a comfortable chair in a place where you won't be interrupted. Take a few deep breaths, shut your eyes, and think of someone, something, or some-place meaningful that you deeply love. Say to yourself, "I love…" whatever you have chosen and experience in your body what that feels like. Sink into that sen-sation and intensify it. Notice what's happening in your body. Typically, you'll be aware of your heart, stomach, hands, arms, or face and in one location or several. When you're finished, write down what you noticed.

Stand up for a minute and shake your arms and legs to get rid of what you've just been feeling. Once you sense you're back at a neutral state, sit down again, take a few more deep breaths, close your eyes, and now prepare to tell yourself a lie. Say to yourself that you hate the person, thing, or place that you were just thinking of. Sink into that sensation and intensify it if you can. Notice what you experience or feel when your body processes something that's not true.

A truth or yes usually feels contented, expansive, warm, tingly, and peaceful. A lie or a no most often has sensations of tightness, constriction, discomfort, restlessness, or itchiness, is gut clenching, and feels closed.

And there it is. This is your body indicating a yes and a no. To verify, check in what you know to be true, for example, about your projects, or colleagues. You'll probably find you experience similar sensations albeit less intensely. You can use this yes or no technique for quick hits when you're trying to get the measure of a person, idea, or recommendation. Just remember to check your intuitions by asking real world relevant questions, particularly if you're getting a no response.

Sometimes you have to explore more deeply, like in this instance.

Imagine you've been offered a new job and you're trying to work out whether to take it, so you want a yes or no intuitive hit. The difficulty with binary questions like this is that the yes or no can change over time and it might be yes for some parts of the job and no for others. For example, the current leader of the team might be a disorganized micromanager, but that the work you'd do would be interesting and you'd learn a lot. To make a yes/no answer more complicated perhaps the boss will leave in six months' time. Because the situation is dynamic, you could intuit a no for the current situation and a yes for six months down the line.

Tip: To help yourself get more clarity in this instance, you might try exploring other attributes, like sooner, easier, pleasant, or difficult so that you get more information. In addition, pay attention to the imagery, words, or feelings that emerge because they're often helpful.

You might then want more clarity about timing as a next step.

Intuiting about time

Time and intuition can be tough because we all have such a mixed relationship and experience of it. For example, when you're standing in line, getting to the front takes forever; when you're having fun with a group of friends, it flashes past. Even more complicated, we often use the word 'timing' to ask both about the right moment for an activity *and* how long it might take.

To find out when something might happen or how long it could take, try the following. Just remember to first of all get clear which question you are asking and interrogate one at a time.

Imagine a clock or watch in your mind's eye. Spin the clock hands if you like analog or imagine scrolling through the hours of the day if you prefer digital. Or you might try hearing an alarm ring. If you're not clear, write down several options and notice where your hand pauses, see what your eye is drawn to, and sense what your feeling of knowing might be hinting at. Then check that wishful thinking isn't getting in the way.

If you're working with a longer time frame, you can do the same thing either with seasons, months, or years. Sometimes I find that random numbers pop up when I'm trying to intuit times, for example, a two or a three and I'm not sure what that applies to. To check in, I'll add the yes/no technique.

Tip: To get better at intuiting time, without looking at your phone or watch, simply ask yourself, "What time is it" occasionally throughout the day. It's such an easy thing to do to grow your accuracy. You can also project forward about what you'll do: for example, "I sense I'll stop working at 7.40 pm and get into bed at 10.25 pm." Without paying any attention to time during the evening, simply check when that happens and if you're right.

When you start to use your intuition around time, consider working with ranges. For example, you might assess whether your feeling of knowing around a project start date is stronger for the next one to three month period, or three to six months. Getting a range right is better than getting a date precisely wrong – and it allows you to grow your confidence.

Sensing energy and managing it

Energy is life. At one level it's a physical matter that fluctuates during the day. But there's a second kind of energy you'll recognize when you use the word itself or "vibes," "atmosphere," and "aura," as in, "He was giving off bad vibes" or "There was a negative atmosphere in the team" and "She's got an aura about her." And by the way, you really don't need to see auras to be able to feel them: when you observe anyone with charisma their very presence turns heads and draws people to them. Just as you're aware when someone's confident, fearful, disinterested, condescending, or bored.

You tend to most notice this kind of energy in high-stakes or stressful situations like when you're participating in a crucial meeting, doing an interview, watching someone give an update about something tough, or during a sale. If you've ever had to pitch an idea, service, or product you'll know that a lot of the debrief afterward isn't so much about what specifically was said, but how everyone reacted, the atmosphere in the room, and the feelings you came away with as your social intuition kicks in.

You'll also be totally familiar with the fact that you feel relaxed around some people but nervous or uncomfortable around others. And that's not just because they are junior, senior, or more experienced than you. It's their energy that you're tuning into which acts like a magnet to attract or repel you. In the former case it's because their energy is appealing and it increases yours, so when you work together, amazing things seem to happen, and work doesn't feel like work. At the other end of the spectrum, you find people whose energy is overwhelming in one of three ways: first, they're always on, dominating what's happening but not in a good way; second, their negativity or contrariness brings everyone right down; or third, they're needy and love the drama.

In all these cases it feels like the very lifeblood is being sucked out of you. And this is important because research shows that feelings are contagious to three degrees, meaning your downer can spread to the colleagues of your colleagues'

colleagues. That happens when you're face-to-face, working remotely, or communicating using social media. Bad vibes not only impact how people feel but what they subsequently think and do. Conversely, when a team is in a good mood you get the right stuff in terms of greater cooperation, collaboration, and work done.

So how do you avoid catching negative vibes and getting dragged down by someone?

If you're going to be physically present, decide beforehand where you're going to sit because being directly opposite your energy drain doesn't help. Try turning your chair so you're three-quarters on to them or sit at right-angled table corners. You're taking advantage of a typical martial arts approach, which is to meet energy and redirect it with small or subtle techniques. By the way, the ancient Chinese practice of Fung Shui has that the most powerful place in the room is looking at the door so you can see who comes and goes.

Then remember that what you intend matters intensely. When you set an intention, you determine what you want to have, feel, or experience. In that respect, intentions catalyze your actions, which in turn lead to the outcomes you want. They become even more powerful if you can share them with others because that allows everyone to direct or redirect their focus. For example, if you set an intention of having a positive results-oriented meeting as you start, and you say that out loud to everyone in the room, you can refer to it when the conversation slips down a rabbit hole.

There are a couple of other techniques like laughter that always help. So does some simple behavior like looking less at any mood hoover; we often mirror the body language and facial expressions of others as we adopt them; less gaze means picking up less negativity. And direct eye contact is a signal that you're paying attention and listening, something you might not want to encourage.

If you do get caught up in bad vibes, consciously notice what's happening and recognize the impact. If you feel your throat constricted, your chest tightening, your stomach sinking, pressure in your head, your feet twitching, slight nausea, or you're just reacting crankily, pay attention. Try mentally redirecting this negativity so that you imagine it flowing around you, not through you; even better, put yourself in an imaginary bubble that nothing can penetrate. What you're aiming to do is detach and maintain your well-being even in a challenging situation.

You can also name what's going on, internally to yourself or out loud depending on your levels of comfort. If you notice other people moving in their chairs and looking away, when your energy vampire starts to speak, that may be the time to make an intervention. Expressing what's happening allows you to start to change things, and you can do that by saying, for example, "Interesting, I'm noticing a real lack of energy in me around this conversation; who else is finding that too?" In that way you're recognizing what's going on and building a coalition at the same time.

If you do find that you've caught someone's negativity during a meeting, something that's easily done if you're a highly sensitive person, suggest a short break. Do a quick body scan for tension, focusing on your jaw, shoulders, and hands, noticing what changes as you breathe into it and let it go. This will allow you to flip your focus to you instead of the other person.

After such an encounter you might find yourself still having imagined conversations with your energy drain, imagining all the things you would like to have said. Don't. Instead, try mentally telling yourself, "We're done," and visualizing a no entry sign. If you really want to give them feedback, do it with a focus on what could be better instead of letting rip with any negative comments you'd like to make.

The benefit of managing any energy drain is that you'll start to protect yourself from people who draw on a precious and finite resource. And that's an important leadership ability as you work on being good tired not bad tired. Good tired is about getting value-add stuff done; bad tired is about dealing with people that exhaust you mentally and physically. What you don't want to do is absorb what they are giving off or indulge them because it doesn't get rid of the problem.

That's people. Then there are those meeting rooms you walk into where the atmosphere is so thick that you feel instantly lethargic and heavy. If you've been in a difficult project team which always meets in the same place, switch up where you get together to see how it impacts team energy. Other than avoiding those rooms, you can change the vibes by moving the furniture, opening windows, adding plants, increasing light, or playing music. Getting people to stand and move makes a massive difference too.

But what about those times when you want to give out maximum oomph and confident vibes because you've got something to say and need to be heard? What often happens is your body pulls energy in on itself for protection, diminishing you and your voice. At that point no one feels your authority or your presence.

To project and amplify your energy, think about what gives you meaning in your job, what provides passion because this boosts strength and power. When you breathe in, feel that passion expand and imagine that happening until it bursts through your pores. Push it out even further until you begin to tingle. If you don't feel anything, it doesn't matter, just imagine it instead. Extend that energy and enthusiasm to everyone in the room, whether you're in front of an audience of five or 5,000 people, and imagine their energy and enthusiasm coming back to you. That's how to create a leadership spotlight centered on you.

If you want, you can also use your breath to draw in red, yellow, or blue. Traditionally, red is your power station and helps you feel solid or earthed; blue is connected to communication; and yellow is for your emotional or intuitive center.

Do this for a few minutes before you start, reminding yourself that you know your stuff and have important information for everyone in the room. Tell yourself you'll be fluent and that answers to questions will trip off your tongue and visualize that happening. Your brain can't process negative information – just watch any child fall over immediately after a parent shouted, "Don't run, you'll trip" at them. Instead, visualize your success and everyone's engagement while telling yourself, "I've got this," because energetically that will boost your confidence, strengthen your spotlight, and draw everyone in.

Tip: To get more used to thinking about energy and how it affects you, try some of the following:

- Throughout your working day, just stop and close your eyes. Notice what's happening to your breath. Are you holding it? Why? What's happening to your body? Where are you tense? What happens if you direct energy there?
- How do others affect your energy? How does it expand or contract? Who do you connect with? Who don't you? What's the difference?
- Observe others' energy. How do you feel around this person? Do they draw you in or push you away? Do you sense they hold back, hold in, or share their energy?
- What happens when you mentally pull your energy close to yourself or push it out to others? How does that change around different people?

Energy is a precious resource that you only have so much of, so you want to use it wisely. When you absorb other people's emotions and moods, you may feel more connected to those around you, which can be a powerful experience. But when your boundaries are down, you can soak up others' stuff that isn't useful to you. When this happens, put a mental bridge between you and the person or imagine yourself holding a mirror in front of you to reflect all negativity. Doing this helps you pull back from being sucked in by negativity on what's being said, which is also helpful. That's how you'll take care of yourself and influence others to pull back too.

And energy is how you make things happen.

Making something happen

When I was 26, I was working in the insurance world, and I used to have regular coffee meetings with an underwriter called Andy Elliott. We'd meet in the Lloyd's of London building and go to the coffee shop known as the Captain's Room. On one of these occasions, we started talking about our futures and Andy said that he loved his job so much that he wanted to be carried out of Lloyd's feet first. I was appalled at the idea. Staying there until the end of my career felt suffocating and out of nowhere, I blurted that I wanted to start a business. I was surprised and amazed by the thought because at the time I had no idea how to do that or what it might be.

Fast forward 14 years. I'm now working as a freelance trainer and facilitator with a few big clients. I'm sitting with my accountant Tanya to go through my year end. She tells me that my turnover is too big, that I need to put what I'm doing into a formal business and take myself more seriously. And I flash back to that coffee morning with Andy and think, "Ah, so this is it." Over the years I'd returned to that thought and I can only describe that I held it lightly.

Here's how CEO and founder of SoaringWords Lisa Buksbaum describes it:

> I just hold things loosely. Think of a rose: if I was to clench it, I'd kill it and hurt myself on the thorns. If you want to feed an idea, or yourself, you have to give it room. You don't stand over a blade of grass saying, "Grow! Grow!" When you let things have room, you help prime the soil for new ideas to blossom and take shape.

As international landscape designer and author Jinny Blom confirms:

> If there's a tinge of desperation people feel it. If something doesn't work, it doesn't matter, and you can find something else to do. If you lean back things happen and that's when you apply the effort.

Leaning back is the same as holding something lightly and then you lean in when things start to happen. When you're too desperate, others pick up on that and it's unappealing. You make something happen by aligning your intent with your actions. In my case that meant leaving a corporate job, starting as a freelancer, creating a value proposition, finding clients, hiring people, and building a successful practice, all of which involve overcoming multiple obstacles and using plenty of common sense. Making dreams come true takes physical energy and effort not just belief. But you'll make them happen if you can use the thought as a guiding star rather than a crutch.

It also involves accepting risk. If you want a bigger job, a leadership role, more money, or your own business you have to accept the risk of not getting it. That means stepping out of your comfort zone, and pushing yourself as you go for your dream.

Here's Nikki Monroe, talent and learning director, talking about how she achieved hers.

I grew up in lower-middle-income family in a one traffic light town in Central Florida. Each year when my high school yearbook was published, I would flip through the shiny, stiff pages and stare in awe of the teenagers who lived in lavish homes on the only ski lake in town. Invariably each year, pages were filled with images of cool girls slaloming or wet-haired boys jet skiing at full throttle across the lake.

I made a conscious decision that when I grew up and had a family of my own, I was going to live on a ski lake so my children could be those fun, popular kids in their town – the polar opposite of how I felt.

Fast forward 25 years and I'm a newly divorced, single mother with a daughter, Olivia, in middle school living off one income. I felt lost, financially devastated, and alone during a difficult time. But someone gave me a pair of old water skis and I put them in a prominent location in my garage so I would see them every time I pulled in as a reminder of my dream. Then in January 2017, I put a down payment on my own small home off a canal leading out to a ski lake, and in April 2021, I bought a small boat and a used wakeboard.

The first few times we went out, Olivia repeatedly fell and got so frustrated and tired. But a little later in the summer when the heat of July in Florida set in, she finally stood up on that wakeboard. Her face was elated with excitement and a giant smile. This rush of emotion welled up inside me as that I couldn't stop grinning with pride so vast that I started to cry involuntarily. As she was climbing back onto the boat, she asked me what was wrong. I said, "Nothing is wrong. In fact, everything is exactly as it should be. You have made my dreams come true in many ways and today is no exception." I'm so grateful that I've been fortunate enough to give my daughter the childhood I always wanted.

It's a powerful thing to hold onto your dreams and envision your future.

Tip: If you want to make something happen, try writing it down. Once is enough and flesh out any details if you have them but don't worry if there's mental fog: total clarity doesn't matter in the origination process. Then think about what would get this off the ground; who would you need to talk to? What would you need in place? That's where you start. And if you can't get there, don't worry, hold the thought gently until you can.

If you've already got an idea and it's feeling hard to you, consider your effort to results ratio and whether that feels OK energy-wise. I don't mean on a daily basis, but an overall check in with your intuition. If it feels right, great; if it doesn't, maybe think about whether you're holding what you're doing more loosely or whether it's the best thing for you right now.

Making something happen is about information and conversations to test and refine your ideas; and at this point, empathy plus plus can help you too.

Empathy plus plus

You already know that empathy helps with intuition because it enables you to figure out what's happening for someone else. Empathy plus plus takes you one step further by applying your feeling of knowing.

In this chapter I've already referred to the imaginary conversations or thoughts you send out to other people when things are difficult. I'll bet you've sent out the thought, "Shut up you're being a bore" in meetings more than once in your life. You'll also most likely mentally rehearse conversations you're going to have or imagined chance encounters. When you're doing empathy plus plus, you do the same, but instead of talking to that person from your perspective, you imagine stepping into their mind and body to understand them better. Meaning that an ideal time to use this technique is when you don't know someone that well, want to understand their intentions or see how they might be experiencing a situation.

Actors do it all the time to become plausible characters: here's Helena Bonham Carter. Notice that she kicks off with intention because, like all these techniques, what you intend always opens the door to making it happen.

Intention is everything and you sow a lot of seeds for it to all come together. I approach a part and a person from different perspectives. Some of it is factual, and I find out as much as I can and read biographies. Some of it is watching them if that's possible. Some of that is having an expert watch with me to decode. So, I'll have a body language person who's really good at seeing things that I wouldn't see and what's going on, physically. And then I'll have a vocal person who does the same. I get their handwriting analyzed and their astrology done to gather as much information as possible.

But at the end of the day, it's intuitive despite all these facts. It's not intellectual, it's an unconscious thing. You've got to find the touchstone, the idiom of that person that gives you a gateway, a portal. I definitely have to find the right shoes to feel right, because you're walking new steps, and the shoes will often dictate it. And it's also an internal world that you're trying to connect with. Like this morning, I was thinking, "I've got to find the inside of my current character." It's a sense, a dynamic, an internal landscape of how this person feels at that time in her life.

By contrast, Princess Margaret's energy when I played her was utterly different. She was somebody who was closed off. And before going on set I felt my way into that sort of energy where you're very, very lonely inside, and where you want to keep everyone away to protect yourself. Anyway, it's lots of different things, but ultimately you go for a feeling. You gather a lot of information intellectually and it becomes like a cloak you can wear. Then I have to suspend my disbelief if I hope to suspend that of others and help them engage with what's a magical act.

If you want to really find out what's going on for someone else and, as Helena says, step into their shoes, you'll need to stop whatever else is happening in your body-mind. That means closing down other concerns, mental conversations, or worries that might be simmering. Then get in touch with this person's core qualities and motivations. For example, you might think about their grit, determination, sharpness, energy, sensitivity, pace, and discernment as you get going.

Then mentally see, hear, and feel the world through their eyes. Notice how to be in their body, to use their faculties, wear their clothes, speak as they do, and have their energy. Then check in with their feelings about this situation or event, as that's the easiest access. After that you can turn to their perceptions and thoughts. How are they experiencing this? What do they want to happen next? What would be the best possible outcome? Rewind or fast forward, pause or replay any part as you do so. Where might the sticking points lie? Which option does your feeling of knowing tell you is the best one?

If you're more auditory, what most speaks to you? If you're more sensory, which option is the smoothest? The juiciest? The hardest? When you've landed on your best working option, intuit what an uninterested observer might think just to check your biases or potential wishful thinking. You can use this technique to see what might play out best in a meeting, with a team, at a customer or client visit, or at a key juncture in any project or decision.

There's another twist on this. That's to "be" the meeting, the team, the relationship, the project or to see what it needs. When I do this, I often get images or symbols that I then need to decipher. For example, once when I tuned into a business before a client meeting, the image that I got in my mind's eye was a Chinese dancing dragon, the type you see at New Year. I know that they represent luck, but this dragon kept dancing up and down the street. I took this to mean that it was worth going to the meeting but that we'd circle around a bit without getting anywhere which is exactly what happened. A big reorganization was taking place, things were very unclear, so the project sponsor wanted to wait. It did, in the end, happen; it just took time.

One of the things you don't want to do is pester anyone about a potential pet project. That's when you can either do a timeline check or see if you can glean anything from your dreams.

Precognitive dreams

Family lore has it that my great-grandmother, who had a reputation for being slightly odd (she once hid behind her own sofa from visitors. When they started gossiping about her, she stood up to remonstrate with them as they fled). Vere, which was her name, would dream of what was happening or was about to happen to my great-grandfather when he was away fighting the Boer War in South Africa.

Sometimes of course, dreams simply reflect the fact that your subconscious mind is making connections while you sleep and incubating answers for you. Here's Jeremy Bowen, international editor at the BBC, describing that:

> I was in Ukraine, putting together a report for the BBC about the first year of the war, one year on. And the problem was how to distil it all down to some interesting human stories, while weaving in the bigger analysis. I was trying to find a path through a lot of material, terabytes worth of pictures, and I wasn't quite sure how to end it.
>
> I had a very vivid dream the night before I had to finish the script. I woke up at about four o'clock in the morning and stumbled around the room looking for a pen, and I found a yellow sticky note. And I wrote down three sentences for my script on that sticky note and stuck it onto my laptop so I wouldn't forget. The next day I used two of them as the last thoughts in the piece I did for the 10 o'clock news.
>
> My conclusion is that somehow the mind is processing stuff when you're sleeping, and perhaps finding a way through, deconflicting and defragmenting your inner disk and working on a problem subconsciously.

But precognitive dreams are different. They give you information about the future which you wouldn't otherwise have, and happen to about one-third of us. For example, James Watson dreamed of a spiral staircase that led to the DNA double helix structure. Dmitri Mendeleev, who formulated the periodic table, wrote in his diary that he'd dreamed it one night, having spent 10 years trying to connect the elements. Niels Bohr, the father of quantum mechanics, dreamed of the nucleus of an atom with electrons spinning round it like planets revolving around the sun. That then inspired his research. But if you think it's only for scientists, Mary Shelley, Edgar Allen Poe, Salvador Dali, and Paul McCartney have also been inspired by their dreams.

And there are famous examples going right back to the book of Genesis. Take Pharoah's dream when seven fat cows were eaten by seven thin ones. That was then followed by seven heads of grain doing the same thing; both were interpreted by Joseph to mean seven years of abundance followed by seven years of famine. So, the dream was in the form of an analogy like those of Watson and Bohr.

They can also be very specific.

Bishop Lanyi's famous and highly detailed precognitive dream occurred on June 28, 1914. Dr Josef von Lanyi was the Roman Catholic bishop of Nagvara, Hungary, and the former tutor of Franz Ferdinand of Austria. The night before the archduke's assassination in Sarajevo, he dreamed that he went to his desk to read his morning mail. There he saw his customary pile of letters but this time, lying on top was one which was black-edged, sealed with black wax, and stamped with the archduke's coat of arms. In his dream, the bishop recognized the writing and opened the letter.

Inside, Lanyi found a picture of the archduke and his wife, sitting in a car. Facing them was the Austrian general, while the chauffeur and another army officer were riding up-front. The street was lined with people, with soldiers standing to attention. Suddenly out of the crowd two young men rushed up firing revolvers. On the back of picture, in the handwriting of the archduke, Lanyi read the following message:

My Lord Bishop:
Dear Dr Lanyi:
I herewith inform you that today, my wife and I fell victim to a political assassination.
We commend ourselves to your pious prayers.
Kindest regards from your
Archduke Franz
Sarajevo, the 28th of June
3.30 A.M.

Lanyi awoke crying, jumped out of bed, and his clock said 3:30 a.m. He immediately went to his desk and wrote down everything he'd seen and read in his dream. About two hours later a servant came in and found him praying. Immediately after that, the bishop held a mass for his dream victims in his chapel, attended by his household and a guest.

The bishop then drew sketch of his dream's assassination scene because he felt there was something strange about it. He had his notes and the drawing certified by two witnesses present and sent an account of his experience along with the sketch to his brother Eduard, a Jesuit priest.

Later that day the archduke was murdered in Sarajevo. The scene resembled Lanyi's sketch even down to two assassins, though initially it was thought there was only one. Bishop Lanyi heard the news at 3:30 that afternoon, 12 hours after his dream. But he wasn't amazed because he'd been convinced all along that he'd experienced more than a normal nightmare.

That was a very literal dream, choc-full of precise detail. Interestingly when precognitive dreams are analyzed, about 40% of them concern events that will happen the following day or that take place shortly after. When you dream about taking an early flight or going into a tough negotiation both of which are actually going to happen the next day, you aren't precognitively dreaming. This is simply your brain processing what's coming next.

If you're interested in developing your precognitive dream ability, set an intention to dream more and put your journal by your bed. When people are asked to remember their dreams, they remember a lot fewer of them and less detail about them than when they write them down. That means recording them as soon as you can. The best dream time is often just before waking or when you're in a transitional state like after your alarm has gone off and you hit the snooze button.

Write down the date, the sounds, words, symbols, emotions, and add any sketches if you feel like it. Don't worry so much about the clarity or fuzziness; contrary to what everyone thinks, neither sharpness of focus nor intensity have much impact on accuracy.

When you've recorded it, reflect briefly on the literal and metaphorical meaning. For example, shortly before I decided to leave my business, I dreamed I'd given birth to an unlovable, lifeless, cold marble baby that was lying face down on the floor. That dream helped me make my decision. Of course, not all dreams are that simple and many of them can feel like jumbled pieces of a jigsaw. That's why writing them down allows you to reflect on and interpret what you get.

Tip: To make more sense of your dreams, go back in your journal and re-read them from time to time. That way you'll start to notice patterns of events and the meaning of your dream symbols.

Precognitive dreams give you information that may not reach your waking mind and it's a fun development process. Dream journalling not only builds self-awareness but potentially enables you to understand and act on life-changing or confirming information.

Then there's a technique called remote viewing, which is in an extraordinary category of its own.

Remote viewing

Recent genetic testing shows that all Indigenous Australians are related to a colonizing population of some 72–100 people who arrived there about 50,000 years ago. That tiny group of people was descended from ancestors who'd left Africa some 20,000 years before. They most likely got to Australia from what's now Timor, arriving in the north because that's the shortest route. They would probably have set off on a type of raft that would have had to travel at least 65 miles across open sea.

Drift modeling shows that accidentally arriving in Australia would have been unlikely any time outside the monsoon, which would have been too dangerous a time to travel. And it would have taken between four to seven days to make the crossing. How did they know where to go? What they'd encounter? What to plan for? A group of that size is a planned and managed expedition, not a haphazard event.

One hypothesis is that, like their descendants, those colonizers knew how to remote view. That involves getting impressions and information about a place, person, event, or thing that exists at a distance and that can't be seen by the viewer. And remote viewing is well known in many other cultures throughout history. For example, in 400 BC, Hindu author and philosopher Patanjali described in his *Yoga Sutras* how a serious practitioner can obtain knowledge of hidden or distant objects using "Divya Drishti," or divine sight. And throughout the world traditional shamanic practice, whether it's performed by South African sangomas or Sami shamans, is all about seeing things at a distance in real time. That's why shamans are also known as "walkers between worlds."

Remote viewing is both a skill and an ability like math. Yes, of course some people are mathematical geniuses, but everyone can add two plus two. After 50 years of research, evidence shows that people who don't think they have any ability at all are frequently the best viewers. And most people do better than chance even when they start – even though current scientific knowledge simply can't explain what they're doing or how they do it.

The term remote viewing was first coined by Hal Puthoff and Russell Targ in the 1970s. They were two physicists who were based at Stanford and working for the US Department of Defense. At the height of the Cold War and before satellite technology, there was intense interest in developing methods to find out what the Russians were up to. The Stargate team, as it was known, ran a 20-year program to learn more and develop the technique. To do this, they had a go at finding shipwrecks, Soviet bombers, and even kidnapped heiress Patty Hearst.

While the theory, earlier experiments, protocols, and results have been criticized and it's a highly controversial technique, there's still something behind it. That's been confirmed by Professor Jessica Utts, a statistician who worked on the Stargate project, and wrote a paper for Congress to look at evidence around remote viewing. By the way, she was also the president of the American Statistical Association in 2016, so she's a heavyweight in her field. What she found were small but consistent effects across studies, experimenters, and labs. Her research showed that most people do better than chance, and some people do much better than that.

So how do you go about remote viewing? Like most intuitive information, very few people clearly see the target they want more information about because it just isn't like watching a movie. It's more about teasing information out of your mind that comes along in bits of images, sounds, feelings, tastes, and sensations even though the process is called remote viewing. If you're getting crisp clear visuals, it's unlikely to be good data.

The most important part of remote viewing is to filter out signal from noise, which is why doing it when your brain is idling and when you're not tired or stressed matters. If you put yourself under performance pressure or worry about getting it wrong, ironically that's exactly what will happen. Because the process was supervised by the military, there is an established protocol to it. But if you're doing this for yourself, not to be a professional remote viewer, short cuts are fine. Nevertheless, there are some useful practices like writing down your output as you work because it helps keep your logical mind out of the way. You'll also be able to sketch any impressions you get, which is often easier than describing them.

It's easiest to develop your skills by using random pictures that you can't see to practice on. You can use online automatically generated photos, apps, or picture cards so you have plenty of fresh material to work with. Try to use photos rather than computer-generated pictures as they are somehow easier. What you do is describe, rather than identify what you sense the images might be. That means using adjectives, like round, heavy, wooden, cool, large, solid, and brown for example.

You do this for three reasons. First, the minute you've identified something, for example, you could put all the above adjectives together and say, "Oh it's a table," then everything afterward will be associated with that table. But the description for a table could equally apply to a stool. If you go with table, you'll be wrong and feel like you failed when all the descriptors are right. You'll build your confidence if you describe rather than identify and doing this also keeps your logical mind out of the way.

Second, research shows that this is more accurate than immediately jumping to what you think a target is. Third, a central tenet of remote viewing is that the fainter the perception, the more likely is to be accurate and the less likely you'll feel sure in what you're intuiting. Those faint perceptions are more easily grasped through description of both things or feelings.

Start by setting aside your concerns about being right, doing something crazy, and any other worries. Suspend any disbelief in what you're doing as you take a minute to focus in on yourself and get centered. Breathe a little until you notice that your mind is buzzing less and connect to the insightful, knowledgeable part of you. Then simply sense what might be there, it's as simple as that.

I recommend working out loud while writing everything down as you go so you give yourself something to correct. For example, "I'm sensing a smooth, round, and manmade object." That might be all you get to start with. As you get more experienced, you can identify more specific attributes. For example, "It seems to be beige, cool to the touch with a solid three-D feeling to it." The idea is to get as much information as possible; you'll know you're done because nothing else turns up.

Then you can check your photo to see how you've done. If you practice a few times, you'll quickly start to recognize when you're intuiting and when you're guessing. Once you develop that understanding, you can try something even wilder that also has evidence-based outcomes; you can remote view future events.

Here's how.

Let's say you want some insights about tomorrow's meeting. Visualize or sense yourself there with everyone around you whether they are working remotely or in the same room. Simply describe what you feel without jumping to conclusions. Don't be too specific and imagine what individuals will do or say because that's how you use your imagination. Tune in instead to what the atmosphere feels like. How engaged is everyone? What's present or absent? What would make a positive difference? What needs to happen to make progress? What's happening for you internally? Notice what else pops into your mind and what you feel with your body rather than trying to identify the scene or the conversation. Start again with the words "I'm sensing…" and you'll be more likely to stay on track.

The beauty of doing this is that you'll be able to get quick feedback on how you did: you only have to wait until the following day.

There's another way to use this technique, which is when you're trying to decide between several and equally viable courses of action. Consider each possible future choice and sit with them in turn, describing it at a future date as if you had selected that option. You notice what you see, hear, and feel with your mind-body as you go through each of your possible alternatives using the present tense. So, you'd say something like, "It's Monday 27 June and I'm driving into my new job; I'm there early as I want to go through my presentation to the senior team one more time. I've been here three months and things are starting to feel much clearer. I'm feeling energized by this new direction." You get the idea.

Notice which option feels more attractive and makes you more animated; if you record yourself, it's often easier to hear that when you listen to what you've said. I often use this as a coaching technique to help coachees make choices because nine times out of 10 it's so obvious. If you can't get clarity, it's because now probably isn't the time to make a decision, so try a timeline to find out when is.

Tip: Don't be surprised if you're pretty good at remote viewing when you start, then you go through a slump where you get it all wrong. That's normal, if disconcerting, and often happens because you want to be right. Take the pressure off yourself and just allow descriptions to come. You can also combine it with the yes/no technique to check what you're getting.

To conclude. Yes, remote viewing is controversial. But given that this is one of the few ways of sensing what's going to emerge and understanding others, it's useful. Moreover, it's a technique you can proactively develop, just like precognitive dreaming. As for organic precognitions, unfortunately you just have to wait for them to turn up.

Organic precognition

By organic precognition, I mean precognitions that you do nothing to encourage, they simply arise. Like remote viewing and precognitive dreaming, they also defy the current laws of physics and psychology. Yet I'm sure you've been driving down a road and known that the car in front was going to swerve before it did. Or that a colleague was going to let you down. Or that someone wasn't going to show up for a meeting. Or that things would simply sort themselves out if you did nothing. Those are organic precognitions which apparently one in five of us experience, and they tend to turn up as either a subtle whisper or a feeling of something quite intense.

If you've experienced organic precognitions, you probably will have:

- Had flashes of thoughts, or waking visions which are confirmed by events that take place shortly afterward.
- Been in mid-conversation with someone and known exactly the non-obvious thing they are about to say.
- Been totally clear that something has taken place without being told.
- Wanted to do something to get out of harm's way.

Here's Paul Boissier, former Royal Navy Chief Operating Officer and ex-CEO of the RNLI, talking about one of his experiences.

I've had several instances like this. When I was captain of a submarine, one night I just woke up. No one shook me, there was no spur to wake up. I was tired, and it was a long way up to wakefulness. I knew the voice in the back of my head said, "Put your boots on and go out to see what's going on in the control room." Submarines dive to periscope – that's when you're right on the surface, you've got to periscope up, you're looking around, but you have very limited vision. Everything is black in the controlling areas and submarine to preserve the night vision. Two o'clock in the morning is a difficult time, but in the pitch black with a bit of roll going on decisions are even harder.

Two of my officers were on watch. They were really sweating because they found themselves right on the edge of a fishing fleet. It must have been somewhere out on the edge of the continental shelf, where fleets tend to congregate. There was a swell, they couldn't really see and as we moved forward, these fishing boats were beginning to surround us. That's dangerous because even if you can see the boats, they're towing an awful lot of high-tension wire and heavy weights probably four miles behind. The officers shouldn't have got into that situation and should have woken me up. Anyway, I was able to sort it out and quietly steer the submarine back out; I could just feel stress go away. We got into clear water again, and I went back to bed.

I've told this to quite a lot of people and a number of experienced captains have said, "I can tell a similar story." When you're just a little bit on edge and your senses are heightened, helpful things happen if you're paying attention. When I was learning to be a submarine captain, the guy who taught us said, "Always, always, always listen to that voice in the back of your head," and I've always tried to do that. Indeed, it's wisdom that I pass on to successive generations of mariners as well.

Precognitions happen around your work, your worries, and your well-being because that's what you're most invested in. They turn up for some people when they are more relaxed and for others when they are under pressure. But most often they arrive as a recognition that something is not what it seems, that something's about to happen, is happening, or there's a need to course correct.

I've also found that precognitions can present severally and as seemingly separate things that are shortly afterward linked together by an event. For example, a few years ago I felt I needed to book a mammogram even though I wasn't due for one; I just had a slight nag in the back of my brain, a subtle whisper to go. Around the same time, twice I had a strong sense of foreboding and got a visual of myself turning the key in my front door, being alone and very upset; I could mentally see myself crying. I mentioned this to my friend and colleague Diane, who came to stay for the weekend; I was worrying that something was going to happen to a close family member.

The day after I'd told her, I went for the mammogram and was diagnosed then and there with breast cancer. The tumor was visible on the screen even to a novice like me. But it was so close to my pectoral wall that I couldn't feel it. I was whisked out of the room to have an immediate biopsy and meeting with the consultant who told me what would happen next.

Reeling, I sat on the steps outside the clinic to cancel that afternoon's meetings, phone my family, and try to collect myself before I rode my motorcycle home. I parked, walked up the path to the front door, put my key in the lock, and my precognitions flooded through me as I entered the house and burst into tears. The two separate precognitions, the one subtle, the other intense, were connected by a real-world event.

This was a precognition and not a déjà vu. A déjà vu, meaning "already seen" in French, involves something which should feel like a new experience because you haven't lived it before. But it doesn't. As a result, they feel fleeting, weird, and unsettling. They typically happen around conversations when you think you've talked about this already or places, when you feel you've already been somewhere. When people are asked, 98% say that they had at least one déjà vu, while 67% say they've had lots. You have more of them when you're tired, stressed, and young because they diminish as you age.

And it's possible to manufacture them.

Since 1959 it's been known that you can provoke déjà vus in patients; Dr Wilder Penfield found out that by stimulating the medial temporal lobe of awake patients during surgery. They told him that they had a sense of knowing what was going to happen, which wasn't surprising. People who have seizures in that area experience déjà vu.

Dr Anne Cleary more recently studied this using virtual reality. She developed dozens of similar scenes using VR to intentionally invoke déjà vu by, for example, creating a bedroom layout which was similar to a shop. And that's exactly what participants then reported. Meaning when you have a certain mix of familiarity and novelty, you'll probably experience a déjà vu and it's a memory phenomenon. Others say that they are due to a lag in neural transmission or a brief glitch in a perceptual experience.

In other words, déjà vus are unlikely to be intuitive experiences. But those times when you have information that somehow can't be rationally explained are.

Given that organic precognitions arise by themselves, how do you have more of them? The best way is not to push, or your creative mind will fill in the gap; instead allow them to emerge. And a great first step is to set an intention that you want more precognitions to be available to you. Then start to notice what's going on around you and pay attention to your internal state. What symbols, sounds, or people pop into your head? What other internal flashes do you get? And when? During any seriously boring meetings, pay attention not to what's said but what you can pick up for yourself and about others. I find that defocusing my gaze or doodling helps me get my rational and creative brain out of the way. And again, write down anything so you can check if you were right. Feedback is the quickest way you learn, and the more you get, the faster you'll learn.

Tip: Precognitions are not vague worries about the future, they are specific and verifiable whether they are positive or negative. But, in that they are organic, all you can do is be open and pay attention to the cues you get. Meditation is an activity which is well documented to help; I'm sure that's because it teaches you to allow, to be in the present, and to notice. Those are precisely the skills you're trying to develop.

In conclusion

On a practical note, now you've read the chapter, flick back to check what resonated for or intrigued you. Try that technique for a couple of weeks to see how you experience it. And if you get stuck, find me online and I'll be happy to help.

Meanwhile you'll have noticed that I refer to intention setting more than once in this chapter, and I wrote about its importance in Chapter 2. Intention corrals your feelings, thoughts, and actions, priming your unconscious brain and intuition as you move toward your goals. With that in mind, whatever you decide to try, set an intention for it. For example, "This month, I'm going to experience useful dreams," or "I'm open to having precognitions this week."

And finally, while precognition in all its forms is scientifically impossible, they happen all the time. Given that they are common and result in privileged, life-enhancing, and occasionally life-saving knowledge, you might as well maximize their use. Personal competitive advantage is hard to come by; if these techniques help you build it, you've got a lot to gain by trying them.

Summary and next steps

Top Take-aways

- There are plenty of ways to extend your intuitive skill-set; trying one new technique at a time is easier than diving into several simultaneously.
- Development is an uneven process: don't be surprised if you make a big leap forward on what you do and then regress a little. That's normal.
- Intentions catalyze everything, so think about what you want and why you want it.
- Information that you access intuitively is exciting but remember to verify what you get to build accuracy and trust in your process.

Read

- Cheung, T., & Mossbridger, J. (2019) *The Premonition Code*. Watkins
- McTaggart, L. (2007) *The Intention Experiment: Using Your Thoughts to Change Your Life and the World*. Free Press
- Orloff, J. (2020) How to sense subtle energy, www.drjudithorloff.com

Watch

- Chang, J. (2018) Qi Gong Routine for Stress, Anxiety and Energy, YouTube
- McCulla, C. (2014) The power of intention, TEDx
- Pestano, B. (2020) Why our dreams could be the key to time travel, BBC

Try

- Joining the International Remote Viewing Association at irva.org
- Getting practice remote viewing resources at https://intuitivespecialists.com/target-pool/
- Checking TikTok or Instagram for short intuition challenges

6 Applying intuition as a leader

When you're leading a team, business unit, or an organization, a lot of what you do is fuzzy round the edges. Meaning you face situations where frequently there are no clear or perfect answers. Without intuition in your data and analysis mix, you're more likely to miss a beat or drop a ball. But it goes further than this. Research done in 2022 showed that 67% of executives say they prefer to make decisions based on intuition and experience rather than data analytics. This chimes pretty perfectly with evidence from data leaders; 66% of chief data officers, say executives ignore organizational data, relying on their gut instead.

Intuition is increasingly recognized as a vital leadership skill because it speeds up your response time, tells you when something isn't right, and stops you from second-guessing your choices. That's particularly true when you have to make tough hiring decisions, help your direct reports then build their own intuitive skills, find and set direction, manage change or transformation, get a team to use their collective intuition, and, finally, recognize when to call it a day whatever the context.

While each topic could have been an entire chapter, what you'll find are top tips from leaders I interviewed coupled with my experience over the past 25 years.

Hiring with intuition

Recruiting great talent is tough, yet it's critical for any leader's success and succession. Despite tons of new digital tools, expensive and long recruitment processes frequently lead to poor hires. That shows up in the numbers that suggest an astonishing 20% of people fail probation within the first 45 days, while between 30–40%, depending on who you ask, only last six months. It's even worse at senior level, where about 60% of leaders are thought to fail or derail.

Why is finding talent so hard? First, the landscape has changed: people, especially millennials, want to work flexibly, and their personal goals and aspirations have evolved. Second, particularly for complex roles with shifting priorities and multiple stakeholders, it's often not clear exactly what skills a job requires. How will you find that great hire if you can't articulate what you're looking for? Third, to rightly address unconscious bias and discrimination, often there's too much faith placed in algorithms and technology.

When you're hiring, of course, your first task is to ensure equality of opportunity and diversity of thinking. Bias has no place in a recruiting process, but intuition should be there. If you're worried about mixing them up, the former is largely about social stereotypes, while the latter is simply your feeling of knowing. It's bias if you keep hiring candidates who look like you; on the other hand, if you challenge an unconscious bias with logic, it usually falls away. But an intuition around a potential hire will persist, even when you dismiss it. If you've ever ignored your gut feel and hired the wrong person, you'll know exactly what I mean: you'll have had that inkling not to go ahead more than once.

The fact is that intuition is ideally suited to situations where there's great uncertainty, time pressure, insufficient data, and many possible solutions, all of which are key attributes of recruitment. And it matters when you're hiring for two reasons. Recent research shows that if you've got experience as an interviewer and use your intuition, you'll recruit better quality people, particularly if the job is complex. In that instance it's hard to nail down both objective interview measures and success criteria: all you're left with is intuition.

Moreover, while obviously you need to assess someone's capability, you really need to know where their interests lie, how enthusiastic they are, how they learn, what flexibility means to them, what their grasp of detail is, how they like to work with others, how they prefer to be managed, and how all of this meshes with you and your needs. Gauging character, attitudes, and motivation is something that by and large isn't amenable to a structured process because there are no hard answers. Psychometrics or character profiles might give you some pointers but they aren't infallible, because if candidates have done a few they'll know how to game them. Your judgment is always the key decider and that's inevitably guided by unexpected comments, little asides, the tenor, and nuances of their interactions with you, the very elements that require intuition, even if it's an unspoken part of the process.

Here's Paula Dowdy, board member and senior executive:

One of the biggest mistakes leaders make is around people. Execs smother their instincts and intuition because they're optimists and like to give people chances. Or they look at a CV and say, "Oh, he went to Harvard, has a medical degree, worked at this big company and his credentials are awesome." But the fit isn't then right, the passion, humility, or collaboration is missing, or the ability to take a team along with them isn't there. When you make a hiring mistake at senior level it's not just about the individual time loss, but about talent beneath and everything that doesn't get done.

Judgment of people in the interview process is vital, and for me it's the tiny things that distill the BS. That's what to dig into when something doesn't feel right.

Paula's spot-on. The biggest mistake that leaders make is not listening to themselves then hiring the wrong person, particularly when under pressure to fill an empty role. Everyone I asked when writing this book had made that mistake, including me.

A solid process and structured interview obviously lead to a better hire as it's easier to compare your candidates. But even when that produces someone suitable, it doesn't mean they'll be a great hire. By their nature, interviews encourage people to exaggerate or boast, and chronic self-promoters often get the most positive evaluations. That partly explains why there is so much preposterous behavior in large organizations: people with serious personality traits can come over as incredibly relaxed, charming, and confident and if your intuition isn't hard at work, you may fail to spot that.

Here's what Bill Liao, entrepreneur, investor, and speaker, does to try and flush them out.

Unfortunately, since joining the investment world I have had to deal with a bunch of psychopaths. Psychopaths have no empathy, and they have no guilt, and they are perfect liars. Perfect. Because they simulate emotion, and they do it from the crib, you may not get any intuitive red flags when you meet them. They're super charming, and apparently very self-aware. But there's one place where intuition works – that is in multi-person interviews.

For example, if you have three people interviewing your psychopath, and one of them is pretending to be or is the key decision-maker, because psychopaths can only truly simulate empathy for one person at a time, the other people in the room will intuitively feel off. They'll sense that something's wrong because they're not getting that connection. The person your psychopath identifies as the boss will, on the other hand, be getting love-bombed to death. That's the best test that I've been able to come out to filter out psychopaths.

Bill is right to be concerned. While the number of psychopaths among the general population is only 1%, one in five corporate leaders have high levels of psychopath traits. While they are clearly not clinical cases, their behaviors include being manipulative, dishonest, volatile, low in empathy but loving power and control; worst of all they are toxic to manage and terrible with their teams.

People with psychopathic tendencies are members of the sinister-sounding "dark triad." That also includes narcissists, who show off and are great at managing first impressions, and Machiavellians, who are happy to lie and kiss up at interview. Even if they don't experience clinical problems, they can cause terrible havoc in their organizations. All of them show coolness under pressure and they love an interview, after all, they're discussing their favorite topic – themselves. Hire one and they'll spend their time putting their needs first, self-promoting, and stalking the corridors of power.

That's why it's important to really probe what you hear particularly around their colleagues and co-workers for whom they will have less empathy or consideration. Notice inconsistencies or discrepancies and pick up on them: people with dark triad attributes are less likely to be consistent, which is where multiple interviews are useful.

Tip: Simply ask yourself during any interview, "What am I seeing and not seeing with this person?" then notice what comes to mind.

When you listen to your intuition, you're more likely to bring in the right people, as telco senior executive Dr Matthews Mtumbuka found:

Recently I was recruiting quality assurance engineers. I was given four candidates to pick two. They were all ranked using a methodology, so I wasn't expected to pick number three or four. But as I was interviewing number four, I felt she was the best candidate. Intuition helps you dig deeper, and that's what I did. I said, "I'll be honest with you, you weren't recommended you were number four, but something tells me you're the best candidate." Naturally she said, "Well I am" and I said, "Can you prove it?" She told me to call this engineer, so then and there I did: she got a great recommendation. To cut a long story short, we changed the outcome and hired her.

She's been amazing: my business has problems with fuel cartels, and she unravelled the biggest one, revealing exactly what was happening. She's been a great hire and that was intuition adding value in the recruiting process. I think it's helpful to mix analytical and intuitive methods for best results.

If you're an expert like Matthews, you can identify the things that will make someone good at their job even if it's hard to articulate exactly what they are.

Tip: At the end of an interview and before chatting to any colleague who might have also been with you, take a breath. Notice what arises when considering this particular candidate. What is or isn't attractive about them? Why? What feelings are you aware of? What images come to mind? Sounds? Impressions? Metaphors? How would you feel about a six-hour car journey with them? Or introducing them to someone you greatly respect?

Even if you're a new manager, bring others in your team into your recruitment process. Not only does it help them acquire this important skill, but they'll develop their intuition in the process as well.

Helping others develop their intuition

One of the biggest tasks you have as a leader is to support the professional development of your team members. You want them, whatever their role, to problem-solve and make decisions as effectively as possible. While of course you'll focus on developing their hard and soft skills, you'll also want them to recognize and use their intuition so that they can make better choices and contribute to the team using their intuitive abilities too.

When you start, you'll find that people who don't think that they are at all intuitive in fact use intuition a lot, they just don't recognize it. Meanwhile colleagues who you think would be highly intuitive sometimes struggle. Whatever they're doing, you can broach the topic by inviting them to consider times at work when they successfully used their intuition; if they can't identify anything, ask for examples in their private life. They don't need to give you specifics, just to recall the experience. What you want to do is highlight that their feeling of knowing is nothing new, it just provides useful information that can help them work faster and better.

Then ask them where their intuition sits. Is it in their bones? heart? guts? brain? hands? blood? A sense of alignment? Expansion or contraction? Or some combination of all of them? Feel free to use any of the descriptions or stories from this book to help you. It's important that you remember what your team member tells you, so that when they want help with a decision or problem, you can use their language and experience a reminder to hook back to.

If they truly don't know, that's something to ask them to start to notice. How do they recognize a good choice? Or that one option is better than another? Is it that something appears more attractive and brighter in their mind's eye? Sounds more appealing in their mind's ear? Or just feels better?

Once someone is aware of their body-mind process, I also recommend sharing stories of how your intuition has worked and not worked for you. That way you're making it safe for someone to try and to fail. Ideally, you then coach someone as they practice the skill using their real-time problems or decisions. You do that by asking questions like:

- What's your gut feeling about this?
- What's is your intuition telling you to do?
- If I wasn't here and you had to decide, what would you do?
- If you were in my position, what do you think I'd say?

Tip: Don't offer immediate answers to their issues even if there's a silence or someone needs to go away and think. If people don't grapple with their own problems, they'll become dependent on you, and you'll become your own bottleneck. In addition, your direct report won't grow their own intuitive muscle or learn to trust their own answers. And having confidence in your own process is the most important part of intuition.

You'll know that the work you're doing is successful when team members start to come to you with decisions that they would like to take based not just on data, but on intuition too. Here's Hal Reisiger, CEO of Cosworth:

I try to foster intuition in our executive team and if members of the executive team really feel strongly about something, even if I feel nervous, I'm ready to offer them what I call a "gimme." That means I don't get it and what they suggest is making my antennae go up. But if they feel that strongly about it, and it's within what I think is an acceptable risk profile, let's do it. I want to encourage a learning-based intuition, where over time as we all get more and more experienced, our intuition gets better and better.

Tip: Encourage team members to use intuition by looking down on a situation as if they were up on a balcony. What's going on? What draws their attention? Appears to be in the dark? Feels better? This shouldn't feel like a tough task, just something to relax into and notice.

Finding and setting direction in life and at work

Finding and setting direction takes place in both personal and professional contexts. The latter will never feel right if the former doesn't, and you'll be much more likely to second-guess what you're doing. That's when it's time to sit down and take stock.

Direction in life

From time to time everyone questions what they are doing and where they are going, particularly around rough times or illness, at the end of a relationship, after being let go, or doing a job that isn't fulfilling. Finding that direction can feel really difficult; then it's important to remember that everyone questions themselves from time to time. Paula McKenzie, CEO of Pizza Hut UK, offers great guidance to find your direction in life.

> *Working out what's important to you is easier said than done. I think there are two ways: one is going to the end of your life, to the 80-year-old you on a rocking chair and ask, "What is true?" It's important to do this multiple times – I was 27 when I first attempted it, and the only things that would surface then were feelings, I couldn't articulate anything else. There was a sense of warmth, which made me then think at I'll buy an apartment, or I spend part of the year in a warm country. I will be a grandmother: at this point I was unmarried and didn't have kids. The third thing that came through is, I'm well-regarded for what I do; I've put a lot of work and time into my career.*
>
> *Those three things helped me make sure I have warmth in my life: I didn't know then quite how much I need that. I also married my boyfriend and had children. My career is a very important to me and so I've kept following that through – I want to fulfill my potential over time. Envisioning the 80-year-old you helps you walk towards what you want to be true.*
>
> *If that's too difficult, start with what feels like – at least from where you are right now – a step in a direction that you sense is good. You might not know where it's going, but it should feel like a step in the right direction in some way. I think if you combine thinking about your direction and feeling your way, you end up with a life that makes sense.*

Tip: When you've done this a few times, notice what your feeling of knowing is telling you. Sense your energy and what feels lighter and brighter. But if you're really stuck and nothing comes to mind, consider this: "if my life depended on it, what would I now do?"

Tip: Projecting yourself into the future to guide you in the present is also a proven way of building resilience. You can deal with a lot more adversity if you know that you're on the right track and that what you're doing is meaningful to you.

Here's how you can put that in place in your work context.

Setting direction at work

Whenever you start a new role, whether you're running a large organization, a small team at the coal face, or simply deciding what project you want to work on next, you're making choices about what's needed and where to best invest your time and energy. And while it's exciting, there's always a frisson and the thought, "Well, where do I begin?"

Whether it's finding organizational direction or kick-starting a project, you have to identify trends, patterns, connections, trade-offs, what's working, what isn't, and potential wins, without getting too bogged in detail or overly worried about how you'll do it. Here's Victoria Wallace, retired non-profit CEO, explaining how she went about finding and setting the direction for the organizations she led, using a technique from the diplomatic service where she started her career.

> *In the Foreign Office [the UK State Department], as a newly appointed head of mission within a month of getting to a new country you had to write a first impressions dispatch. That meant taking stock and setting out what you thought the current situation and the priorities were. And it's a really useful discipline.*
>
> *I did it in every job I took on after I left because I realized that when you start a new job, you have all this information coming at you in a very unfiltered way. You've got a lot of people putting their case for things that they've wanted changed or that they hate. You have to distill it all down very quickly, but at the start you have much more ability to see clearly. You can do so without prejudice because you don't know much about the place and you're picking up this stuff in a very raw and natural way. You're having to make some gut-related visceral decisions about what's important, what to accept, and what to move forward with.*

If you wait six months to define where you're going, or six weeks to get a time-sensitive project off the ground, you're prevaricating. Your team will be restless and, because everyone hates a vacuum, people will start to jostle for their preferred options. Mostly it's fear of doing the wrong thing that gets in the way, but it's much better to decide and move on, rather than spend forever trying not to make a mistake.

That's at the start of a new job or project. Then there are the times that you'll want a reboot or reset. When you notice that your organization or team is caught up in excuses for why change is too hard, or you hear, "We tried that before," or "It will never work around here," check with your gut if you need to act. Leaders often put this off because it involves confronting what you see and talking about fault lines. Those are intense conversations, and because of that, they often take place far too late or are avoided altogether.

On the other hand, if your team is simply stale, you need new input. Encourage everyone to meet people in adjacent or partner industries, go to conferences they wouldn't usually attend, research a new topic, or do a short program at business school, and share their new knowledge. Bring people, facilitators or speakers, into meetings and wrap their thinking into the conversation. It's engaging with new material that generates ideas and intuitions, not just sitting listening to it.

That's also why it's important to talk to employees at the sharp end of your business because you'll learn so much more as vice admiral, ex-CEO, and board member Paul Boissier points out.

> As a leader it's important to open your mind and get information from everywhere. Don't just sit at your desk but walk around, go out, visit, and listen to people. it's amazing what you hear. You don't just hear their life stories, you hear about how they're all getting on with their colleagues, what their perceptions are of the work that you as the boss are doing, how things play out or could be better. You get so many more invaluable feeds into your decision making.

Tip: When you meet with people you don't usually interact with around your organization, you start to pick up on weak signals, those early warning signs of an impending problem, or trivial throwaway details that unlock important intuitions. They're the intuitive puffs of smoke crossing your internal horizon. When two or three of those come together, they indicate that you've got a signal not mere noise and are invaluable if you're sensing that you need a new direction or simply to course correct. If you're not sure what the signals might mean, try putting them into various stories. Then consider which story makes most sense to you before sharing it with someone else.

Tip: If you're trying to make choices about direction and your head is full, or you're feeling emotional, take a break because both will override your intuitive abilities. Then try summarizing the pros and cons of any options you've generated while checking with your feeling of knowing as you do this. See what you notice.

One thing is sure: whatever path you take and wherever you work, you'll have to manage change and deal with transformation: the world moves too fast for anything to stay static.

Managing change and transformation

Every organization everywhere tackles the same massive headache. That's how to deliver today's product or service better through defined projects which is change management. And at the same time they are getting ready for big tech advances, regulatory shifts, new social needs, and emerging competition. This is transformation – reinventing the way an organization does business through a series of complex interdependent initiatives. This combination means employees face simultaneous incremental and radical adjustments to the way they work.

Both are ideally suited to intuition where patterns and themes are emergent, and timing is critical. Wait too long and you miss the moment and risk being left behind. Move too fast and at best people can't keep up, at worst they get overloaded, burned out, or quit because they can't take on anymore. Go too slow and you get just the same, but because people are bored and fed up dealing with unresolved problems.

Pace is something that applies to all individuals, teams, and organizations and represents the speed at which you make progress and achieve your goals. Obviously, pace is dynamic because it depends on what's going on internally and externally, but it isn't about the complexity of what you're doing or the approach you take. It's more about the ability to deal with what's new and unfamiliar in a consistent solutions-focused way.

At an organizational level, pace is strongly connected with the management style of the core leadership team, particularly its leader. Every organization has a pace tolerance sweet spot which not only has to do with the senior leadership team but also the culture and behaviors that are valued. For example, the pace of a start-up will be very different to that of a bureaucracy.

Dame Louise Makin, ex-CEO of BTG Pharmaceuticals plc, chair and board member, explains how she sees it:

One of the things you do as a CEO is set the pace and that's a particularly important part of your job. The organizations I'm involved with are always moving – hopefully forward. Pace setting is something I realized and honed because you can either overtask or undertask and both are equally as bad. I use intuition a lot there.

Obviously, I gather data, but I have an image in my mind of a surfer when a wave is just getting to the top and it's almost breaking, but not quite and sometimes it seems to go on for ever. That image of course has nothing to do with the data, but my intuition is that this is the time to really push on the next question, on the next level, so let's paint a picture of that. Then I invite people to go there.

Louise's perfect wave is a fantastic metaphor for organizational readiness which means that the moment is right to introduce the next steps. But knowing that takes intuition because some people and teams will be ready and willing, while others never will be. There are winners and losers in every change or transformation.

To think about readiness, consider these coaching questions:

- How energized do employees feel to me?
- Hand on heart, can I get my key players to truly come with me?
- If we push on now, what will we gain? And is it worth it?
- If we push on now, what will we lose? And is that worth it?

Then think about what signs would indicate that you're moving too fast, too slow or are in a Goldilocks zone, so you can gauge pace. And of course, you'll need to listen to your people if they tell you they are struggling; here's CEO Hal Reisiger again:

One time, I was a new VP of Ops at this company and this whole situation was a train wreck. I wanted to fix everything at once, and thought it was no problem. One of the guys on the team came up to me, and he says, "I've got to be honest with you. Your brain is moving faster than any of us can execute. We're so far behind you, we just don't get how you want to do all this." I said, "OK" – because for me when people give you feedback, you sort things out.

We ended up prioritizing the improvements, and actually it worked out great. I'm constantly reflecting on those past experiences because I want my team to learn from them.

Hal's correct on two counts: what you're aiming for is a pace that maintains motivation and momentum while considering everyone's capacity to get stuff done. And sharing your experience helps others learn and means they don't need to make your mistakes.

Tip: On the flip side of the coin, if you're bogged down and need to generate pace, remember that while everyone may need a voice in the process, not everyone has to agree. When you're having discussions about direction or pace, dive into options and choices because robust discussion creates a sense of energy. Moreover, you create alignment if you check you're seeing issues from all angles.

Tip: People also complain a lot about doing difficult things, but they love having done them – a bit like a workout. Where intuition is really helpful is in understanding if there are real pain-points or it's just grumbling as everyone gets to grips with the next change process.

You'll get the best results when managing change or transformation when you bring your team in and leverage everyone's intuition.

Leveraging team intuition

The idea of group intuition is a relatively new one even though intuitions often happen when you're with other people. Team intuition isn't about brainstorming. It's about an emergent and collective understanding or decision generated through conversation between group members. That fresh approach only happens when everyone gets together.

There's a great body of new research showing that intuition in team settings brings a bunch of benefits. That includes recognizing threats and opportunities more easily, working together more effectively, managing turbulent conditions better, interpreting information faster and more efficiently, as well as increasing shared knowledge. It also helps with the human side of teamwork. Studies show that using collective intuition improves everyone's experience of a team, leads to greater feelings of empowerment, and builds more trust – including when working virtually.

Most excitingly, team intuition can give you sustained competitive advantage because it can be applied to strategy, the knottiest of issues. Just to be clear. This isn't about ignoring data or evidence. It's about combining intuition with analysis and intentionally using both as a group to arrive at quality decisions, as Fabrice Beaulieu, chief marketing and sustainability officer at a FTSE 10 corporation, illustrates:

A few years ago, I had a reinvention job to do on a business unit, and I had this intuition that going back to what we'd done in the past wasn't going to work. There were all these little signals that the Zeitgeist had changed: people were worrying about ingredients, worrying about transparency, and starting to talk about plastic. I took a group of leaders to Cambridge University, and we started to understand better why sustainability was the right space to be looking at.

Just as we were getting into this sustainability journey, I also thought that the teams needed to build extra muscles on digital. I got a recommendation from someone who told me, "You need to see this professor at IMD in Lausanne as he approaches digital very differently." We created another program for leaders where this professor took us through concrete cases showing how forward-looking businesses transform. We had a collective epiphany there because all these digital stories started with a redefinition of the purpose of the company. All of them had thought through the difference they wanted to make and used technology – digital to bring that to life.

The Cambridge journey and the IMD journey came together meaning we recognized that sustainability was the challenge we had to crack (and a big opportunity), the purpose our North star, and digital a powerful enabler. It had a massive influence on where we took our brands and business.

This team and their organization emerged with a new strategic direction from using both intuitive and rational processes. If teams rely on analysis alone, they often get bogged down in irrelevant data; if they rely on just intuition, they don't take relevant information into account. The point is to oscillate intentionally between both. If you adopt this practice as a team principle, you're more likely to catch possible contradictions, and to avoid bias because you keep resetting what you're doing. Best of all you're more likely to develop new combinations that everyone can intuitively check on.

When teams combine intuition and analysis, they are more successful because they make the best decisions, and there are multiple papers outlining that. Intuitions that come from a team leader or subject matter experts are helpful when there's a crisis and you want a speedy decision. But the risk is that individuals don't take the group with them; if things don't work out, they'll be the ones carrying the can.

The good news is that team intuition can be developed and leveraged. To make it happen, you first need to create the context for it.

Creating the context for intuition to flourish in a team setting

As a reminder, when anyone around you talks about their opinions, feelings, senses, insights, heart, gut, shares doubt or danger, or uses words like "maybe," "should," and "would" to describe outcomes, that's most likely their intuition speaking. And you want it in the room to enable better decisions, but you can't force it. Nevertheless, there are two main drivers that help: you need to know each other well enough, and everyone needs to feel they can speak up. Both are fundamentally about trust; the former in each other, the latter in a team's process.

Trust matters. You don't get real with someone you don't know, or at least until you have found some shared values or common goals. While you're gauging someone's or a group's trustworthiness, you tend to self-edit, meaning you don't share potentially important information. And I don't necessarily mean the big stuff: often it's more about weak signals which often stack up to indicate something much more important. Building trust means spending time together to hear each other's skills, strengths, and stories. These interactions matter because, as Professor Uri Hasson has shown, and as I mentioned in Chapter 1, they build shared inter-brain activity between different listeners.

But it goes even further than that. Here's one experiment that had three stages to it. First, participants lay in an fMRI scanner to watch part of a TV show with exciting plot twists. Second, one person was recorded recounting what they'd seen while being scanned again. Third, people who hadn't seen the show then listened to that recording while in a scanner. You'd think that watching a video clip, remembering, or imagining it are very different processes but in fact, scientists found shared patterns of brain activity.

This brain-syncing effect also takes place when people intentionally cooperate. For example, it's been seen between pilots in joint flight simulations, when individuals are asked to collaborate in a lab, and even when people are simply told, "You are part of the same team." And recent research shows that it also happens – no surprise – when working online. What it results in is better performance, greater empathy, more rapport, increased feelings of connectedness, and enhanced engagement. You feel on the same wavelength, because you are.

It means that leaders who remind people that they are a team, and take the time to get to know each other are more likely to create the conditions for group intuitions to arise. That's the first driver.

Here's the second.

You'll always hold back if you don't feel psychologically safe. Psychological safety means simply knowing that you can be you in a group. You won't be put down for speaking up, you can ask silly questions without worrying about looking stupid, and that you can say what's on your mind. You know if you make a mistake, it won't be held against you. When I'm coaching a team, any leader who tells me, "They don't work well as a group" is often saying, "We haven't yet got a climate of psychological safety." Psychological safety enables constructive disagreement between team members as well as encouraging everyone to share and exchange information.

If you've got a hunch but don't feel you can put it into the room, you won't have collective conversations that generate the best insights, ideas, or decisions. Sitting on your hands and holding your tongue generally means you've prioritized feeling comfortable over risk-taking. If you do this, you'll probably notice that there's a gap between what you feel and what you say. But if everyone does this, you'll leave your meetings feeling dissatisfied because you won't have real conversations or won't do genuine work. If you're not willing to share half-formed ideas that catalyze new ones, it's unlikely you'll be a high-performing team: Google's research back in 2016 showed that psychological safety is the one thing that the best teams have in common.

Tip: If you want to ensure psychological safety, all you need to do is adopt some straightforward behaviors. These involve sharing airtime equally, everyone contributing, showing empathy for how others are feeling, admitting what you don't know, no interrupting, and summarizing to show you've heard. If you think about it, it's the behavior you'd expect of anyone you want a decent relationship with. It doesn't mean being nice, and it's fine to disagree but it is about trying to keep your ego out of the room. It also involves building self-awareness so that if you're a team leader, people don't read your stress or seniority as, "I don't want to listen to this person."

You can get everyone to help with psychological safety if, when sharing ideas, everyone prefaces what they say with, "This isn't a fully formed idea" when that's the case. It stops other people from criticizing and encourages everyone to build on ideas instead.

Tip: When getting to know each other, don't just share successes, also share failures and near-misses because vulnerability is bonding. And share some simple stuff too, like favorite foods, restaurants, pets, vacations, and outings because similarities create connection.

Once you know each other and collaborate well enough, and that's something you'll judge by gut, then can start to work intentionally with intuition.

Combining collective intuition and analysis

If you're going to get a team working on any problem, you need to start by making sure you're tackling not just the right issue but the right question. Way too often groups jump in without taking the time to clearly articulate and agree the precise question they are answering. If you're lucky, it emerges during the process and, if you're unlucky, well, further down the line. As an aside, when I'm coaching teams, I can spend hours working on the right questions. But if you don't get them right you waste time and frustrate people.

Let's imagine you've nailed your question. Whether you're working on strategy or sorting out a thorny operational problem, you are going to get contrary information which will cause tension. For example, you might have two equally good solutions to a problem, three equally great markets to open up, or your data tells you one thing but intuition another. It's easy in these cases for people to take sides, arguments to get entrenched, and rows to ensue.

If you want to avoid fallouts, it's important not just to discuss choices which is what usually happens, but to think through scenarios and allow time to intuit consequences. In practical terms that means doing a lot of "if ... then" thinking. If there are some gritty conversations, great, because that's how you refine ideas and get better outcomes. The result of working like this is that it's easier for everyone to accept decisions and live with them without getting defensive or wanting payback next time. Moreover, this is the real work of a team and what makes it gel.

Once you've done that and got options and possibilities on the table, it's the time to make a deliberate switch between analysis and intuition. The benefit is that you'll be more likely to avoid groupthink or bias and get to a quality decision. Here are a few helpful questions to get everyone's juices going: people don't need to answer all of them; they are simply prompts.

- What are you feeling or sensing about our options?
- What's your gut telling you?
- What weak signals, symbols, or analogies come to mind?
- What do you want to share right now?

Tip: If you prefer, you can also start any decisional meeting with an intuitive check-in around the options before you analyze them. Doing this means you get some useful working hypotheses which you can prove or disprove with analysis. Just remember to get the most influential team members to speak last, because the social pressure they exude can suppress others' correct intuitions.

Tip: Before jumping into individuals' intuitive perceptions, I recommend having a few minutes' quiet reflection. That way everyone can more easily work out what their intuition is telling them. Then invite everyone to share specific sensations, thoughts, physical reactions, or impressions with each other. This should spark more conversation, which will take everyone to another level. You can then summarize what's been said as you move into your next stage of your analysis.

Keep intentionally switching between analysis and intuition, returning to the questions listed above until you feel you are done, or the decision is obvious.

Tip: At the end of your meeting, it's interesting to also reflect on the overall switching process to generate further personal and collective insights.

The best thing about working in this way is that the quality of the conversation changes in a remarkable way. And when that takes place what you instantly get are much tighter relationships between team members: I've observed that happening so many times. It's also worth remembering that all discussions and decisions will evoke feelings and sensations whether you like it or not. And those feelings and sensations evolved for a reason: to find answers. When you leverage this as a group, you have powerful, valuable, and bonding way of working that delivers first rate decisions.

It's a pity that this is so often wasted.

Calling it a day

I'm sure that, even if your career has been relatively short, you've seen zombie projects, programs, or even business units that shouldn't exist. And I'm guessing that you've also worked with people who should have been fired. Perhaps, like me, you've also hung on to a job for too long. But when is the right moment to pull the plug on a project? To let someone go? To quit a job? That's when you need intuition around timing.

Take projects. Zombie projects which will never go anywhere, are evidence of sunk cost, emotional attachment, and perhaps a dash of ego getting in the way of sensible decisions. There's a ton of research showing just how much leaders are loath to kill failing programs or disband teams even when there are more profitable new opportunities. Often executives or sponsors with a track record of success think that it will all work out fine if only everyone put more effort in. But if you were to ask everyone in the team individually, "Should this project continue?" you'd get a resounding, "No." This disconnect means cash and morale going down the drain as work staggers on over weeks, months, and even years. During that time, the team will most often try to tackle the question, "How do we save this project?" not "How do we kill it?"

Here's Jana Bennett, who I interviewed when she was president of A+E Networks History channel.

> *I've failed more than I've succeeded but no one sees that. You have to trust your judgment when making big strategic decisions, and sometimes you have to put*

your babies – programs or projects – out on the mountainside to die. That's very hard when a lot of effort and money is behind them. When you say no to one thing, you say yes to something else.

And that's the point. To think about what you're saying no to if you continue and what you'd be saying yes to if you stop. Failing projects suck the joy out of work, make you feel stuck, less creative, and trapped, while waiting for something to change never makes anything better. If you think a project needs canning, imagine how you'd feel working on something that truly added value for you and your organization. In contrast, project forward another 18 months and think about continuing to do the same thing. What repeated conversations would you be having with close colleagues, friends, and family? What would your biggest regret about either choice be? Tune into what your body-mind knows as you think through your options. If you're not clear, flip back through Chapter 5 because most of the tools in it will help you explore what your intuition is telling you.

If you are going to bite the bullet and call it as you see it, think through different ways of achieving your project's original objectives. Regardless of your opinion, the more helpful and positive you are, the easier it is for everyone around you to hear what you have to say.

That's projects. Then there's firing someone. Every leader I've ever coached at some point has hung onto a bad hire for longer than they should, trying to make it work. I've done it too. You can see that your team member's performance isn't up to scratch, you take on or divide up some of their tasks, and invest much more time than you'd like in helping them succeed. And they still don't get it. So, you agonize about what to do. Do you fire them? Is now the right time? Is someone better than no one especially if there's a hiring freeze? What will it cost to keep them? Or to get rid of them? How will you get through the next major deadline and the one after that? What's the current and future impact on the team?

It's a particularly hard decision if someone is just bumping along. There's nothing terrible, no sackable offense has taken place, but you certainly don't see anything great in terms of what they deliver. So, you wait, hoping for things to improve. Perhaps you collect impressions from colleagues and stakeholders, which is a good thing to do because it will help guard against any bias you might have. Then you give more feedback and coaching. Well, here's the steer. If you have an inkling, also known as an intuition, that you should let your employee go, you're probably right.

Tip: You know for sure that this person should leave if you think this imaginary situation through. Visualize your employee coming to tell you that they've been poached then consider just how hard would you fight to keep them. Or in fact would it be a terrific relief? Now picture your dream team. Hand on heart, can you say that this employee is truly part of it? Then think about how heavy it feels to carry this person on a scale of 1–10 and how light you'd feel if they weren't there. Finally, imagine what your partner would say if you came home and said you'd bitten the bullet and had a tough conversation. Are your nearest and dearest just as fed up with your employee as you are?

If there's good research showing that people hang onto weak employees for too long, both psychology and economics reveal that most people tend to stay too long in a job. And when you stay too long, it's easy to get in the way of your intuition.

Here's ex-CEO Victoria Wallace again.

> One of the reasons I left Leeds Castle after 10 years was that I stopped trusting my own intuition. It was such a cyclical business and however much I loved it, we were, for example, planning next year's Christmas before we'd done this year's. Even if I thought the hunch for this year would work, we could never really be sure, and we'd just have to double down on it to see.
>
> With time I didn't trust my intuition as much as I had, and I would second guess myself. I don't know whether that was out of boredom by the fact that I'd talked about and rejected ideas, or I'd done it all before. I think I made less good decisions at the end than I did at the start when I knew when something was or wasn't right.

If you've started to second-guess yourself and been in a job a while, it may be time to think about your next steps. Typically, we put it off recognizing all the hard work that lies ahead. And we worry about what others will think of us, tied up in the idea that winners never quit – which is tosh and faulty thinking. The most successful people have quit, failed, or changed course to get somewhere better. And framing something as quitting isn't helpful; I much prefer to think of this as knowing when to move on or pivot in your career.

As James Fearnley-Marr, senior communications executive, says:

> I really don't like the phrase "Never give up." It's vacuous and bad advice. If I'd tried to be a professional football player and someone said, "Never give up," that would have been terrible because I wouldn't have made it. Sometimes it's right to give up, to walk away and recognize this is going nowhere. Or not where you wanted. It's your guidance to pivot, and that's how you move towards your own success.

Of course, the best time to look elsewhere is when everything's going well. New opportunities have a different feeling to them when you're positive and optimistic than when you're bored and fed up. Moreover, it's easy to rush into a suboptimal choice if you've been let go, so it's worth knowing what a great opportunity feels like when your energy and enthusiasm are in good shape.

What's the right moment to leave, other than noticing that your intuitions are off? It's time to go if that's coupled with a lack of enthusiasm and energy for the business or finding that achieving your goals is less relevant to you. If you get out of bed with a sinking sensation, without experiencing any joy or fun in your day, it's the right moment to leave. If you're canceling meetings because you can't be bothered or if you feel that you're stagnating and not doing anything new, start looking for another role. If you're in constant fights with your boss or your team and feel unhappy without seeing a way out – all of these are indicators that now's the moment to find something else. It's a winning strategy to stop the fight and the good news is that it's associated with better health, less stress, and more sleep.

That's all well and good if you know you want out. But what if you're unsure about taking a new direction or a role elsewhere? Or feel you can't because of financial responsibilities you might have? In cases like this, here's what Paula McKenzie advises:

> *Give yourself a phase, a research and development phase, say to yourself, "I am going to take six months, six weeks or six days – time to form a view and make a decision." It takes the pressure off deciding tomorrow, the next day, or the day after. And it stops you driving you, your family, friends, and loved ones mad with, "What do you think, what do you think?"*

> *In my last role, I had to decide to relocate to Dallas. It was a huge life decision. I gave myself six to nine months to figure it out, and I reached my conclusion. You distil down to what's important and how you're going to make the decision by, like a scientist, examining the variables. Look at them, go research them, talk to people, visit, try everything on to understand what you think. And get in touch with your head-heart as you sit with it all. By just really living with it for a bit, you see what you're gravitationally pulled to and suddenly everything slots into place.*

That gravitational pull is your intuition. It may take you a bit of time and that's fine. What isn't, is stressing out unable to decide because that won't contribute to your success. Success is the by-product of investing in what gives you joy.

You could also consider Steven Levitt's work. He's the economist who wrote *Freakonomics* and a few years ago he built a website for people struggling with big decisions. The most common question was, "Should I quit my job?" To start with, everyone had to answer a series of questions to check that they truly couldn't decide and would be happy to live with the results of a virtual coin flip. At that point, the coin got flipped and their choice was made for them. All the participants were followed up two and six months after their decision. Individuals whose coin toss told them to quit were more satisfied with their decisions and happier at both two and six months later, than those who'd been told to stick with the status quo.

Tip: If you're uncertain about quitting or canning any project, firing an employee, or leaving your job, ask yourself, "What's the worst that could happen?" And then, "How likely is that?" Check in with your feeling of knowing as you ponder both questions. Once you've done that, project forward to what might happen if you do nothing and what the best outcomes might be if you take action. You should feel a pull from one direction or the other.

Just remember that if you're hesitating about calling something a day, it's highly likely that that's the right thing to do.

Conclusion

Being a leader right now is hard. While others will have expectations of you, you'll have much bigger ones of yourself as you put out fires and problem-solve multiple tricky issues that come out of nowhere. Your success will ultimately rest on the decisions you make either alone or with others. Some of them will be easy, others much less so, which is why intuition matters as an additional tool. It helps you make better decisions in less time particularly when there aren't obvious choices.

But it's not just about better decisions, it's also about actively avoiding bad ones because there's clear research that shows that suppressing intuition leads to worse results whether you're an individual or a team. When you're using your intuition well, you avoid crises, pick up on confusion, recognize discomfort, and become more confident in yourself.

However, sometimes everyone loses sight of what should come naturally. When you're struggling as a leader and feel that you can't get a handle on what to do, that's when to turn to your intuition. It's always there to serve you, and it's one of the most vital and unique components that makes you, you. Use it to build your leadership competitive edge.

Summary and next steps

Top takeaways

- Hiring others is ideally suited to using your intuition. And if you have a hunch that someone won't work out, listen to it.
- Finding and setting direction is often easier when you come to something without too much knowledge and you're forced to use your intuitive skills.
- Pacesetting depends a lot on the culture and a leader; too fast and too slow are equally bad, while both rely on intuitive feel.
- Team intuition depends on knowing each other well and good group processes. When you problem-solve together, try moving intentionally between intuition and rational analysis for the best results.
- Most people don't listen to their intuition early enough when it comes to canning a bad project, firing someone, or leaving a job.

Read

- Campbell, A.F. (2016) Considering a big change? Go for it says evidence from 20,000 coin flips, *The Atlantic*
- Codou, S., Williams, D.W., & Fuller, R.M. (2022) The forms and use of intuition in top management teams, *The Leadership Quarterly*
- Fuller, J., et al. (2023) 40 ideas to shake up your hiring process, *Harvard Business Review*

Watch

- Barlett, S. (2021) Why quitting is important for success, BBC
- Eberhardt, J. (2020) How to check your unconscious bias, Global Goals
- Hasson, U. (2016) This is your brain on communication, TED

Listen

- Grant, A. with Edmondson, A. (2022) Is it safe to speak up at work?
- Qadar, S. (2021) Machiavellianism, and the "dark triad" of personality, ABC podcast
- Winfrey, O. (2022) Trust Yourself, Trust Your Power, Trust Your Intuition

7 Consciousness and its role in intuition

Consciousness is vital to the intuitive experience because what's unconscious and unavailable emerges into your awareness as an intuition. Moreover, there's an important interplay between intuition and unconscious thought. Loads of studies have shown if you put a tough problem aside to incubate, you get better answers. Meaning your unconscious plays an important role, not as the coke-head misogynist Freud said, as a repository of all unacceptable thoughts, but as a coordinator and integrator of large amounts of information. When the answer's ready, it moves into your consciousness, and you respond to it. And that happens in a way that ranges from fuzzy and hard to grasp, to feeling like a punch and clear as daylight.

How else do you experience this range?

Take fleeting intuitions that feel like they are on the fringes of consciousness. They tend to be less clear when you're overloaded or tired or your mental chatter is buzzing; signals get drowned out because you don't have the capacity to notice them. You can only become consciously aware of something when it's captured your attention and that happens when you experience something new, sudden, physical, or emotional, all of which are harder to perceive when you're out of energy.

The opposite of that is voluntary attention which is all about deliberately deciding what you want to focus on and for how long. Meaning you concentrate deliberately on the inner signals your mind or body sends you. Doing this allows you to become more attuned and sensitive to your intuitions.

That your intuitive experiences show up as a continuum isn't surprising because consciousness follows similar patterns. That means understanding your conscious states, recognizing, and experimenting with them can only help your intuitive abilities.

Without getting too precious about a definition, by consciousness I mean a constantly shifting personal awareness or perceptions of your thoughts, feelings, sensations, impressions, intuitions, and environment. Because consciousness allows you to access intuition, I'm going to look at two of the big answered scientific questions: where does it come from, and how does it work in different contexts?

So, here's a non-exhaustive take on both.

Recap and expansion

You already know from Chapter 1 that intuition seems to fall into three theoretical groups. There's personal intuition, which consists of what happens internally within yourself; that includes for example expert or moral intuition. This seems to be the result of the synchronization of self-organizing systems within our bodies. Those systems start with electrons, molecules, brain and organ coordination, working through to biology, physiology, and psychology. These hierarchical systems come together as part of a process that moves from unconscious to consciousness, and results in intuitions.

Then there's interpersonal intuition, which seems to encompass what happens between friends, family, and close colleagues. It's also based on your internal self-organizing systems but with the added principle of a strong enough connection that ensures you and others synchronize in a specific way: we know this from fMRI scans and it's also evidenced by behavior. You'll see the results, for example, in highly productive teamwork and those incredible coincidences when people seem to be connected at a distance.

Finally, there's extra-personal intuition, which includes non-expert intuition and precognition. Maybe, as others like Jung have suggested, there's an as-yet-unknown but synchronizing mechanism at work here too which we can't yet perceive as it's beyond our three-dimensional capacity and current scientific understanding. Yet we get hints that it's at work when we have precognitive dreams or anticipate future events. This isn't new: 2,000 years ago Plato said that our reality may be only a fragment of a greater reality based on our limited ability to perceive the world with five senses.

But Plato doesn't sit well with the Western world's scientific approach. That assumes that our underlying reality is a nihilistic universe which has no meaning or purpose. And this applies to you too. Everything is down to a chance accident, and consciousness essentially emerges from what's physical. That's a pretty depressing worldview but it's the central tenet of what's called materialism or physicalism.

At the opposite end of the philosophical spectrum is idealism. This suggests that consciousness is everywhere, that it's primary, that the universe has purpose, and that our minds are part of something greater than ourselves. Idealism perhaps chimes better with many people's lived experience and suggests that we could be independent, interconnected, and interdependent at the same time which is exactly how intuition seems to show up.

In short, intuition seems to suggest self-organizing systems that start with oneself, extends to others, and ultimately seems to transcend time and space.

In what way might consciousness help clarify this?

How is consciousness experienced?

Because the experience of consciousness is intensely subjective, the only way to describe it is as a series of analogies. For Aristotle, consciousness was like a theater; for William James, the American psychologist, writing in the 1890s, it was like a river or a stream, which Buddhists also think; for David Chalmers, the philosopher, it's a movie that seems to be playing all the time in our heads.

But it can be experienced in many ways depending on your biology.

Kim Arnold, a communications and marketing consultant, finds it more of an abstract watercolor with colors and feelings: the yellows are bright and energetic, the blue-grays, calm and thoughtful. She has grapheme color synesthesia, so while she isn't hearing colors, tasting shapes, or feeling sounds, her lived experience is pretty different to most of us.

> When I was about 12, I was talking to my brother and I said, "You know how letters have colors in your head?" And I realized at that moment that not everyone saw things in quite the same way as I do, associating colors with letters, numbers, names, and words. For example, A is red, B is blue, C is yellow, and that hasn't changed; my brother tested me over a 10-year period and they were all the same.

> Sometimes I see a color with the word; sometimes the word is that color; sometimes it's very bright and sometimes it's hazy with bleached edges. It can also be quite a mix of colors: your name for example is pinky-purple.

> When I'm fresh, the colors are more vivid, but I use it to my advantage – the color connections make it easy to remember stuff. I do a lot of writing, and in the planning process, I often sit down in front of a whiteboard with a whole bunch of different marker pens and use color for inspiration as well.

The only way the rest of us would experience these amazing color associations would be with hallucinatory drugs.

When you indulge in weed, mescaline, LSD, magic mushrooms, MDMA, ayahuasca, and ketamine, colors seem brighter, and boundaries appear to merge. That's because areas of the brain which don't usually communicate, do so under the influence of these drugs.

But you don't have to take drugs; meditation can also lead to unusual experience. For example, yoga or Zen practitioners do specific exercises designed to break through ordinary consciousness to lose a sense of self. Practitioners describe their bodies merging with time and space into a single conscious experience, without borders, body awareness, or boundaries. They move out of a personal sense of awareness into an extra-personal one.

This is how Zen teacher, poet, and author Henry Shukman finds it.

> *The collapsing of boundaries is difficult to describe because you have to go through it to know it. But it is the sense that suddenly I have of not being isolated and never have been. It's as if there's another dimension. I'm used to being a 3-D person in a 3-D world, and suddenly I've found this other dimension that connects everything, that cuts through everything, so everything is participating in it.*

> *It's a sense that rather than my body being contained by my skin bag, my body is for example the sofa on the other side of the room, the rooftops, and the trees outside. It's like one body. It's not like I'm just a little part of it and I'm not separate from it. What I really am is just all of it. That's where boundaries have vanished. And it's not like we've got to get things to merge or something; it's more like the thing in us that makes us feel separate has temporarily evaporated. Then what's revealed is that we're part of everything. But that's weak, because there is this other level of our reality, in which we're already everything.*

> *It is fantastic to find it, because all our troubles are erased; all our troubles are predicated on being the separate thing. I believe it's a bona-fide level or register of consciousness. But even calling it consciousness isn't strong enough, because it is in fact a level of reality.*

The idea that everything can merge is a notion way beyond science's current understanding of consciousness; in fact, most scientists would deny that it exists. And yet it's something that practiced meditators, like Henry, regularly achieve.

By the way, even if mastery isn't your aim, research shows that meditation not only improves anxiety and mood disorders but leads to lasting brain changes at structural and functional levels. And this can happen after a mere 40 days of regular sitting. Moreover, meditation is known to help intuition because it calms the mind, allowing you to notice what you become conscious of.

And just like meditation, practicing intuitive thought improves it, something that's been known since the 1980s. That you can learn and get better at both shows that your conscious experience is something malleable because you can alter and change it.

Lucid dreaming belongs in the same bucket.

Lucid dreaming, hypnosis, and placebos

Science still can't really explain why we dream. But a major assumption in research terms has been that when you sleep you aren't conscious. Lucid dreams, which happen to about 20% of us, are a bit different. In a lucid dream, you know you're dreaming but can control what's going on, almost like an internal virtual reality. And experienced lucid dreamers can even indicate to researchers when they're lucid dreaming by moving their eyes left-right-left-right as rapid eye movement (REM) sleep starts. Amazingly, they can also even direct their dreams.

Here's how hypnotherapist Michael Carson describes it.

> I've had a lot of lucid dreams since I started hypnosis. I had one when I exactly saw the face of the person who would be teaching me the next day. It was a bit of a telepathic experience in fact. I had been anxious about attending a course, thinking everyone would be more experienced and knowledgeable than me. I went to sleep and was aware that I was dreaming. The course leader was telling me to come and that he was glad I was participating, that it would be good for me and for the others who would be there. The next day when I saw him, I was amazed because he looked just like he did in my dream.

> I use lucid dreaming with intention and write down things I want to work on. I do find that issues get resolved and a shift happens. I think it's the intention, if it's consistent and congruent with your goals, that your unconscious takes and works with. There's a communication happening in the unconscious – consciously.

Michael's experience is typical of lucid dreamers as it shows knowledge of facts, reasoning, and self-awareness, unlike ordinary dreams.

When I was writing about lucid dreaming, I decided to have a go; I found a YouTube video that explained that we are more likely to lucid dream after our third sleep cycle early in the morning. It also outlined how to tap two fingers gently while falling asleep. That night, I suddenly realized I was in a lucid dream as I was tapping my fingers on an old-fashioned Victorian gas light while standing in a darkened street. More curiously, I was awaiting a response. The YouTube instructions said to put a hand through an object or jump up and down to check that I was dreaming, and then to direct my dream both of which I unfortunately forgot to do.

Lucid dreaming is interesting because the dreamer is neither 100% awake nor 100% asleep, so it's a curious hybrid state in terms of consciousness. Plus, there are definable and measurable differences from waking and REM sleep, when normal dreams occur, and that's been confirmed by EEG analysis.

Hypnotism is yet another route to modified consciousness and, perhaps because it's directed by someone else, falls into the interconnected category of consciousness. And it's almost impossible to hypnotize someone who doesn't like you or doesn't want to be hypnotized, suggesting that interpersonal connection matters in the process.

Under hypnosis your sense of time disappears and your focus narrows making you more receptive to suggestions that lead toward personal goals. There are studies to show that it works to manage anxiety, stress, sleep, migraine, post-surgical recovery, childbirth, eating disorders, alcoholism, and even replacing analgesia during surgery. And none of this a merely a placebo effect.

But let's not diss placebos.

Placebos mean your mind convinces your body that a fake treatment is the real deal. And they can be just as effective as meds. Placebos have been found to work for pain, insomnia, nausea, fatigue, and even Parkinson's. Amazingly, even when people know they are taking a placebo, a significant number still experience a positive effect. That was shown in an experiment where participants felt less pain when given a blue cream and clearly told that it didn't contain any analgesics.

All this means is that there isn't one setting for consciousness: it can be directed, guided, and changed. And if you can do that with consciousness, you can do it with all kinds of intuition. What matters is improving what you notice, interpret, and remember along with an understanding of what makes it function better or impacts it for the worse. To do that, it's worth considering how consciousness shows up in unusual circumstances to see what you can glean from them.

These extraordinary circumstances are perhaps more useful to consider than brain neurology because whatever locations and circuits are involved, scientists can't explain how a mental experience emerges from a physical one. You can't prove what you're thinking or feeling, regardless of the areas that light up when you have an fMRI scan. I must take your word that you like or loathe a colleague, or that you think my idea dreadful or fabulous; all your brain will show is intense activity in similar areas for those very different reactions.

Nor can science yet describe how you can be conscious when there are no physical signs of it.

Consciousness isn't just when you're conscious

Someone in a coma shows no signs of being aware or awake and they have minimal brain activity. When they're in a vegetative state, they may open their eyes, but they aren't conscious as you or I would understand. They can't speak, move intentionally, show emotion, or communicate. But back in 2006, Adrian Owen, a neuroscientist at Cambridge University, did fMRI tests on a woman who had been in a vegetative state following a car accident. She was asked to imagine both playing tennis and walking through her home. Amazingly, the same areas of her brain lit up as in healthy patients, meaning that she was showing signs of consciousness. Since that research, about 10–20% of patients in a coma have also been found to have some level of consciousness. What this implies is that consciousness doesn't have switch-like properties that you turn on and off but instead is a kind of continuum.

Near-death experiences (NDEs) also cast a potentially very challenging light on some of the assumptions around consciousness. They happen most typically to people in cardiac arrest, who are near drowning, have attempted suicide, or experience birth or operative complications; most often they are lifeless for periods lasting between two and 10 minutes.

In this short time, there's no breathing, no pulse, no heartbeat, no reflexes, nor any demonstrable brain activity. That's because when the heart stops beating, within a second the brain stops working and the body stops functioning; for example, you can stick your fingers down someone's throat because the gag reflex isn't there anymore. Their eyes don't react to light, and they don't breathe.

After 15 seconds, the EEG flatlines, which means there's no electrical activity in the cortex. This is the beginning of the death process, and the only way to reverse it is to resuscitate the patient within those first 10 minutes.

Now traditionally consciousness is thought to be a product of brain function. Yet with no brain function whatsoever, about one in five people who've had an NDE also have experiences which they can describe afterward. That includes seeing what's happening to their body, reporting on conversations that took place, and recognizing the instruments that were used to treat them.

How?

In 2001, cardiologist Dr Pim van Lommel published research in the *Lancet* detailing a prospective study that he and his colleagues had carried out. A prospective study first documents the presence or absence of what's being investigated, then a patient comes in exhibiting symptoms; afterward they're asked about their experiences. Dr van Lommel had wanted to investigate his patients' NDEs and verify if their experiences were due to lack of oxygen, side effects of drugs, hallucinations, fear of death, or false memory syndrome.

The study found that around 20% of patients reported similar NDE elements: their pain was gone, they had no feeling in their bodies, they could see their own resuscitation, and report on critical details that were later corroborated. Most importantly, he found that there was no pharmacological or physiological explanation for their accounts.

Here's how Monica Hernandez, gardener and cook, described what happened to her:

I have three daughters all of them born in USA. When I had my youngest Camila, I had an incredible experience. All my daughters were born naturally so I was always aware of what was happening. But after giving birth to Camila, I was taken to the recovery room where usually there were from four to eight women recovering from childbirth, all of them medicated except me.

In the recovery room, nurses push your stomach to be sure that all the afterbirth comes out and when it does, they send you to your room. I was in that process, and I asked the midwife looking after me when was I going to my room. She told me I was doing great, that I was ready, and she was calling to get me taken to my room.

Then suddenly, I find myself in a dark tunnel and I can see a brilliant, beautiful silvery light at the end. It is life, love, euphoric, pleasure, happiness, oneness, everything that I was needing. It's hard to describe. But I immediately I think about my three beautiful daughters, and I realize that I can't stay, I must go back.

I return to consciousness, and I can only raise my right arm (my left arm is connected to an IV); a nurse sees me, lifts the cover, sees that my stomach that is huge, and when she pushes, all I hear is "flop squish." Next thing I know, I am out of my body, up on the ceiling watching what is happening and seeing everything. The nurse is panicking saying, "There's no blood pressure!" The other two nurses come running with fluid for the IV; they start inserting more drips to get fluid into me.

One of the nurses is shouting, "Code blue, code blue." I see a doctor running in. He says, "What's happening?" There's blood everywhere and the nurse answers, "She had a blood clot, I don't know how; she was fine a minute ago." I hear all this from up outside my body, seeing it below.

When I'd had enough fluid, and after they'd brought all the kit to bring me back and used it, I was then snapped back in my body; I opened my eyes and said, "What's happening?" The nurse answered, "Natural childbirth and Valium 5000!" But that experience was life-changing.

Monica's story is of course fascinating. But I also noticed my response to her; I found her very credible and moving. Talk to anyone who's had an NDE, and you'll probably be astonished and amazed too. But it leaves a puzzling question: in what way was she conscious? Your opinion will of course depend on your worldview: if you're rooted in the scientific approach, an NDE might be anathema to you, while if you're more attracted by personal experience you're perhaps more open to it.

Pim, who has studied thousands of NDEs, believes that consciousness is not a function of the brain. It can't be if someone unconscious is able to "see," "hear," and "feel" when all their senses are clinically unavailable to them. He believes it must exist somewhere else outside the human body, which is a profoundly different way of thinking. Here's what he said:

Consciousness is a non-local reality where time and space do not play any role. It's not in or of the body or mind; it's fundamental, primary, beyond time and space and everywhere. Like the Cloud. Say there are x billion websites and videos. They are always there but you need an encryption instrument to receive it. Downloading one doesn't preclude the others existing; it's the same with consciousness. There's a non-local information exchange and you receive information not by your senses or by your body. And when you've been through an NDE, the threshold of your consciousness changes permanently.

The parsimony principle is fundamental to all science and says that you choose the simplest scientific explanation that fits the evidence. Other than, "They were making it all up," which doesn't account for reported actions and

144

repeated conversations, the simplest explanation for NDEs is that an element of consciousness exists outside the physical body.

Interestingly, some theoretical scientists like Andrew Lohrey and Bruce Boreham suggest that perhaps the entire universe might be non-local, meaning that it's interconnected, integrated, and holistic. Perhaps that explains how extra- or interpersonal intuitions show up – those occasions when people shouldn't be able to know something but nevertheless, they do. Much like Western medicine can't explain Chinese meridians in acupuncture or prana in Ayurvedic tradition, are there unobserved channels or links that connect us to people with whom we have a close emotional relationship?

Take Taleah and Tiva Samaru, identical twins who know what's going on for each other when the stakes are high. Taleah, a procurement specialist, describes both a mental and a physical connection.

We both lived in Trinidad and Tobago, and then Tiva relocated to the United States about 10 years ago. Because we'd been at home together, living in the same space it wasn't as noticeable that we were that in tune. It was much clearer when we were separated. There are two things that happen; first, I get this feeling that maybe I need to check in. It just starts in my mind, and it keeps telling me to call, to touch base and see if everything's alright because mentally I'm feeling I need to.

If it's a physical thing and she's sick, that manifests physically for me too. My stomach can be hurting for no reason but then I realise and find out she isn't well. And it happens for her too. Tiva will message me and say, "My head was hurting today" and I'll say, "That's because I'm coming down with flu."

Here's how Tiva, an early childhood specialist, describes her connection.

Taleah had a really traumatic incident when we were teenagers. My parents actually asked me if I knew what was going on – I thought they meant telepathically. I said, "No," but in reality, I was feeling very, very sick in the guts, this profound uneasiness, but a very overwhelming sense of it. It was more of a conviction, maybe how a mother would feel about her child, but I felt it even deeper than that, because I knew something was wrong. They asked me if she was dead. I said, "No, she's not dead." The fact that I just knew symbolizes a connection.

There have been other times, like when she was about to go into labor with my nieces. I was getting unexplained random pains that were like period cramps, though my period wasn't due. I just knew. The reason it stands out is because she was on the East Coast at the time, and I was on the West Coast, but I was living her reality of the pains as she was experiencing them. I knew my nieces were there before she messaged me saying that they had been born.

Thousands of cases like this have been reported but these mental phenomena can't be quantified or localized.

Transplant patients may have something to add to the topic because they often feel they acquire some of their donors' personalities. Research papers reveal how these patients experience changes in food preferences, music, emotions, and even identity that align with their donors' lives. For example, Tim E described having a heart transplant from a 22-year-old donor in 2021. He was 59 at the time of the transplant and noticed on his return from hospital that unlike before, he wanted to chew gum, something he's never done, and use his right hand a lot. Both of these were attributes of his donor – Tim has been left-handed all his life.

Paul Pearsall and Gary Schwartz, who've published research on heart transplant patients, argue that these post-operative coincidences between donors and recipients are too detailed to be down to chance. They suggest that memory may not just lie within the brain and that cellular memory somehow plays a role. We know from immunology that cells retain memory; one hypothesis is that cells retain information from the organ's previous owners. But how that turns into a conscious experience is far from clear.

Then there's terminal lucidity or end-of-life rallies when people who really shouldn't show signs of consciousness somehow do. Medical professionals report that people with severe brain trauma or diseases, like advanced Alzheimer's, dementia, or glioblastoma, often appear to gain the power to communicate or even to have meaningful conversations shortly before they die when they haven't been able to talk for days, weeks, months, or even years. Autopsies confirm that these patients shouldn't have been able to communicate and yet they do.

Maggie Bisset, an end-of-life nurse consultant, describes one such experience.

I was called to intensive care where a woman had profound problems in terms of kidney failure and sepsis. She was going to die very soon indeed – we're talking about in the next hour or two: I knew that because of her breathing.

She murmured when you touched her but not in a coherent way. I sat with her and asked the staff, "Is there anyone who should be here familywise?" As soon as I said that her breathing become much more labored. The nurse with her said,

146

"We've been trying to get her son, he's on his way but his train got stuck. We think he'll be here in about an hour and a half." I explained, "Your son is on his way, he's having a delay on the train," and started to talk about the outside world. I said, "I'm going to stay with you because I want to and I get the impression that your son coming is crucial to you." She did another kind of moan. And I thought my goodness, how does this woman even communicate with us using her voice?

That hour was the longest hour because she really deteriorated and was shutting down, dying. Finally, he arrived and burst into the room saying, "Mum, I'm here." She just let out one of those amazing moans and opened her eyes. There was a flicker of a smile. At that moment, because we had the monitor on to check her pulse, she died. He sat on the bed and took her hand as we watched her pulse fade.

I don't think we understand people when they are in an unconscious state of mind because our understanding of consciousness is quite narrow. We as nurses see these meaningful coincidences at the end of life even when people are less conscious and approaching death. I like the metaphor of an archipelago: we're all a cluster of islands. I'm one, you're another but if you draw the water away, we're all deeply connected.

How consciousness operates at this point is far from obvious. It simply reiterates the fact that when it comes to consciousness and by extension intuition, there are many unanswered questions. Perhaps quantum mechanics, the study of how the universe operates at a subatomic scale, has possible answers to contribute.

Is consciousness a property of everything?

Your understanding of consciousness and reality is based on your perceptions of how your world works, so it's highly personal and subjective but it's likely to be consistent. Yet in a subatomic structure, a wave can be a particle, or a particle can be a wave. This is known as wave-particle duality and is so bizarre that it's almost unbelievable.

This is why.

Pick up a stone; it can only exist in one place at one time, just like a particle. Throw it into water and you get a wave, which, unlike a stone, can exist in many places at once. You know this by just seeing a wave breaking on a shoreline.

In experimental conditions, colliding particles bounce off each other, colliding waves pass through each other and emerge unchanged. But overlapping waves cause the trough of one to overlap with the crest of another, leading to areas where the wave either disappears altogether or becomes stronger. This is known as diffraction.

Here's where it gets challenging.

When experimenters fire atomic particles between two slits, in the famous "double slit experiment," you don't see two neat clusters just as if you'd thrown a bunch of pebbles through them. In "observed" experiments, even when the observer is an electronic detector, you get diffraction patterns just as if waves had been fired through the double slits.

And when you fire electron waves through the slits, they don't deposit energy over the entire surface of a detector; the energy is deposited at a point as if it were a particle.

So, waves behave like particles and particles behave like waves, and the more there are observers, the stronger the effect. Hence Erwin Schrödinger's famous thought experiment, where a cat in a box is simultaneously dead and alive until an observer has a look.

This is extremely challenging to our notion of reality because although subatomic particles are inanimate, they are behaving and responding to forces. And they are moving in different ways in different experimental conditions.

One conclusion that some researchers have come to is that there may be a kind of quantum consciousness which is part of the fundamental structure of everything. This is what's known as panpsychism which hypothesizes that consciousness is woven into the fabric of the universe. Most usefully it combines an explanation of what we know to be true about our experience of consciousness with quantum physics. It posits that while humans have lots of consciousness, quarks, electrons, and photons have only a tiny bit. The amount available depends on an organism's complexity.

Take fungi.

Fungi respond to the environment, seek food, solve problems, and defend themselves. All that is a kind of intelligence. You can't have intelligence without awareness, whether you call it consciousness or not.

Trees are similar.

Trees communicate using miles of mycelium, the underground network of threads from which mushrooms grow, as their pathways connect. They use mycelium to feed each other, swapping helpful nutrients, and even sharing carbon. If it's sentience of some kind, isn't it consciousness of some kind too?

Insects also are capable of sophisticated, learned behaviors that would be recognized as consciousness if a human behaved similarly. It's the same for octopuses, crows, fish, and coelacanths. Darwin concluded from studying worms that there was no absolute threshold between lower and higher animals. But it's almost impossible to research the extent to which other species have subjective experiences, which we understand consciousness to be.

What about taking it a step further?

The idea that your laptop has a mental life and can have an existential crisis is ridiculous, much less a photon. But accepting a range of consciousness from simple to complex is an idea that's now more mainstream and picks up on what Buddhists, Amazonian Indians, First Nations, and First Peoples have always thought: that everything is interconnected and has a life force. As Oxford University archaeologist Professor Chris Gosden says:

> If we asked everyone in the world, the vast majority would believe that the universe is sentient. Those of us who don't believe are the odd ones out.

Panpsychism speaks to our experience. When you become conscious of your thought, "I must call Anne" who you haven't talked to for a year and seconds later you see her number pop up on your mobile because she's calling you, it's hard not to think we're interconnected in some way and that interpersonal intuition is at work.

How else might quantum mechanics explain consciousness?

Fourteen billion years ago after the Big Bang, we ended up with a universe filled with particles. While most of our cells regenerate, many of the particles that make up those cells have been around for millions of millennia. Our hydrogen atoms were produced in the Big Bang, and our oxygen, nitrogen, and carbon atoms were made in burning stars. That's the ultimate recycling program.

We're not only made of particles, we also meet them all the time. For example, cosmic rays or high-energy radiation from outer space smacks into the atmosphere constantly; the sun bombs us with neutrinos which whizz through our bodies at a rate of about 100 trillion a second.

Meanwhile we know that when two of these subatomic particles become entangled on a quantum level, they share one or more properties such as spin, polarization, or momentum. That effect continues no matter how far apart they are in space or time, even on a cosmic scale. And amazingly, in 2019, scientists in Glasgow took the first photo of pairs of photons showing that they were entangled, so it's more than simply a mathematical proposition.

And it doesn't just show connection.

Entanglement also means that a change in one particle instantly creates a simultaneous change in the other. Einstein described this as "spooky actions from a distance" because it suggests an underlying reality that defies explanation. But it could support the possibility that consciousness might be both inside and – more controversially – outside the body, just like Pim van Lommel suggests.

The problem with entanglement is that it's incredibly fragile and short-lived as it's currently understood. Entangled particles are easily disturbed by their surroundings, and their entanglement is reduced by the slightest interaction with the environment, even if entangled particles can currently be found several kilometers apart.

But it leaves some interesting questions. Could entanglement occur in patterns? Can the mind somehow sense those patterns? For example, research indicates that robins may use entangled effects to "see" the Earth's magnetic field as they migrate. Perhaps quantum entanglement illustrates one of the most important parts of quantum mechanics: it's extraordinary and there's a lot that's still unknown.

What about quantum tunneling as a way of understanding consciousness and intuition?

Quantum tunneling is a terrible name for a fascinating phenomenon that doesn't involve any tunnels or openings. It describes how a particle like an electron can move through a solid barrier despite not having energy to do so, violating all the principles of classical mechanics. When electrons tunnel, they simply appear on the opposite side of a barrier.

Fascinatingly, quantum tunneling may play a role in DNA mutations; research is underway to see if hydrogen atoms jump from one strand of the double helix before they separate, thereby leading to modified structures. If that's the case, it would be very important and exciting.

There's another ongoing experiment based on the idea of quantum tunneling that's coming up with some pretty crazy results. Hold on to your hat for something extra peculiar, even stranger than animals running away in advance of earthquakes.

The Global Consciousness Project, created at Princeton and started in 1998, seems to show that certain events can affect the data output of computers. What these researchers have done is to set up 70 random number generators (RNGs) that produce a totally unpredictable sequences of zeros and ones. This data is then transmitted back to a central archive which then examines it for correlations. If you're interested, go to noosphere.princeton.edu to see it working in real time.

What they've found is that when a notable event occurs that has the same emotional impact on millions of people at the same time, the global network of RNGs seems to become subtly structured in a statistically significant way. In short, feelings appear to impact data output. Is this a unified field of consciousness? Or interpersonal intuition? Possibly. But the actual process for how multiple mental states affect a hardware system is unclear. Critics of course talk about cherry-picking appropriate data but it's extraordinary however you look at it.

What else might provide some clues?

String theory was developed as a mechanism to resolve the incompatibility between general relativity and quantum mechanics. Here on the Earth, we only can perceive and work in three spatial dimensions: up/down, left/right, and forward/backward. But back in 1919, Theodore Kaluza proposed that there were additional dimensions we can't see. Today, super string theory proposes a world of 10 or 11 dimensions, some of which are said to be curled up at microscopic level, while others are larger, for example, space and time. The theory states that there are no elementary particles, but tiny vibrating strings.

According to the theory, the fifth and sixth dimensions are where the notion of possible worlds arise. Other researchers consider that consciousness is the fifth dimension: when it's theoretical everything's up for grabs.

What do we really know? Well, string theory could be the ultimate brilliant theory of everything, or just a beautiful mathematical model. Because right now there's no research which proves or disproves it.

Another interesting if fringe quantum angle was developed in the 1990s by Stuart Hameroff and Roger Penrose. They speculate that microtubules in the brain's neurons are involved in the emergence of consciousness. Recent experiments in the past couple of years have shown hints but not conclusive evidence that this may be the case.

To conclude, quantum mechanics has been inextricably linked with consciousness since its birth; quantum physicists of the 1960s, some of whom were known for getting high on LSD, tried to use it to explain telepathy and altered states of consciousness. But well-known theoretical physicist Professor Jim Al-Khalili says:

Let me make this very clear: if you think that quantum mechanics allows for psychic phenomena, ESP, intuition, and coincidence, then you'd better take a proper course in quantum mechanics. The fact is that while we are now discovering that quantum mechanics may indeed play a role in biology, it is really confined to the behavior at the atomic scale inside cells. Two electrons that are spatially separated can be quantum entangled, but this is a delicate state existing inside a single biomolecule in a cell. We cannot extrapolate the idea to say that it then, for example, explains why twins seem to be aware of each other when apart because their conscious states are quantum entangled. That's woo woo pseudoscience.

So, the jury is out whether quantum mechanics and consciousness have anything relevant to say to each other, and if so, exactly what. The same therefore applies to intuition.

An inconclusion

We're still left wrestling with the scientifically inexplicable, including meditators' experiences of merged boundaries, lucid dreaming, NDEs, end-of-life rallies, precognitions, and transplant recipients changed characteristics to name a few. We've seen that it's possible to experience consciousness very differently and that when unconscious or barely conscious people have experiences that appear to transcend time and place.

We've also seen that there's a scale to consciousness ranging from less to more, that some people experience it very differently to others, and that perhaps it can exist without brain function. If that's the case, it and the intuitions which spring from it, must then *be* somewhere.

It's also clear that when we experience personal and interpersonal intuitions, they arise out of hierarchical self-organizing systems. The former takes place within and between your body and mind, while the latter between one or more people in the form of brain synchrony. If these self-organizing systems exist in two intuitive spheres, why would this process simply stop when that sphere was extended? Of course, this is a hypothesis, but perhaps it offers a possibility into how intuitions can arise about anything and anyone regardless of distance. As a reminder, this is something that has long been an accepted occurrence among indigenous peoples.

Researcher Dr Sam Parnia, a leading expert on the study of cardiac arrests and NDEs, has an interesting and helpful analogy. He likens his research to that done on electromagnetism. We know it's all around us even though we don't have the receptors to pick it up. But a hundred years ago there were no tools to measure it; today we know it's there because our phones and TVs work. But just as our phones and TVs don't produce the content we consume, perhaps the brain doesn't either.

Where and what does, is yet to be discovered.

Returning to the two questions posed at the start of this chapter; have they been answered? In a word, no.

What we've seen is that there are no absolutes when it comes to consciousness or intuition because there are too many unknowns. But there are some interesting avenues that might lead to more answers. Right now, panpsychism has a lot to offer because it seems to elegantly account for the reality of our experiences. Microtubules could be an answer, but we need more evidence. And while locating consciousness outside the brain may be a long shot, if you're interested, follow the AWARE II study that Sam Parnia is leading.

Which leaves us with what should we think about the intuitive part of the conscious process. Maybe the main point is to be open to the experience, particularly when it seems informative and meaningful to you – regardless of how it comes about or where it might be located.

Summary and next steps

Top takeaways

- Consciousness is how we know ourselves and our worlds; it matters because it's how we become aware of intuitions.
- Skilled meditators, lucid dreamers, transplant patients, and those who've had near-death experiences have very different experiences of it.
- Some researchers hypothesize that consciousness or an element of it must be located outside the human body, but we can't currently perceive that.
- Quantum mechanics is unlikely to play a role in understanding consciousness other than perhaps metaphorically.
- Idealism and panpsychism seem to offer explanations that better match our perceived reality.

Read

- Anil Seth (2021), *Being You: A New Science of Consciousness*, Faber
- Suzanne Simard (2021), *Finding the Mother Tree: Discovering the Wisdom and Intelligence of the Forest*, Penguin
- Pim van Lommel (2011), *Consciousness Beyond Life: The Science of Near-Death*, HarperCollins

Watch

- David Chalmers' TED talk on consciousness
- Netflix: Surviving Death, Episode 1; Fantastic Fungi
- MIT open course on Consciousness

Listen

- Browse Theconsciousnesspodcast.com
- BBC Sounds, Panpsychism: Is Everything Conscious?
- https://blog.oup.com/2021/07/the-neuroscience-of-human -consciousness-podcast/

Conclusion

When you make a difficult decision or come across a complex situation, you're going to have an emotional, physical, and intuitive response to it because you're hard-wired to. That's something you can never turn off. And you wouldn't want it any other way because that reaction is important information, whatever age and stage you're at. Given that it's there, you gain everything by learning to use it superbly.

In fact, the payback can be tremendous.

Having read this book, you now know that more responsiveness, more flexibility, better decisions, improved organizational performance, and greater revenues are all associated with intuitive decision-making. But it doesn't mean chucking the data out. It means working to have intuitions about your analyses and analyzing your intuitions to arrive at the best answers. That's because, as Zak Brown, CEO of McLaren, says:

> Sometimes intuition tells you something and then you go get the data which validates what you're thinking. And then there are other times when you see some data which brings to life what you're thinking. They can come in either order.

Yes, it takes understanding and practice, but if you're envisaging a career as a senior leader or CEO, developing this skill is a must. No one will tell you that intuition helps propel you to the top, but if you want quick and accurate choices that side-step pitfalls and create value, honing your intuition is essential. This is particularly true today when so much is changing and there often isn't a playbook. Relentless change also means constantly reinventing yourself and your business because everything is always new – and when that's the case, intuition becomes even more crucial. Moreover, it's the one thing that artificial intelligence will never be able to replicate.

Finally, it always helps when you're accompanied on your journey. Award-winning music, media, and digital entertainment executive Julie Pilat advises:

> *You need community to nurture you and your intuition as you learn. I have friends and a group of people that know my industry and who are a little more anchored in what I do, that I can bounce things off. I feel safe saying, "The craziest thing ever just happened" and then talking about it with them and without self-editing. I think that's important because intuition can be very specific or feel so far out that sometimes you'll even second-guess yourself. If you're too close to something, sometimes you need another take on it. They're your witnesses to you and your process as well as being your sounding board.*

Not everyone is fortunate enough to have those witnesses or that sounding board. So, here's an open invitation to a LinkedIn group that will offer you a community, resources, and a place to share your experiences: https://www.linkedin.com/groups/12708820/ or just check out Intuition at Work: Making Better Decisions, and you should find us.

I look forward to meeting you there.

Toolkit to tackle 10 top blocks

When you're working with intuition, it's easy to get stuck from time to time. The point is to recognize what's going wrong so you can put it right. Interestingly, I got completely stuck when writing this section of the book. That's because I had to put myself right into each challenge as I wrote about, and doing that wholeheartedly got me totally in my own way. The only useful part was recognizing that at least the blocks were accurate.

To get the most out of this toolkit, and to avoid gold-plating any block like I did, I recommend simply turning to what you're working on and only reading that section. If you feel you've got a mix of a couple, read what you're drawn to because that's your intuition working for you.

Here's what you'll find in this toolkit:

1. I don't make the time to try
2. I'm not getting anything
3. I can't tell if it's intuition or bias
4. I really want a specific result
5. I've got a lot of doubt and I'm second-guessing myself
6. I'm struggling with a gut vs analysis conflict
7. I'm uncertain whether it's fear, anxiety, or intuition
8. I'm worried that ego is getting in the way
9. I don't know whether this is about me or someone else
10. I'm getting a bunch of misses

You'll notice when you turn to the section that applies for you, I've switched the headings to be as positive as possible. That's because the minute you start thinking negatively, you get dragged down and blocked some more.

1. Creating the time to try

What you'll find

When you're dealing with this block, you'll probably:

- Put off trying today making semi-promises to yourself that you'll do it tomorrow
- Turn to trivia instead which doesn't add a lot of value
- Fail to schedule time with yourself

Why it happens

You know it but you don't do it, something that I've always called the knowing-doing gap. Like eating well, drinking less, and exercising more. Behavior change is hard. An activity may only take a few minutes but there are always competing priorities; doing something easy and concrete like replying to an email instead of even trying, will give you an immediate dopamine hit, that delicious feeling of satisfaction and accomplishment when you knock something off your to-do list.

But if you've decided that you want to use your intuition more or better and find you just aren't tuning in, maybe there's an underlying discomfort or worry to face. After all, doing something new is often frustrating particularly if something doesn't come easily. And when you're a novice you change your self-perceptions because you're a beginner yet again.

Second, you might be worried that your intuition will make you face some uncomfortable facts. For example, that you don't enjoy your job, that your boss is unsupportive or incapable, your products or services are overpriced, and your colleagues dull. That's entirely possible. I'm guessing that rational thought has done that for you in the past too, exposing things you'd rather not know or might not want to recognize. While that's understandable, it doesn't resolve anything. Problems don't simply go away by themselves; like a dripping tap, they just get worse. And in the end, if we don't act, we often get pushed there by someone or something else. Meaning you can tackle it now, or when it's even tougher. Up to you.

How to deal with it

Start by reframing your mindset and tell yourself, "I'm on my way to getting better," or "I'm improving an important skill," or perhaps "learning something new is exciting." Whatever works for you. But please avoid the thought, "I can't do this" or any self-criticism which is just demotivating and most likely untrue, particularly if you're reading this.

Then decide that you can invest three to five minutes a day in working with your intuition; you really don't need a lot of time. Make it as simple as connecting with yourself before switching your laptop on and focusing on what the day will bring or how what you've done might land. Or taking a break to do this before an important call. If you prefer, try noticing what comes to mind at the end of your day. It could be as quirky as the pepper grinder in a café at lunchtime, a sticky note on your desk, or someone who was late to a call. Think about what those things might mean to you, and notice where your mind next goes. All you're doing is relaxing, downshifting your energy and paying attention. Go back to Chapter 2 if you need a quick review of your process. Jot anything down in your journal so you can come back to it and keep yourself honest about your accuracy.

Tip: Any thoughts telling you're a lazy person for putting off using your intuition aren't intuitive. Your intuition will never blame you; it's just a small quiet voice that's there to help and guide you. And remember that you don't need to be in the right mood or at the right place to access intuition. It's simply a matter of stopping, minimizing distraction, and focusing.

Tip: Take yourself out and go somewhere new. Set the intention that you'll come back with something helpful on the intuitive front, then just enjoy what you're doing without looking at your phone. Put yourself in the moment as much as you can, and notice what then pops into your mind about any issue you're trying to solve. This is what allowing is all about. Don't worry too much about distractions as they may be part of any solution; just notice how you feel about them.

2. Pushing through a dry patch

What you'll find

When you believe that however hard you try on the intuitive front, you're not getting anywhere, you'll probably notice that you:

- Experience frustration or bewilderment
- Start to doubt yourself
- Feel that you want to give up

Why it happens

Forget movies and Netflix series. Intuition isn't like a bolt of lightning that hits you on the side of your head while you're face settles into an expression of shock or amazement. It's a whole heap more subtle for starters. So then the question becomes how are you protecting and encouraging your intuitions. You can do a mini self-audit by checking in with the following:

- Am I really giving myself the time to tune in, to pay attention, and fully sense my mind-body?
- Have I been building a close and ongoing relationship with my intuition?
- To what extent am I aware of my intuitive cues?

If you're pressurizing yourself and forcing an issue, it's hard to sense and make sense of your perceptions; taking your foot off the pedal will be a lot more helpful.

If, on the other hand, you've answered yes to all the above questions, before you jump into being annoyed with yourself, remember that sometimes it's right to do nothing. If that's the case, you evidently won't get a hit, so any irritation is misplaced and might drown out your feeling of knowing. Instead, try to recenter yourself and check whether letting something be is your best option.

How to deal with it

The most important thing is to look at what you're working on from a different angle. Try curiosity as an approach, and remember that if you're in a highly emotional state that won't help either. When you try too hard, you don't allow your intuition the space to respond, let alone for you to hear it. You can de-pressurize yourself by intuiting the feeling of an interaction or the sense of your day. Get playful by intuiting the outcome of sports events, tracking stock prices or anything totally without stress or consequence.

Once you sense you've let yourself off the hook, you can also try to unlock your intuition by asking yourself, "If I were to know, what would the answer be?" or "If I was to ask my closest friend, what would their answer be?" This slight change of angle can often release your internal flow.

Analogies can be another great way to help you tune in intuitively. They consist of similes and metaphors which enable you to find new ways of looking at a problem while at the same time enabling you to move away from any inner churn. Similes uses the words "like" or "as" to draw comparisons and are generally easier to find than metaphors. Here are some well-known examples: "she's like a dog with two tails"; "he's got a voice like a foghorn"; "she's tough as nails"; "it's as clear as a bell." To find one, just keep asking yourself, "What's that like?" and pushing yourself until you find something that's takes your understanding to a deeper level.

Here's how you'd use the technique. If you think a situation is difficult, you'd then ask yourself, "What's it like?" And then you might hit on, "It's like being stuck in mud." Then check in that that feels right to you. You'd then mentally explore a way forward by asking yourself, "Well what do I now need to get unstuck and who could help me?"

A metaphor, on the other hand, swaps out one word or concept for another. At work you often hear, for example, "That's explosive," "He's venting," or "Don't boil the ocean." These phrases are so overused that they're now clichés. A meaningful metaphor involves something deeper, that's more expansive, like this one that that arose for CEO and SoaringWords founder Lisa Buksbaum:

> *I managed a lot of people in my first career in advertising but one of them was a dud. He was handsome and telegenic but dopey and super lazy. He was getting by doing as little as possible. Suddenly, when I was thinking about him, I saw this image in my mind's eye like Jesus carrying that 500-pound cross. It's crushing him and at that moment I understood that I was carrying this 6ft 2 inch guy on my back. That said everything. I realized I had to go to my boss and say I was done covering for him, done with carrying him. It came to me with such visual clarity. Ask yourself when you get these images, "What's this about, what's this trying to say to me?*

Tip: If analogies or metaphors don't come to you, you can also try turning on a TV in your mind's eye; sit down on a comfortable chair in and mentally switch it on. What's happening on the screen? What do you see if you fast forward? Switch channels? Add different actors? You can try the same with a radio or podcast if you prefer. Either are great ways of checking in with what you know.

Tip: if you really can't find an analogy, go to an AI tool like ChatGPT and ask it to give you a few examples. Pay attention not to the result, but to your reaction to the result. What do you notice? And what does that then lead to?

3. Checking if it's intuition or bias

What you'll find

While there are hundreds of biases, I'm going to deal with the one that gets most confused with intuition – confirmation bias. That involves looking for evidence to reinforce thinking patterns, while ignoring anything that doesn't fit. It becomes a problem because it closes your mind to better options.

If you're confused about whether you've got an intuitive hit or experiencing confirmation bias, you'll probably:

- Have niggling feelings of uncertainty and doubt
- Aren't sure whether to trust yourself
- Defer deciding

The problem with confirmation bias is that it leads to selective attention, overconfidence, poor decisions, and costly outcomes. You'll recognize it if you or anyone around you has been:

- Searching for information to confirm what you know
- Cherry-picking data that adds to existing beliefs
- Interpreting information to confirm your thoughts
- Remembering facts that support your position
- Discounting contradictory evidence

If you're now worrying whether you're dealing with something other than confirmation bias, go back to Chapter 1 and read about how intuition differs from other kinds of thinking.

Why it happens

So, a thought or feeling emerges and you wonder, "Is this intuition or simply how I've made a previous decision?" And you're right to question yourself because it could be your Reticular Activating System (RAS), the name for a bundle of nerves at your brainstem which is responsible for wakefulness, ability to focus, fight-flight response and how you perceive the world. It acts like a gatekeeper, filtering out unnecessary information and explains why when you learn a new word, you then start hearing it everywhere. Or why you can tune out a crowd full of talking people, yet immediately snap to attention when someone says your name. Or think about buying a red mini and suddenly see them at every junction.

The RAS takes what you're focusing on and creates a filter for it, sifting through what's incoming and presenting you with the stuff that matters to you. It also looks for information that validates your beliefs, so for example, if you think you're bad at networking, it's probably true. If you think you're efficient getting through your to-do list, you most likely are. Meaning that your RAS is also what lies behind confirmation bias, our tendency to reinforce previous beliefs.

How to deal with it

The first step is to admit that we all have biases and the more shortcuts we take, or the more tired we are, the more likely they are to appear.

You'll know that it's confirmation bias and not intuition if you are only willing to choose what you've selected before. One instructive experiment backed this up by showing that failed intuitive decision-makers were willing to learn from their mistakes and make new choices. That contrasted with participants making non-intuitive choices: they didn't change what they did because they were operating out of bias.

If you feel an internal resistance or reluctance to commit to any action, you can best protect yourself from bias by adopting decision-making principles which you always apply; it's something that the most effective decision-makers do as Dame Louise Makin, ex-CEO and Board Chair, describes:

> *I have a few but important operating principles: that the enterprise can always be better; do everything properly – make it excellent – and be your best self. These principles have helped guide me and make choices in all my roles.*

Other principles that can help you avoid bias might include managing risk within defined parameters, setting out to always create value, or protecting people first. Or do your own thinking instead of following others. Or being honest with colleagues about what's influencing you as you go about your decisions.

The most important principle of all is bringing in diverse thinking when you're making a tough call. That's because people unlike you notice patterns that you don't. When dissimilar people work together, they start to join the dots in unconnected fields more quickly, and that elevates everyone's intuitive ability.

And research confirms that diverse teams do better: individuals become more aware of how they think, start to process information more carefully and that results in better decisions.

That's all very well and good when you're dealing with yourself but what about when you recognize it in others?

Here's Dr Kate Macintyre, senior public health social scientist:

> *Back in the early 2000s I was funded to do some research about HIV orphans. The results of our study showed that these HIV orphans were better off than non-orphans which went against everything that this foundation was putting out there. But if you had a child or several children, and you were dying, would you place those children with your better off or your worse off sister? These orphans were outdoing the others on every measure.*
>
> *This foundation tried to stop my research from being published, saying that the methodology that we'd used was flawed. It was their bias overriding evidence which funders and donors would have been sensitive to – I was furious. But I was about to emigrate to Kenya and my intuition was not to fight as it would have sucked up a huge amount of time and energy.*

Kate called it right. Sometimes the best thing you can do is to walk away. If someone else is biased and data won't shift their position, then that's probably your best option.

Tip: First, just asking yourself if confirmation bias is at play is helpful because it makes you reassess and check. Second, if you want to understand more about your biases, visit https://implicit.harvard.edu/implicit/selectatest.html and click into social attitudes. You'll find a series of interesting non-judgmental tests to check out.

Tip: If you think you might be discounting or ignoring information, which is what happens when confirmation bias is activated, get out and talk to a couple of people with different perspectives. They can help you develop new hypotheses which you just can't do by yourself.

4. Being open to outcomes

What you'll find

When you dearly want something to happen and are too attached to an outcome, you might:

- Have strong feelings that certain things are right or wrong
- Use "need," "should," "must," and "have to" language
- Discount or ignore useful intuitions
- Lose your commitment, engagement, and passion along the way

Why it happens

From time to time we all get over-invested in wanting something that will never come to fruition. I've certainly got hooked by this unhelpful block. But we live in an uncertain world; things seldom go as planned, people let us down, and stuff changes all the time. Outcomes can be affected by too many variables that have nothing to do with you and Covid has certainly reinforced that understanding.

Even knowing that we don't control outcomes, tunnel vision still can take over. When that happens, it's easy to neglect yourself and others as you push toward the impossible, ignoring the intuitive clues that you would normally notice.

And if you do recognize what you get, because these intuitions don't lead in the direction you want, you'll be more likely to reject them and continue down an unhelpful path. Others might have told you things will work out differently, but you'll probably won't listen to them either. Obviously, this never results in success, happiness, or joy.

How to deal with it

Noticing that your energy is being drained disproportionately to the event or its consequences is a great first step. Interestingly, while distraction is a reasonable short-term fix, really letting go can be more useful. That means releasing right into disappointment, frustration, irritation, sadness, or anger because negativity often dissipates when you take some deep breaths and dive right in, focusing on whatever area of your body is feeling tight and tense. As you do this, you'll reduce any fight or flight response especially if you notice air moving from your nostrils to lungs and observe the pause between breaths.

You should then feel calmer, which is a bunch more helpful than being aggravated or suppressing your feelings. It isn't about giving up; it's about releasing emotionally unhealthy or unhelpful thoughts, and yes, that may take a little time and repetition. When you've done that, ask yourself what you could now most usefully focus on and see what pops up for you, checking in with your mind-body that you're right. Then you can refocus on any intuitions that you might have been ignoring up until now to assess how big a change you need to make.

Tip: Try switching your focus to the process around what you're doing instead. That process can consist of anything from a simple set of actions to a complex project plan, but it gives you tangible focus. You always have some influence or control over your actions and a good process can help you get to a better outcome – but not always.

If working on the process doesn't apply to your situation, then pivoting probably does, and that's often the best practical answer. Your intuition is a great guide in those moments as biotech general manager Mark Robinson found:

> *I was actually about to be promoted in my last company to the job that I had always wanted. I was in the interview process, and it felt like this was going to happen. But there was a requirement which said I'd need to move my family to Switzerland and live there to do the job. That was a lot of heartache. We discussed it, and my wife said, "We can do it. If you want it, we can do it, we can go." Then it just came down to what does my gut say? Do I want us to move? And the answer was no, it's not going to happen. I had to make one of the hardest phone calls of my life and say, "I'm going to pull out."*
>
> *That then triggered the question of "If my dream job, the job that I've been working to get for the last 10 years, isn't open to me, what does that mean?" And at that point, my current organization rang and offered what really I'd been looking for.*

It often takes courage to say no to something, but when you do, it's amazing how often a better option opens up.

Tip: If you realize you are overly attached to an outcome, as a way of letting go, visualize cutting any ties that connect you to the person or situation. It helps pull back attention or energy that you might be wasting, and which are valuable but finite resources.

5. Feeling confident in and acting on what you get

What you'll find

When you're dealing with self-doubt or want to stop second-guessing yourself, you'll probably:

- Mistrust your feeling of knowing
- Hesitate or fail to act on what you later realize is right
- Sabotage your accurate intuitions

By examining these three outcomes you can see that this block shows up as a continuum that has a progressively unhelpful consequences. So, it's important to nip it in the bud to get the big calls right.

Why it happens

When intuition feels effortless or an answer too way out, it's easy to worry that you're making it all up, to question what you get or intellectualize it all away. But we're all making it up, all the time! That's all any of us ever do. Before you get too hard on yourself, there are positives to self-doubt. It shows that you care and that's part and parcel of being a thoughtful and kind human being. People with no self-doubt tip over into arrogance which seriously unhelpful when it comes to intuition.

It's also worth recognizing that you're more likely to experience self-doubt when you're hungry, angry, lonely, or tired. If that's the case, fix your physical needs first so they don't get in the way.

But here's the big problem with self-doubt, regardless of how it arises. Most often it doesn't stop with the thought itself but drags along frustration and stasis, draining your energy and preventing you from moving on. With so much on offer and switchable in a digital world, it's easy to waste time hunting down a better option and end up discounting your intuition in the process.

The result is you end up questioning yourself while you mentally chew over options and choices. But one thing we know about rumination is that it's bad for your mental health.

How to deal with it

Instead of worrying about what might be wrong, think about what might be right. Then list and reflect on some previous successes. You'll certainly have had a few to show, and they prove that you know what you're doing.

And accepting that life is a tangled business helps too. Worry is a dreadful waste of energy and perfectionism is a terrible disrupter of your inner peace. Getting an intuitive hit that you then ignore or discount impacts your self-confidence, and if you contradict yourself in one area of life, you'll probably do it in another: that's also not great for your mental well-being.

If you get a strong sense of discomfort, lean into it. Notice it. Witness that it's there. Ask it what it wants you to know and decide on how long you can live with it. Give yourself a defined period, for example 48 hours, and then take action. Positive self-talk is a way to support yourself during your time of reflection, as in, "I've got this, I'm just checking with myself, then I'll be good to go." Ignoring it won't make it go away and ironically can make you more anxious and harsher with yourself.

Another option is to try going against your intuition and experiment as Mark Dean CEO of En Masse did.

I've experimented in a low-risk way when I haven't been sure. Someone came into my life commercially who I had this very strong inkling was not a genuine, authentic person, and would say what was needed to manipulate me, knowing what a values-based person I am. It was just a feeling. But then I did a logical assessment, and I thought that I could be wrong. So, I took a low risk way to go into this, eyes open, and give this person a chance.

I structured the relationship in full confidence that if my intuition was correct, I was protected. And it did go wrong – I was right. The little experiment just proved to me two things. One, my intuition is real. Two, when I trust in it and act upon it rather than just use my head, I know that things will work out for me.

Tip: Articulate what you're feeling and share it with others, as in, "The data looks solid, but I've got worries about it. Might there be something behind that? And does anyone else feel the same?" That allows you to dig into what might be behind your intuition, enlist others, and arrive at the best course of action.

If you can't do that, try focusing on these questions:

- What will help me feel that I'm doing the right thing?
- What's my very best next step?
- How would a close friend or mentor react?
- How do I make the most of this?

As you answer these questions, tune into your body responses, and feel what you have most energy for. That's most likely to be your answer.

Just to add a note of realism here: I doubt you will ever feel 100% confident in an intuition because you know that nothing is ever totally certain, and life isn't constructed in black and white but the gray zones. But there again, you probably wouldn't bet your life on a spreadsheet built on a bunch of assumptions. Go back to what your gut is telling you, recognizing that you may not like the answer. If you're still uncertain, use the sticky note technique in Chapter 3 and then sleep on it.

Then accept that this is much more about being OK with being wrong, being OK with vulnerability and accepting your humanity. When you do this, you allow everyone around you to be human too. What a gift.

6. Working through a gut vs data conflict

What you'll find

When you're dealing with this block, you'll probably:

- Feel torn
- Flip between choices
- Play for time

Why it happens

It's just a fact that all decisions have an element of feeling attached to them. Sometimes that feeling will be aligned with the data and analyses in front of you, and sometimes it won't be. And yet you still have to make a call and then it's likely your mind starts to spin as you struggle with your dilemma.

This conflict between data and intuition is a hurdle you will face time and again. When I asked Hal Reisiger, CEO of Cosworth, what he did in such situations, he unhesitatingly said he went with his intuition and drew my attention to the speed of his answer. He also said:

> *Data is very important, but data is a snapshot in time. Data is what you know today. But if you want key strategic decisions, in this dynamic world, tomorrow is very different — you can count on it. If my head and heart, which is how I define my intuition, are telling me one thing and the data is telling me another, I don't hesitate and, in a nanosecond, I use my head and my heart. I'll be wrong sometimes, but it's within a risk profile that I deem appropriate.*
>
> *What enables my intuition to a great extent is pure outright determination. I will take determination over education and experience every time, so if I've got a*

combination of intuition that says to do something and determination, it's going to come out right most of the time.

This leads straight to how to tackle a data-intuition conflict.

How to deal with it

There are two important points to note in Hal's analysis. The first is around a risk profile, which structures any decision in terms of resources, time, and money. Risk profiles help contain any decision so that it feels more manageable and, like principles, are a great discipline when the pressure is on.

The second is determination. Determination represents the energy behind your decision; whatever you have the energy for is most likely the best direction of travel because it will carry you through the challenges you'll inevitably face. It doesn't mean that you'll face anything less difficult, it will simply give you the oomph to push through.

Here's how it might work in practice. Say this is about firing someone for poor performance. You can see that their work isn't up to standard but having someone is better than no one, particularly if you happen to be in a hiring freeze. Your intuition says to let them go but your rational brain doesn't want to put more pressure on the team.

The fundamental problem is that a dilemma with only two options is always hard to solve, so check that that there isn't a third way. In this case for example, could you take a different approach to managing this employee? Swap out their responsibilities? Exchange their role? Put them on a different project? Give them more training and coaching? Or if you want them gone, could you share out responsibilities within the team and increase everyone's compensation? If there's no more money, could you give everyone time instead?

Continuing with the above example, if there is no third way, validation of either option is your next step. To do that, getting back into your body helps overcome this block, because sitting in your head is how you make it worse. When you feel connected with your body and your intuitive process, feel what the next three months would be like with or without this person. And the next six. What burden would the rest of the team carry over those time periods? What would the consequences of that be? Which option do you have more energy for? If you're still unclear, sleep on it and try again. And be honest with yourself; to what extent are you shying away from having a few difficult conversations and managing an awkward situation?

Tip: You can adapt these questions for most data-intuition challenges you may face. Ideally, you write them down then feel your way through each one paying attention to your responses. That way should generate some clear answers for yourself

Tip: One important technique to try is to intentionally switch gears between analytical and intuitive thinking. That means you go back to the data to help your intuition interpret what it all means and create a virtuous thinking cycle. For best results, research shows that you start with intuition and then move into analysis as this appears to help the deliberative process. That's because you won't be biased by what the data tells you. Once you've seen the data, you can change your mind, showing yourself that bias isn't getting in your way, and then tune into your feeling of knowing.

7. Identifying fear, anxiety, and intuition

What you'll find

When you're dealing with this block, you'll probably:

- Have tangled thoughts and feelings
- Struggle to find a way forward
- Feel unnecessarily negative about yourself or a situation

Why it happens

When you are time-poor, under pressure, tired, or stressed out it's hard to work out what's really going on internally. Even if you find the space, allowing clarity to emerge in these circumstances is almost impossible particularly if you feel overwhelmed by intense feelings. That's when it's good to have thought about and understood your different inner processes so you recognize them. If you haven't done that, don't worry.

How to deal with it

Your first step is to understand how fear, anxiety, and intuition show up because when you compare and contrast them it's easy to spot the differences. Intuitions most often are feelings and nudges of "this is right and that's wrong." They tend to come to you to put you on a better path and will keep reappearing if you don't pay attention and the situation stays the same.

While fear, well that's like an internal alarm going off as your blood pressure rises, your heart hammers, and your body starts to sweat. There's an intensity to fear, coupled with measurable biological and emotional markers that you don't find with intuition; that's because your body is preparing you to fight, flee, or freeze. Fear peaks and wears off fast as you take action to find relief.

Anxiety, while less intense, also carries an emotional charge and often occupies a lot of brain space as it spreads its tentacles into other areas of your life. It frequently comes with a bunch of "what ifs," certainly not a quiet feeling of knowing. You'll notice physical changes with both fear and anxiety; your breath is likely to be faster; you might feel light-headed; perhaps you'll be restless or ill-at-ease but it's likely to be hard to focus on something else. Intuition allows you to direct your attention elsewhere; anxiety won't let you off the hook.

Both fear and anxiety can have their roots in instinct or intuitions, but getting stuck in negative feelings will absolutely block your intuitive sense. By the way, it's easy to confuse intuition with fear when you're trying to get answers to something you're already stressed out about. But when you're in a highly charged state, you're more likely to project any fear onto the most difficult things around you. That's the time to check whether you're telling yourself stories and thinking creatively not intuitively, so review that section in Chapter 1. Then remember that if you're worrying or focusing on what could go wrong, imagining negative outcomes, or using very harsh or critical language particularly with yourself, it's not your intuition.

For example, imagine you sent your boss an email recommending a course of action, and you don't hear back from her. You then start thinking, "She didn't like what I said. So, she thinks I'm no good. I must have offended her; she'll tell everyone, they'll think I'm an idiot, and I'm sure to be fired." This kind of storytelling is called catastrophizing; you're embellishing as you leap from one made-up possibility to another.

When you catastrophize, it's easy to go beyond logic and become fully immersed in your anxious brain noise. That's when to take a short time-out; even a few minutes will help. Simply center yourself, focus, and breathe. Breathing will bring your emotions and heart rate down, reducing signs of stress and allowing you to regain some sense of self-control. I like to intentionally send breath down to my feet because that helps me slow down and notice what's happening. Once you feel less heady or less "full" emotionally and physically, then you can investigate what's really going on.

Tip: Notice which thoughts are carrying your feelings; just observing and naming them helps dial them down. When your mental froth has reduced, you can then ask yourself two important questions. "Is this true?" and "Is it useful?"

Take for example not hearing from your boss. You'd ask yourself, "Is it true that your boss is going to fire you because they haven't replied to your email?" If it's true, there'll be some data and evidence. If there's none, it's not true. So, is it then useful? Well, anything that clutters up your brain and prevents you from doing other things is certainly not helpful. To further challenge and coach yourself, consider how someone you respect would see the situation; what would they say?

Then consider whether fear and anxiety have been pushing you to act to relieve your emotional state. In the above case you might be tempted to send another email or text. That's the time to sit with yourself and hypothesize as many reasons as you can for why your boss hasn't got back to you. Maybe she has other more important priorities, or a tough time with her partner, or another senior leader leaning on her. If you're curious about why, you're more likely to be open to your intuition and to find a new story.

At work you're often going to be in tough anxious-making situations because solving problems, which is what work is all about, is hard. If you focus on what's true and useful, you'll avoid fear and anxiety as well as making faster progress.

Tip: Whatever situation you're in, check alignment between head, heart, and gut then project that forward by a week, a month, or a relevant time frame. Will you still be feeling the same at a future date? If not, then consider that your drivers might be fear or anxiety. What other voice can you hear behind all that noise? And what is it saying to you?

8. Moving beyond ego

What you'll find

When you're dealing with this block, you'll probably:

- Find it hard to hear your intuition
- Get distracted by a harder more frantic voice
- Feel tense about a situation

Why it happens

Your ego is incredibly useful as it's there to protect and to keep you safe. It gives you confidence in challenging situations, the ability to stand up for yourself, the drive to do things you might fear, and the wherewithal to move on without guilt. But it isn't useful when it shouts down new ideas, spins out a bunch of "what ifs" and judgments, or holds you back. Quieter intuition gets drowned out or overridden.

Here's Mark Dean, CEO of En Masse, again:

> *I once went into a business relationship which I shouldn't have because I ignored my intuition and my ego got in the way. The grand plans, the excitement of the vision, it was all about splendor, big thinking and I got swept up in it.*

> *I was working hard on everything that needed to be done, doing all the problem-solving but all felt very hard. I couldn't sleep, I rapidly lost weight and before anything went truly sideways, I realized, "This isn't right." My friends and family were asking me, "Is something wrong, do you need to get some tests?" worrying that I was ill. I think my body was telling me to stop ignoring my intuition and to stop my ego taking over.*

> *One day, I had a brief call and my heart fell into my gut; I just knew that the game was up, and it would all be over very quickly. I didn't know how that would happen but a month later I had the opportunity to walk away, and I did. The relief was tremendous.*

How to deal with it

One of the first things to do is to identify what you're thinking. It's ego if you are ignoring any niggle and thinking you can manage or control the situation with "I" statements. For example, "I can turn that project around." Or "I can get this back on-track" or "I can change their thinking." Then ensuing work feels hard and difficult, bringing little joy. There's anxiety or tension around what we're doing which can have a physiological effect like it did for Mark. That often includes headaches, backaches, and minor injuries.

When you work with your intuition, yes, the work may be hard, but it feels purposeful, directed, and that there's internal alignment between the head, heart, or gut. You know it's ego when you're driven by insecurity, big thinking, or overconfidence; intuition is a simple, steady, and peaceful knowing and you'll sense an energetic difference between them. The energy you'll have around intuition is less frantic and goes deeper than ego energy which can feel like it's jumping up and down shouting loudly.

If you do get it wrong, you know ego's been in the mix when like Mark, you have a terrific sense of relief when you walk away. You'll also experience the same sense of relief when you stop having to deal with the ego of others.

Here's Divya Eapen, Chief Risk Officer, talking about why she left a business.

When you decouple decisions from expertise and feedback you can go very wrong. At that time, the CEO and the board had hired people that had a lot of experience but when it came to the big decisions and really tough calls, it all went back to this leader's experience and personality. The board encouraged his behavior rather than challenging it. I think there was the assumption that "I'm smarter, I've built this, I've fixed this before, I'll fix it again," and the CEO didn't recognize the uniqueness of the situation or the available skillsets and experience around him. It was as if we were all singular points who were never bought together to take advantage of everything we knew and find a way forward. He seemed to feel it was his problem to fix rather than a collective one.

I knew there was an issue with information flow, and the week I resigned I found two new things that had been signed or agreed without the leadership team being aware. If you're not going to trust your team, you don't need one. You should just do it on your own and simply not waste everyone's time and energy. There was an extreme sense of self-belief, coupled with a view that others needed to be protected – a Superman complex which in the end played out badly for everyone.

When a Superman complex shows up, leaders don't believe they can fail, and they have an unhealthy sense of responsibility. And Divya is right to say that it's a critical flaw if you make big decisions without taking expertise or feedback into account. Most of the corporate downfalls you see start with ego getting in the way precisely because others aren't brought in or listened to.

Tip: It's ego if you think that you're the only person who can deliver, that you're the smartest person in the room, that you always need to win, that your judgment is the best, and that you can never show doubt or weakness. An easy way to challenge yourself is to consider, "Is this healthy or unhealthy behavior?" and "How does this serve me and everyone around me?"

Tip: The most successful, interesting, and biggest of big-shots I've met or worked with don't act out of ego. They don't need to.

9. Recognizing what's mine or someone else's

What you'll find

When you're dealing with this block, you'll probably:

- Pick up on the feelings of others very easily
- Experience sensations which don't seem to relate to your current situation
- Feel overwhelmed by intensely emotional situations

Why it happens

If you're a sensitive and emotionally intelligent person (for more, review Chapter 3) who spends time around anxious or antsy people, you'll appreciate how easy it is to pick up on their feelings and then experience them yourself. If you've ever felt your skin crawl with embarrassment on behalf of someone else, you'll know exactly what I mean. You'll also recognize emotional contagion, which is the human tendency to match not only what someone's feeling but also their behavior or even their posture when you interact with them. Go to any bar and watch two people for a few minutes: they'll probably be sitting in mirror positions, and when one person changes, the other will follow. You can also see emotional contagion in teams where a couple of key people's moods and behaviors impact a whole group and how they work together.

We're hard-wired to catch feelings from others, and even an emoji will do it because we're so intensely social. That's great when times are positive, or you want to bond with someone but it isn't so effective if you want to avoid bad stuff which isn't yours. And it will be no surprise to learn that intense negative emotions like fear and anxiety are more contagious than positive ones because recognizing threats in our environment is a basic survival skill. But when overplayed, fear and anxiety stop you from thinking straight, and instead of protecting you, they become harmful; being unnecessarily flooded with cortisol is bad for your long-term health.

How to deal with it

It's almost impossible to be intuitive when you're caught up in any intense emotional state because it distorts your thinking. You might first need to find better equilibrium by:

- Standing up and shaking it out physically so you stop embodying what you feel.
- Removing yourself from the source of the anxiety to get back to a useful baseline.

- Breathing more slowly to refind some equilibrium.
- Examining something you can see through the window like a tree, and fully focusing your attention and curiosity on that until you feel calmer.
- Paying attention to parts of your body that don't experience stress, like your feet, behind your knees, or the crook of your elbow while also slowing down your breath. Focusing on your tight chest or clenched stomach can just heighten anxiety.
- Concentrating on managing the next few minutes not the next few months.
- Going for a walk, doing yoga, taking a shower, or going for a swim. Anything physical always helps if you're in a heightened state.

Once you're calmer, if it isn't clear whether a feeling belongs to you or someone else, ask yourself, "Where is this coming from?" or "Who owns this?" Cut eye contact with anyone if you're in a shared space, so you can focus on intuiting an answer.

Tip: You can also try imagining what you're feeling as a cloud; move it around in your mind's eye and see who it feels most comfortably attached to. Notice how it expands or contracts as you move it from person to person.

Tip: If you get a sense that a feeling isn't yours, just mentally detach yourself from it and imagine putting a screen, fence, or shield up around you. What you're doing is teaching yourself to disengage, and if you do it every time, it will become an automatic reaction.

Second, if someone around you is angry, frustrated, or nervous, deliberately slow down your breathing. The contagion effect means you should be able to lead them to a calmer state, and that will help you manage in the moment.

10. Getting a miss or series of misses

What you'll find

When you're wrestling with this block, you'll probably:

- Be surprised or wrong-footed by the way things work out
- Start to doubt your feeling of knowing and begin to second-guess yourself
- Pressurize yourself and make more mistakes

Why it happens

You're human, with all the glorious imperfections that this entails, so you're going to get some misses. But it can be very disconcerting when you get a string of them because it can knock your confidence. That can happen when you can't be your authentic self because you're spending time with people whose judgment you worry about and whom you don't feel safe with. If a large part of your day involves being tense and hyper-vigilant, you won't have much room for intuition.

Time-pressure is a second big factor when it comes to intuition; when you're a leader there are plenty of people pushing you to make immediate decisions. Lack of time means you may not pay enough attention to the situation, your internal or weak signals. Here's one anonymous CEO talking about a decision which illustrates that point.

> *We did one acquisition which was not good. I had a niggle at the time, but I overrode it because I felt we needed to do it for momentum. In looking back at the facts, I relied too much on somebody who was new in role. The person who had been there previously I really trusted, and I just transferred that trust to him.*

That isn't lack of intuition but overriding what you know to get something done.

How to deal with it

Staying mentally and physically fit is a great first step as Dame Louise Makin, ex-CEO and NED, explains:

> *One thing I realised quite quickly as CEO is that I need to keep myself in the best possible shape to make good judgments. I quite quickly got over the guilt of "I'm going to go a Pilates class" or deciding to work at home or go away for a few days. Understanding how I kept myself in the best space to access intuition, make the best judgments and let it flow was critical.*
>
> *It's instrumental to monitor when you're out of balance and to do all the things that put you back into your best possible shape to be the best version of yourself because that's what you're paid to do.*

Second, if you find several misses showing up consecutively, go back to Chapter 2 to review your process and use your journal to answer these questions:

- What was the miss?
- What was the context?
- What happened?
- What got in the way?

Third, consider if you might have been projecting. That means taking thoughts, faults, or feelings that you dislike about yourself and attributing them to someone else. You jump to false conclusions or assumptions about others, mistaking them for intuition when it's really all about you. For example, you might be irritated by a colleague because you're stressed and overwhelmed by what's going on at home. In that way, projection is as if you're dumping all your belongings on someone else's desk and then blaming them for it being untidy. That's the time to find some equilibrium and check where an intense feeling belongs.

Finally, if you get a string of misses and feel your intuition is off, go for what's small but make it less specific. Instead of intuiting that someone will, for example, be wearing red shoes, which is very precise, feel the right moment is to say something in a meeting, sense when it's a good time to drop past someone at work or call them, and look at your wardrobe and decide what would be energizing to wear today. As you make those choices, notice what's going on for you internally, what your attention is being drawn to externally, and be observant of all those cues.

Tip: If you assume your intuition will be there it's more likely to show up, as the expectation effect shows. And check out the short exercises which come next so you practice enough in low-risk situations.

Tip: Keep a conversation going with your intuition; ask it what it needs and how it's doing. Feel when it's more present and more absent. Encourage it to show up, and thank it when it does. Anything you have a strong relationship with is bound to work better.

Conclusion

There are plenty of ways that you can trip over your intuition, and this isn't an exhaustive list. But if you've read even a few sections of this toolkit, you'll have noticed that negativity is a greater blocker of your intuitive abilities. Meaning, fear, anxiety, irritation, pressure, overwhelm, and frustration get in the way. That chimes with research done by Weston Agor back in the 1980s. He asked leaders about times when they thought they'd followed their intuition but got it wrong. What he found was that self-deception, pretense, wishful thinking, over-investment, ego, stress, and emotional pressure had been mistaken for the real deal.

It's much easier to hear the whisper of intuition and avoid traps when you feel grounded, refreshed, and clear-minded and have taken some time for yourself. If you feel really stuck on the intuitive front, start with some self-care first.

Whatever blocks you face, there are some that will recur more regularly for you and others you'll never experience. Start to notice where you stumble the most and what helps you recover, and note that down in your journal. The more you build that muscle, the quicker you'll teach your unconscious mind what you want, and sooner or later you'll overcome that issue for good.

If, however, you get really stuck and can't seem to break through, go to LinkedIn, find me or our intuitive group, and message us with your question.

Intuitive exercises

Remember that if you try from a place of pressure or high emotion, you're more likely to go wrong; relax and use curiosity instead.

Quick and specific hits

- You get an invoice. Before you open the envelope or email, intuit the amount owing.
- You go to fill up your car; how much gas will you buy?
- You're driving down the highway; which vehicle is going to pull out? Or exit?
- You're traveling somewhere; what time might you arrive?
- You are at the checkout of any store; how much will your purchases cost?
- Say the time out loud before you check your phone or watch.
- If you get a hit to call someone, just do it and check what's happening for them.
- If you feel you need to meet someone you don't yet know, do it.
- If you get a positive feeling from someone and like their energy, tell them and find out more.
- If you look at your food and don't want to eat it, don't. Check in with others who ate it afterward.
- If you feel drawn to doing a class or attending a conference, go for it. Pay attention to who you meet and how you feel afterward.
- Notice the energy when you walk into a room. What does it tell you? See who agrees with you and why.

Use Instagram or TikTok to find intuitive additional exercises.

Additional more work-focused options

- Speak up in a meeting without self-editing and get feedback on what you said.
- Project forward to your next meeting: what's the atmosphere going to be like? What outcomes do you think you'll achieve? Where might you land up?
- Write a closed question down on a piece of paper and get two sticky notes. Write "yes" on one sticky note and "no" on the other, and attach them side-by-side under your question. Come back an hour later and see which sticky note you want to underline and which one you want to throw away. Remember, the correct answer may not be the one you really want.
- If you feel irritated in a work situation, check in with your intuition to see what's off. Start to notice patterns.
- If you're uncertain which option to select because several seem plausible, project into the future as if each one had happened. Fully engage with all the detail. What do you notice about each in terms of feelings, sensations, and thoughts?
- If you feel under pressure to decide, allow yourself a set amount of time to truly feel what you want. An intuitive decision even if it's a no, will feel lighter, righter, and more aligned.
- If you're struggling to commit, use Alexander the Great's technique. He would ask himself how much and what evidence it would take to abandon the current plan.

Bibliography

Introduction

Agor, W.H. (1986) The Logic of Intuition: How Top Executives Make Important Decisions. *Organizational Dynamics* 14(3), 5–18

Edelson, M. (2015) The Science behind Going You're Your Gut. *Johns Hopkins Magazine*, https://hub.jhu.edu/magazine/2015/spring/heuristics-going-with-your-gut/

Julmi, C. (2019) When Rational Decision-making becomes Irrational: A Critical Assessment and Re-conceptualization of Intuitive Effectiveness. *Business Research* 12, 291–314.

KPMG (2018) https://home.kpmg/xx/en/home/insights/2018/02/in-digital-world-do-you-trust-the-data.html#

Kump, B. (2022) No Need to Hide: Acknowledging the Researcher's Intuition in Empirical Organizational Research. *Human Relations* 75(4), 635–654, https://doi.org/10.1177/0018726720984837

Maidique, M.A. (2011) Decoding Intuition for More Effective Decision-making. *Harvard Business Review*, https://hbr.org/2011/08/decoding-intuition-for-more-ef

Majority of Business Decision-Makers Say Human Insights Should Precede Analytics (2014) *Marketing Charts,* https://www.marketingcharts.com/customer-centric/customer-engagement-44153

Marinos, G., & Rosni, N. (2017) The Role of Intuition in Executive Strategic Decision Making, https://lup.lub.lu.se/luur/download?func=downloadFile&recordOId=8915229&fileOId=8915230

McKinsey (2022) Human Capital at Work: The Value of Experience, accessed 24.04.2023, https://www.mckinsey.com/business-functions/people-and-organizational-performance/our-insights/human-capital-at-work-the-value-of-experience?cid=eml-web

Medvegy, Z., Raab, M., Tóth, K., Csurilla, G., & Sterbenz, T. (2022) When Do Expert Decision Makers Trust Their Intuition? *Applied Cognitive Psychology*, EarlyView.

Mikels, J.A., et al. (2011) Should I Go With My Gut? Investigating the Benefits of Emotion-Focused Decision Making. *Emotion* 4, 743–753.

Powell, J.E. (2020) Why Gut Instinct Still Dominates Decision Making. TDWI, https://tdwi.org/Articles/2020/10/01/BIZ-ALL-Why-Gut-Instinct-Still-Dominates-Decision-Making.aspx?Page=2

PWC (2014) Executives Rely More on Experience and Advice Than Data, https://www.pwc.com/im/en/assets/document/big-decisions-data-analytics-sept-2014.pdf

Sadler-Smith, E., et al. (2021) Identifying the Linguistic Markers of Intuition in Human Resource (HR) Practice. *Human Resource Management Journal*, https://doi.org/10.1111/1748-8583.12410

Tsetsos, K., Chater, N., & Usher, M. (2012) Salience Driven Value Integration Explains Decision Biases and Preference Reversal. *PNAS* 109(24), 9659, https://doi.org/10.1073/pnas.1119569109

Woiceshyn, J. (2009) Lessons from "Good Minds"; How CEOs Use Intuition, Analysis and Guiding Principles to Make Strategic Decisions. *Long Range Planning* 43(3), 298–319.

Chapter 1

Adinolfi P, & Loia F. Intuition as Emergence: Bridging Psychology, Philosophy and Organizational Science (2022). *Front Psychol.* doi: 10.3389/fpsyg.2021.787428

Akinci, C., & Sadler-Smith, E. (2019) Collective Intuition: Implications for Improved Decision Making and Organizational Learning. *British Journal of Management* 30, 558–577, https://doi.org/10.1111/1467-8551.12269

Bechara, A., Damasio, A.R., Damasio, H., & Anderson, S.W. (1994) Insensitivity to Future Consequences Following Damage to Human Prefrontal Cortex. *Cognition* 50(1–3), 7–15, https://doi.org/10.1016/0010-0277(94)90018-3

Bechara, A., Damasio, H., Tranel, D., & Damasio, A.R. (1997) Deciding Advantageously before Knowing the Advantageous Strategy. *Science* 275(5304), 1293–1295, https://doi.org/10.1126/science.275.5304.1293

Bolte, A., Goschke, T., & Kuhl, J. (2003) Emotion and Intuition: Effects of Positive and Negative Mood on Implicit Judgments of Semantic Coherence. *Psychological Science* 14(5), 416–421, https://doi.org/10.1111/1467-9280.01456

Bos, A., van der Leij, M.W., & van Baaren, R.B. (2009) Predicting Soccer Matches after Unconscious and Conscious thought as a Function of Expertise. *Psychological Science*, https://doi.org/10.1111%2Fj.1467-9280.2009.02451.x

Chou Locke, C. (2015) When It's Safe to Rely on Intuition (and when It's not). HBR, https://hbr.org/2015/04/when-its-safe-to-rely-on-intuition-and-when-its-not

Cszsentmihalyi, M. (1990) *Flow, The Psychology of Optimal Experience: Steps Toward Enhancing the Quality of Life.* New York: Harper Collins.

Dane, E., & Pratt, M.G. (2007) Exploring Intuition and Its Role in Managerial Decision Making. *Academy of Management Review* 32(1), 33–54.

Denworth, L. (2023) Brain Waves Synchronize when People Interact. *Scientific American*, 52–7, https://www.scientificamerican.com/article/brain-waves-synchronize-when-people-interact/

Dijksterhuis, A., Bos, M.W., van der Leij, A., & van Baaren, R.B. (2009) Predicting Soccer Matches after Unconscious and Conscious thought as a Function of Expertise. *Psychological Science*, https://doi.org/10.1111%2Fj.1467-9280.2009.02451.x

Eichler, R.L., & Halseth, J.H. (1992) Intuition. *Social Work with Groups* 15(1), 81–93, https://doi.org/10.1300/J009v15n01_07

Eisenhardt, K.M. (1999) Strategy as Strategic Decision Making. *Sloan Management Review* 40(3), 65–72.

Femke, S., Ten Velden, F.S., Daughters, K., & De Dreu, C.K.W. (2017) Oxytocin Promotes Intuitive Rather than Deliberated Cooperation with the In-group. *Hormones and Behavior* 92, 164–171, https://doi.org/10.1016/j.yhbeh.2016.06.005

Foss, L. (1999) The Necessary Subjectivity of Bodymind Medicine: Candace Pert's Molecules of Emotions. *Advances in Mind-Body Medicine* 15(2), 122–134, https://doi.org/10.1054/ambm .1999.0161

Friedemann Smith, C., et al. (2022) Building the Case for the Use of Gut Feelings in Cancer Referrals: Perspectives of Patients Referred to a Non-specific Symptoms Pathway. *British Journal of General Practice* 72(714), e43–e50, https://doi.org/10.3399/BJGP.2021.0275

Gerrie, H., accessed 17.03.2022, https://neuroscience.ubc.ca/our-second-brain-more-than-a-gut -feeling/

Hardman, T.J. (2021) Understanding Creative Intuition. *Journal of Creativity* 31, https://doi.org /10.1016/j.yjoc.2021.100006

Honorton, C., & Ferrari, D.C. (1989) "Future Telling": A Meta-analysis of Forced-choice Precognition Experiments, 1935–1987. *Journal of Parapsychology* 53, 281–308.

Järvilehto, L. (2016) Intuition and Flow. In L. Harmat, F. Ørsted Andersen, F. Ullén, J. Wright, & G. Sadlo (eds.), *Flow Experience*. Cham: Springer, https://doi.org/10.1007/978-3-319-28634-1_7

Kandasamy, N., Garfinkel, S., Page, L., et al. (2016) Interoceptive Ability Predicts Survival on a London Trading Floor. *Scientific Reports* 6, 32986, https://doi.org/10.1038/srep32986

Kershaw, T.C., & Ohlsson, S. (2004) Multiple Causes of Difficulty in Insight: The Case of the Nine-dot Problem. *Journal of Experimental Psychology: Learning, Memory, and Cognition* 30(1), 3–13, https://doi.org/10.1037/0278-7393.30.1.3

Kirkebøen, G., & Nordbye Gro, H.H. (2017) Intuitive Choices Lead to Intensified Positive Emotions: An Overlooked Reason for "Intuition Bias"? *Frontiers in Psychology* 8, https://doi. org/10.3389/fpsyg.2017.01942

Kutch, L. (2019) Can We Rely on Our Intuition? *Scientific American*, https://www. scientificamerican.com/article/can-we-rely-on-our-intuition/

Lufityanto, G., Donkin, C., & Pearson, J. (2016) Measuring Intuition: Nonconscious Emotional Information Boosts Decision Accuracy and Confidence. *Psychological Science*, https://doi.org/10.1177/0956797616629403

Maidique, M.A. (2011) Decoding Intuition for More Effective Decision-making. *Harvard Business Review*, https://hbr.org/2011/08/decoding-intuition-for-more-ef

Matthews, R. (2020) *Science Focus*, https://www.sciencefocus.com/the-human-body/a-gut-feeling-meet-your-second-brain/

McCraty, R., Atkinson, M., & Bradley, R.T. (2004) Electrophysiological Evidence of Intuition: Part 1. The Surprising Role of the Heart. *Journal of Alternative and Complementary Medicine* 10(1), 133–143. https://doi.org/10.1089/107555304322849057

Mikels, J.A., Maglio, S.J., Reed, A.E., & Kaplowitz, L.J. (2011) Should I Go with My Gut? Investigating the Benefits of Emotion-focused Decision Making. *Emotion* 11(4), 743–753, https://doi.org/10.1037/a0023986

Mobbs, D., et al. (2015) The Ecology of Human Fear: Survival Optimization and the Nervous System. *Frontiers in* Neuroscience, https://doi.org/10.3389/fnins.2015.00055

Raami, A. (2015) Intuition Unleashed: On the Application and Development of Intuition in the Creative Process. Aalto University Publication Series, https://aaltodoc.aalto.fi/handle /123456789/15347

Radin, D.I., & Sclitz, M.J. (2005) Gut Feelings, Intuition and Emotions: An Exploratory Study. *Journal of Alternative and Complementary Medicine* 11(1), 85–91.

Sadler-Smith, E. (2023) *Intuition in Business*. Oxford: Oxford University Press.

Sadler-Smith, W., & Burkey-Smallet, L.A. (2014) What Do We Really Understand about How Mangers Make Important Decisions? *Organizational Dynamics*, http://dx.doi.org/10.1016/j .orgdyn.2014.11.002

Samba, C., et al. (2018) The Impact of Strategic Dissent on Organizational Outcomes: A Meta-analytic Integration. *Strategic Management Journal* 39(2), 379–402.

Samba, C., Williams, D.W., & Fuller, R.M. (2022) The Forms and Use of Intuition in Top Management Teams. *The Leadership Quarterly* 33(3), https://doi.org/10.1016/j.leaqua.2019 .101349

Sinnott-Armstrong, W., Young, L., & Cushman, F. (2010) Moral Intuitions. In J.M. Doris (ed.) & Moral Psychology Research Group, *The Moral Psychology Handbook*, pp. 246–272. Oxford: Oxford University Press.

Storm, L., & Tressoldi, P. (2020) Meta-Analysis of Free-Response Studies 2009-2018: Assessing the Noise-Reduction Model Ten Years On. *Journal of the Society for Psychical Research*, https://doi.org/10.31234/osf.io/3d7at

Vincent, V., Guidice, R., & Mero, N. (2021) Should You Follow Your Gut? The Impact of Expertise on Intuitive Hiring Decisions for Complex Jobs. *Journal of Management & Organization*, 1–21, https://doi.org/10.1017/jmo.2021.9

Walsh, C.W., Collins, J., & Knott, P. (2022) The Four Types of Intuition Managers Need to Know. *Business Horizons* 65(5), 697–708, https://doi.org/10.1016/j.bushor.2021.12 .003

Wergin, V.V., Zimanyi, Z., Mesagno, C., & Beckmann, J. (2018) When Suddenly Nothing Works Anymore within a Team – Causes of Collective Sport Team Collapse. *Frontiers in Psychology* 9, 2115, https://doi.org/10.3389/fpsyg.2018.02115

Wong, M. (2014) Stanford Study Finds Walking Improves Creativity, https://news.stanford.edu /2014/04/24/walking-vs-sitting-042414/

Zak, P.J. (2017) The Neuroscience of Trust. *Harvard Business Review*, https://www.emcleaders .com/wp-content/uploads/2017/03/hbr-neuroscience-of-trust.pdf

Zander, T., Öllinger, M., & Volz Kirsten, G. (2016) Intuition and Insight: Two Processes That Build on Each Other or Fundamentally Differ? *Frontiers in Psychology* 7, https://doi.org/10 .3389/psyg.2016.01395

Zander-Schellenberg, T., et al. (2019) It was Intuitive, and It Felt Good: A Daily Diary Study on How People Feel When Making Decisions. *Cognition and Emotion* 33(7), 1505–1513, https://doi.org/10.1080/02699931.2019.1570914

Chapter 2

Agor, W.H. (1986) The Logic of Intuition: How Top Executives Make Important Decisions. *Organizational Dynamics* 14(3), 5–18, https://doi.org/10.1016/0090-2616(86)90028-8

Gambetti, E., et al. (2020) You Are Right, You Are Wrong: The Effect of Feedback on Intuitive Thinking. *The American Journal of Psychology* 133(4), 473–485, https://doi.org/10.5406/ amerjpsyc.133.4.0473#

Harwig, K. (2000) *The Advantage*. Spring Press.

Hogarth, R.M. (2010) *Educating Intuition*. The University of Chicago Press.

Sadler-Smith, E. (2010) *The Intuitive Mind*. Wiley.

Shanteau, J. (1992) Competence in Experts: The Role of Task Characteristics. *Organizational Behavior and Human Decision Processes* 53, 252–262.

Woiceshyn, J. (2009) Lessons from "Good Minds": How CEOs use Analysis, Intuition and Guiding Principles to Make Strategic Decisions. *Long Range Planning* 42(3), 298–319.

Chapter 3

Alkozei, A., et al. (2019) Increases in Emotional Intelligence After an Online Training Program Are Associated With Better Decision-Making on the Iowa Gambling Task. *Psychological Reports* 22(3), 853–879, https://doi.org/10.1177/0033294118771705

Amabile, T., et al. (2002) Time Pressure and Creativity in Organizations: A Longitudinal Field Study. *Harvard Business School Working Paper, Number 02-073.*

Barford, K.A., & Smillie, L. (2016) Openness and Other Big Five Traits in Relation to Dispositional Mixed Emotions. *Personality and Individual Differences* 102, 118–122.

Beaty, R.E., et al. (2016) Personality and Complex Brain Networks: The Role of Openness to Experience in Default Network Efficiency. *Human Brain Mapping* 37, 773–779.

Chaffey, L., Unsworth, C., & Fossey, E. (2012) Relationship between Intuition and Emotional Intelligence in Occupational Therapists in Mental Health Practice. *The American Journal of Occupational Therapy* 66, 88–96, https://doi.org/10.5014/ajot.2012.001693

Damasio, A.R., Everitt, B.J., & Bishop, D. (1996) The Somatic Marker Hypothesis and the Possible Functions of the Prefrontal Cortex. *Philosophical Transactions: Biological Sciences* 351(1346), 1413–1420, http://www.jstor.org/stable/30691

Dane, E., & Pratt, M. (2007) Exploring Intuition and Its Role in Managerial Decision Making. *Academy of Management Review* 32(1), 33–54

Downey, L.A., Papageorgiou, V., & Stough, C. (2006) Examining the Relationship between Leadership, Emotional Intelligence and Intuition in Senior Female Managers. *Leadership & Organization Development Journal* 27(4), 250–264.

Dunn, B.D., et al. (2010) Listening to Your Heart: How Interoception Shapes Emotion Experience and Intuitive Decision Making. *Psychological Science* 21(12), 1835–1844.

Fischer, D., Messner, M., & Pollatos, O. (2017) Improvement of Interoceptive Processes after an 8-Week Body Scan Intervention. *Frontiers in Human Neuroscience* 11, https://www.frontiersin.org/article/10.3389/fnhum.2017.00452

Fukukura, J., Ferguson, M.J., & Fujita, K. (2013) Psychological Distance Can Improve Decision Making under Information Overload via Gist Memory. *Journal of Experimental Psychology: General* 142(3), 658–665, https://doi.org/10.1037/a0030730

Garfinkel, S.N., et al. (2015) Knowing Your Own Heart: Distinguishing Interoceptive Accuracy from Interoceptive Awareness. *Biological Psychology* 104, 65–74, https://doi.org/10.1016/j.biopsycho.2014.11.004

Gibson, J. (2019) Mindfulness, Interoception, and the Body: A Contemporary Perspective. *Frontiers in Psychology* 10, https://www.frontiersin.org/article/10.3389/fpsyg.2019.02012

Grynberg, D., & Pollatos, O. (2015) Perceiving One's Body Shapes Empathy. *Physiology & Behavior* 140, 54–60, https://doi.org/10.1016/j.physbeh.2014.12.026

Holzer, P. (2017) Interoception and Gut Feelings: Unconscious Body Signals' Impact on Brain Function, Behavior and Belief Processes. In H.-F. Angel, L. Oviedo, R.F. Paloutzian, A.L.C. Runehov, & R.J. Seitz (eds.), *Processes of Believing: The Acquisition, Maintenance, and Change in Creditions*, pp. 435–442. Springer International Publishing AG, https://doi.org/10.1007/978-3-319-50924-2_31

Kara-Yakoubian, M., Walker, A.C., Sharpinskyi, K., Assadourian, G., Fugelsang, J.A., & Harris, R.A. (2022) Beauty and Truth, Truth and Beauty: Chiastic Structure Increases the Subjective Accuracy of Statements. *Canadian Journal of Experimental Psychology/Revue canadienne de psychologie expérimentale.* Advance online publication, https://doi.org/10.1037/cep0000277

Khan, E., Riaz, M., Batool, N., & Riaz, M. (2016) Emotional Intelligence as a Predictor of Decision Making Styles among University Students. *Journal of Applied Environmental and Biological Sciences* 6(4S), 93–99.

Lewicki, P., Hill, T., & Czyzewska, M. (1992) Nonconscious Acquisition of Information. *American Psychologist* 47(6), 796–801, https://doi.org/10.1037/0003-066X.47.6.796

Liebermann, M.D., et al. (2011) Subjective Responses to Emotional Stimuli during Labelling, Reappraisal and Distraction. *Emotions* 11, 468–480.

Liebowitz, J., et al., If Numbers Could "Feel": How Well Do Executives Trust Their Intuition? *VINE Journal of Information and Knowledge Management Systems* 49(4), 531–545, https://doi.org/10.1108/VJIKMS-12-2018-0129

Metzinger, T., & Windt, J.M. (2015) What Does It Mean to Have an Open MIND? In T. Metzinger & J.M. Windt (eds.), *Open MIND*: 0(GI). Frankfurt am Main: MIND Group, https://doi.org/10.15502/9783958571044

Niles, A.N., Craske, M.G., Lieberman, M.D., & Hur, C. (2015) Affect Labeling Enhances Exposure Effectiveness for Public Speaking Anxiety. *Behaviour Research and Therapy* 68, 27–36, https://doi.org/10.1016/j.brat.2015.03.004

Paul, A.M. (2021) *The Extended Mind*. Houghton: Mifflin Harcourt.

Plessner, H., Betsch, C., & Betsch, T., eds. (2008) *Intuition in Judgment and Decision Making*. Lawrence Erlbaum Associates

Riaz, M.N., Riaz, M.A., & Batool, N. (2012) Personality Types as Predictors of Decision-making Styles. *The Journal of Applied Behavioral Science* 22(2), 100–114.

Sayegh, L., Anthony, W.P., & Perrewé, P.L. (2004) Managerial Decision-making under Crisis: The Role of Emotion in an Intuitive Decision Process. *Human Resource Management Review* 14(2), 179–199.

Sheldon, K.M., & Lyubomirsky, S. (2006) How to Increase and Sustain Positive Emotion: The Effects of Expressing Gratitude and Visualizing Best Possible Selves. *The Journal of Positive Psychology* 1(2), 73–82, https://doi.org/10.1080/17439760500510676

Sinclair, M., & Ashkanasy, N.M. (2005) Intuition: Myth or a Decision-Making Tool? *Management Learning* 36(3), 353–370.

Smillie, L. (2017) Openness to Experience: The Gates of the Mind *Scientific American*, 28(6), 151–8.

Smith, A.J., Thurkettle, M.A., & dela Cruz, F.A. (2004) Use of Intuition by Nursing Students: Instrument Development and Testing. *Journal of Advanced Nursing* 47, 614–622.

Sobkow, A., et al. (2018) The Structure of Intuitive Abilities and Their Relationships with Intelligence and Openness to Experience. *Intelligence* 67, 1–10, https://doi.org/10.1016/j.intell.2017.12.001

Wilding, M. (2022) How to Stop Overthinking and Start Trusting Your Gut. *Harvard Business Review*, https://hbr.org/2022/03/how-to-stop-overthinking-and-start-trusting-your-gut

Yip, J.A., Stein, D.H., Côté, S., & Carney, D.R. (2020) Follow Your Gut? Emotional Intelligence Moderates the Association between Physiologically Measured Somatic Markers and Risk-taking. *Emotion* 3, 462–472, https://doi.org/10.1037/emo0000561

Zamariola, G., et al. (2019) Relationship between Interoception and Emotional Regulation: New Evidence from Mixed Methods. *Journal of Affective Disorders* 246, 480–485.

Zimmerman, A. (2021) Teams Grow Stronger When Managers Show Openness and Vulnerability. *LSE, Business Review*, https://blogstest.lse.ac.uk/businessreview/2021/07/22/teams-grow-stronger-when-managers-show-openness-and-vulnerability/

Chapter 4

Arfini, S., Bertolotti, T., & Magnani, L. (2020) The Antinomies of Serendipity How to Cognitively Frame Serendipity for Scientific Discoveries. *Topoi* 39, 939–948, https://doi.org/10.1007/s11245-018-9571-3

BBC Interview with Frank Prentice 1979, https://www.facebook.com/watch/?v=153343056073894

Beck, J. (2016) Coincidences and the Meaning of Life. *The Atlantic*, https://www.theatlantic.com/science/archive/2016/02/the-true-meaning-of-coincidences/463164/

Beitman, B. (2016) *Connecting with Coincidence, the New Science for Using Synchronicity and Serendipity in Your Life.* Health Communications Inc

Beitman, B.D. (2022) *Meaningful Coincidence: How and Why Synchronicity and Serendipity Happen.* Park Street Press.

Burger, E.B., & Starbird, M. (2005) *Coincidences, Chaos and All That Math Jazz: Making Light of Weighty Ideas.* Norton.

Burt, R.S. (2010) *Neighbor Networks: Competitive Advantage Local and Personal.* Oxford University Press.

Burt, R.S., & Soda, G. (2017) Social Origins of Great Strategies. *Strategy Science* 2(4), 226–233, https://doi.org/10.1287/stsc.2017.0043

Busch, C. (2020) *The Serendipity Mindset. The Art and Science of Creating Good Luck.* Riverhead Books.

Busch, C. (2022) Towards a Theory of Serendipity: A Systematic Review and Conceptualization. *Journal of Management Studies*, https://doi.org/10.1111/joms.12890

Clarke, R.D. (1946) An Application of the Poisson Distribution. *Journal of the Institute of Actuaries* (London) 72, https://www.cambridge.org/core/journals/journal-of-the-institute-of-actuaries/article/abs/an-application-of-the-poisson-distribution/F75111847FDA534103BD4941BD96A78E

Copeland, S. (2019) On Serendipity in Science: Discover at the Intersection of Chance and Wisdom. *Synthese* 196, 2385–2406, https://doi.org/10.1007/s11229-017-1544-3

Cunha, M.P. (2005) Serendipity: Why Some Organizations Are Luckier than Others. *FEUNL Working Paper 472*, http://dx.doi.org/10.2139/ssrn.882782

Diaconis, P., & Mosteller, F. (1999) Methods for Studying Coincidences. *Journal of American Statistical Association* 84(408), 853–861.

European Commission (2010) *Special Eurobarometer 340: Science and Technology.* EBS Report No. 340. Brussels: European Commission.

Johansen, M., & Osman, M. (2020) Coincidence Judgment in Causal Reasoning: How Coincidental Is This? *Cognitive Psychology* 120, https://doi.org/10.1016/j.cogpsych.2020.101290

Johanssen, F. (2012) When Success Is Born Out of Serendipity. *Harvard Business Review*, https://hbr.org/2012/10/when-success-is-born-out-of-serendipity

Lubowitz, J.H., et al. (2018) Two of a Kind: Multiple Discovery AKA Simultaneous Invention is the Role. *Journal of Arthroscopic and Related Surgery* 34(8), 2257–2258.

Mackey, C. (2015) *Synchronicity: Empower Your Life with the Gift of Coincidence.* Watkins.

Mackey, C. (2019) *The Positive Psychology of Synchronicity.* Watkins.

Makri, S., Blandford, A., Woods, M., Sharples, S., & Maxwell, D. (2014) "Making My Own Luck": Serendipity Strategies and How to Support them in Digital Information

Environments. *Journal of the Association for Information Science and Technology* 65(11), 2179–2194, https://doi.org/10.1002/asi.23200

Mares, L. (2021) Unconscious Processes in Psychoanalysis, CBT, and Schema Therapy. *Journal of Psychotherapy Integration.* Advance online publication, https://doi.org/10.1037/int0000276

Marlo, H., & Kline, J.S. (1998) Synchronicity and Psychotherapy: Unconscious Communication in the Psychotherapeutic Relationship. *Psychotherapy: Theory, Research, Practice, Training* 35(1), 13–22, https://doi.org/10.1037/h0087805

McCay-Peet, L., & Toms, E.G. (2015) Investigating Serendipity: How It Unfolds and What May Influence It. *Journal for the Association of Information Science and Technology* 66(7), 1463–1476.

Ross, W., & Vallée-Tourangeau, F. (2020) Microserendipity in the Creative Process. *Creative Behavior,* https://doi.org/10.1002/jocb.478

Tversky, A., & Kahneman, D. (1974) Judgment under Uncertainty: Heuristics and Biases. *Science* 185(4157), 1124–1131.

Uscinski, J., et al. (2022) Have Beliefs in Conspiracy Theories Increased Over Time? *PLoS ONE* 17(7), e0270429, https://doi.org/10.1371/journal.pone.0270429

Van Elk, M., Friston, K., & Bekkering, H. (2016) The Experience of Coincidence: An Integrated Psychological and Neurocognitive Perspective. In K. Landsman & E. van Wolde (eds.), *The Challenge of Chance, The Frontiers Collection,* https://doi.org/10.1007/978-3-319-26300-7_9

Wiseman, R. (2003) The Luck Factor. *Skeptical Inquirer* 27(3), 1–5, http://richardwiseman.com/resources/The_Luck_Factor.pdf

Chapter 5

Aspy, D.J. (2016) Is Dream Recall Underestimated by Retrospective Measures and Enhanced by Keeping a Logbook? An Empirical Investigation. *Consciousness and Cognition* 42, 181–203, https://doi.org/10.1016/j.concog.2016.03.015

Barsade, S.G. (2020) The Contagion We Can Control. *Harvard Business Review,* https://hbr.org/2020/03/the-contagion-we-can-control

Barsade, S.G., et al. (2018) Emotional Contagion in Organizational Life. *Research in Organizational Behavior* 38, 137–151, https://doi.org/10.1016/j.riob.2018.11.005

Bem, D.J. (2011) Feeling the Future: Experimental Evidence for Anomalous Retroactive Influences on Cognition and Affect. *Journal of Personality and Social Psychology* 100(3), 407–425.

Bird, M.I., et al. (2018) Palaeogeography and Voyage Modeling Indicates Early Human Colonization of Australia Was Likely from Timor-Roti. *Quaternary Science Reviews* 191, 431–439.

Bošnjak, P.M., et al. (2018) Many Faces of Déjà Vu: A Narrative Review. *Psychiatria Danubina* 30(1), 21–25, https://doi.org/10.24869/psyd.2018.21

Cardeña, E. (2018) The Experimental Evidence for Parapsychological Phenomena: A Review. *American Psychologist* 73(5), 663–677, https://doi.org/10.1037/amp0000236

Cheung, T., & Mossbridger, J. (2019) *The Premonition Code.* Watkins.

Fallon, J.H. (2015) Foreword. In E.C. May & S.B. Marwaha (eds.), *Extrasensory Perception: Support, Skepticism, and Science. Vol. 1: History, Controversy, and Research,* pp. ix–xv. Santa Barbara: Praege.

Fowler, J.H., & Christakis, N.A. (2008) Dynamic Spread of Happiness in a Large Social Network: Longitudinal Analysis over 20 Years in the Framingham Heart Study. *BMJ* 337, a2338.

Goldenberg, A., & Gross, J.J. (2020) Digital Emotion Contagion. *Trends in Cognitive Sciences* 24(4), 316–328, https://doi.org/10.1016/j.tics.2020.01.009

Gollwitzer, P.M. (1993) Goal Achievement: The Role of Intentions. *European Review of Social Psychology* 4(1), 141–185, https://doi.org/10.1080/14792779343000059

Haraldsson, E. (1985) Representative National Surveys of Psychic Phenomena. *Journal of the Society for Psychical Research* 53, 145–158.

Lange, R., Schredl, M., & Houran, J. (2000) What Precognitive Dreams Are Made Of: The Nonlinear Dynamics of Tolerance of Ambiguity, Dream Recall, and Paranormal Belief. *Dynamic Psychology: An International Interdisciplinary Journal of Complex Mental Processes*, https://goertzel.org/dynapsyc/2000/Precog%20Dreams.htm

Lee, J.H. (2007) Remote Viewing as Applied to Futures Studies. *Technological Forecasting & Social Change*, https://doi.org/10.1016/j.techfore.2006.09.001

Mossbridge, J., Tressoldi, P., & Utts, J. (2012) Predictive Physiological Anticipation Preceding Seemingly Unpredictable Stimuli: A Meta-analysis. *Frontiers in Psychology* 3, 390, https://doi.org/10.3389/fpsyg.2012.00390

Mossbridge, J.A., & Radin, D. (2018) Precognition as a Form of Prospection: A Review of the Evidence. *Psychology of Consciousness: Theory, Research, and Practice* 5(1), 78–93, https://doi.org/10.1037/cns0000121

Müller, M., Müller, L., & Wittmann, M. (2019) Predicting the Stock Market: An Associative Remote Viewing Study. *Zeitschrift für Anomalistik* Band 19(2019), S.326–346, DOI: 10.23793/zfa.2019.326

Parra, A., & Argibay, J.C. (2013) Anomalous Remote Diagnosis: Mental and Motor Psi Impressions under Iconic Representation of the Person-Target. *Journal of Parapsychology* 77(1), 123–130.

Radtke, E.L., et al. (2020) Personality, Stress, and Intuition: Emotion Regulation Abilities Moderate the Effect of Stress-Dependent Cortisol Increase on Coherence Judgments. *Frontiers in Psychology* 11, https://doi.org/10.3389/fpsyg.2020.00339

Roe, C. (2021) Small Wonder: Effect Sizes in Parapsychology. *The Magazine for the Society of Psychical Research* 1, 4–5.

Schmidt, S., Schneider, R., Utts, J., & Walach, H. (2004) Distant Intentionality and the Feeling of Being Stared At: Two Meta-analyses. *British Journal of Psychology* (Pt 2), 235–247, https://doi.org/10.1348/000712604773952449

Smith, C.C., Laham, D., & Moddel, G. (2014) Stock Market Prediction Using Associative Remote Viewing by Inexperienced Remote Viewers. *Journal of Scientific Exploration* 28(1), https://journalofscientificexploration.org/index.php/jse/article/view/6...

Utts, J. (1991) Replication and Meta-analysis in Parapsychology. *Statistical Science* 6(4), 363–403.

Utts, J. (1999) The Significance of Statistics in Mind-Matter. *Research Journal of Scientific Exploration* 13(4), 615–638.

Wahbeh, H., Radin, D., Mossbridge, J., Vieten, C., & Delorme, A. (2018) Exceptional Experiences Reported by Scientists and Engineers. *Explore* (NY) 14(5), 329–341, https://doi.org/10.1016/j.explore.2018.05.002

Wargo, E. (2021) *Precognitive Dreamwork and The Long Self*. Rochester, Vermont: Inner Traditions.

Yu, R. (2015) Stress Potentiates Decision Biases: A Stress Induced Deliberation-to-Intuition (SIDI) Model. *Neurobiology of Stress* 3, 83–95, https://doi.org/10.1016/j.ynstr.2015.12.006

Chapter 6

Akgün, A., & Keskin, H. (2021) Team Intuition and Creativity in New Product Development Projects: A Multi-faceted Perspective. *Journal of Engineering and Technology Management* 62, 101660, https://doi.org/10.1016/j.jengtecman.2021.101660

Akinci, C., & Sadler-Smith, E. (2019) Collective Intuition: Implications for Improved Decision Making and Organizational Learning. *British Journal of Management* 30, 558–577, https://doi.org/10.1111/1467-8551.12269

Barraza, P., Perez, A., & Rodríguez, E. (2020) Brain-to-Brain Coupling in the Gamma-Band as a Marker of Shared Intentionality. *Frontiers in Human Neuroscience* 14, https://www.frontiersin.org/articles/10.3389/fnhum.2020.00295

Boddy, C.R. (2015) Organisational Psychopaths: A Ten-Year Update. *Management Decision* 53(10), 2407–2432, http://dx.doi.org/10.1108/md-04-2015-0114

Bolte, A., Goschke, T., & Kuhl, J. (2003) Emotion and Intuition: Effects of Positive and Negative Mood on Implicit Judgments of Semantic Coherence. *Psychological Science* 14(5), 416–421, https://doi.org/10.1111/1467-9280.01456

Boulter, L. (2021) *How so Many Toxic Employees Ascend to Leadership*. Palgrave Macmillan, https://doi.org/10.1007/978-3-030-65025-4_4

Claxton, G., et al. (2013) Hubris in Leadership: A Peril of Unbridled Intuition. *Leadership* 11(1), 57–78, https://journals.sagepub.com/doi/10.1177/1742715013511482

Codou, S., Williams, D.W., & Fuller, R.M. (2022) The Forms and Use of Intuition in Top Management Teams. *The Leadership Quarterly* 33(3), https://doi.org/10.1016/j.leaqua.2019.101349

Cunha, M.P., Rego, A., Clegg, A., & Lindsay, G. (2015) The Dialectics of Serendipity. *European Management Journal* 33(1), 9–18, https://doi.org/10.1016/j.emj.2014.11.001

Dane, E., & Pratt, M.G. (2007) Exploring Intuition and Its Role in Managerial Decision Making. *Academy of Management Review* 32, 33–54.

Dayan, M., & Elbanna, S. (2011) Antecedents of Team Intuition and Its Impact on the Success of New Product Development Projects. *The Journal of Product Innovation Management* 28(s1), 159–174.

Edmondson, A. (1999) Psychological Safety and Learning Behavior in Work Teams. *Administrative Science Quarterly* 44(2), 350–383, https://doi.org/10.2307/2666999

Eichler, R.L., & Halseth, J.H. (1992) Intuition. *Social Work with Groups* 15(1), 81–93, https://doi.org/10.1300/J009v15n01_07

Eisenhardt, K.M. (1999) Strategy as Strategic Decision Making. *MIT Sloan Management Review* 40(3), 65.

Evans, A.M., & Rand, D.G. (2019) Cooperation and Decision Time. *Current Opinion in Psychology* 26, 67–71, https://doi.org/10.1016/j.copsyc.2018.05.007

Fuller, R., Vera, D., Samba, C., & Williams, D. (2021) Virtual Team Decision Making: The Value of Team Intuition and Its Enabling Media Capabilities. *Academy of Management Proceedings* 1, 14345.

Greenhalgh, T. (2002) Intuition and Evidence-Uneasy Bedfellows? *British Journal of General Practice* 52(478), 395–400.

Hasson, U., et al. (2012) Brain-to-Brain Coupling: A Mechanism for Creating and Sharing a Social World. *Trends in Cognitive Sciences* 6(2), 114–121, https://doi.org/10.1016/j.tics.2011.12.007

Hill, D., & Scott, H. (2019) Climbing the Corporate Ladder: Desired Leadership Skills and Successful Psychopaths. *Journal of Financial Crime* 26(3), 881–896, https://doi.org/10.1108/JFC-11-2018-0117

Hogan, R., & Hogan, J. (2008) Assessing Leadership: A View from the Dark Side. *International Journal of Selection and Assessment*, http://dx.doi.org/10.1111/1468-2389.00162

Holt, D.T., et al. (2007) Readiness for Organizational Change: The Systematic Development of a Scale. *Journal of Applied Behavioral Science* 43(2), 232–255.

Jett, Q., & Brown, A. (2002) *Collective Intuition: The Formation of Shared Experience for Rapid Problem Solving in Innovation Teams.* Houston: Working Paper.

Keil, M., et al. (2007) Reporting Bad News on Software Projects: The Effects of Culturally Constituted Views of Face-Saving. *Information Systems Journal* 17, 59–87, https://doi.org/10.1111/j.1365-2575.2006.00235.x

Kuusela, H., Koivumäki, S., & Yrjölä, M. (2020) M&As Get Another Assist: When CEOs Add Intuition to the Decision Mix. *Journal of Business Strategy* 41(3), 57–65.

Levitt, S.D. (2021) Heads or Tails: The Impact of a Coin Toss on Major Life Decisions and Subsequent Happiness. *The Review of Economic Studies* 88(1), 378–405, https://doi.org/10.1093/restud/rdaa016

Medvegy, Z., Raab, M., Tóth, K., Csurilla, G., & Sterbenz, T. (2022) When Do Expert Decision Makers Trust Their Intuition? *Applied Cognitive Psychology* 36(4), 748–57.

Miller, C.C., & Ireland, R.D. (2005) Intuition in Strategic Decision Making: Friend or Foe in the Fast-paced 21st Century? *Academy of Management Executive* 19, 19–30.

Nuthall, P.L. (2022) Assessing the Core Variables of Business Managers' Intuitive Decision Ability: A Review and Analysis. *Behavioral Sciences* 12(11), 409, https://doi.org/10.3390/bs12110409

Prietule, J.M., & Simon, H.A. (1989) The Experts in Your Midst. *Harvard Business Review* 67, 120–134.

Reinero, D.A., Dikker, A., & Van Bavel, J.J. (2021) Inter-brain Synchrony in Teams Predicts Collective Performance. *Social Cognitive and Affective Neuroscience* 16(1–2), 43–57, https://doi.org/10.1093/scan/nsaa135

Royer, I. (2003) Why Bad Projects Are so Hard to Kill. *Harvard Business Review* 81(2), 48–56, 123.

Salas, E., et al. (2010) Expertise-Based Intuition and Decision Making in Organizations. *Journal of Management* 36, 941–973.

Samba, C., et al. (2018) The Impact of Strategic Dissent on Organizational Outcomes: A Meta-analytic Integration. *Strategic Management Journal* 39(2), 379–402.

Samba, C., Williams, D.W., & Fuller, R.M. (2019) The Forms and Use of Intuition in Top Management Teams. *The Leadership Quarterly* 33(2), 101349.

Schneider, L. (2021) The Weight of Scope, Pace and Practices or Organizational Change during Evaluations of Acceptance of Organizational Change. Electronic Theses, Projects, and Dissertations, p. 1253, https://scholarworks.lib.csusb.edu/etd/1253

Sinclair, M., et al. (2010) Affective Antecedents of Intuitive Decision Making. *Journal of Management & Organization* 16, 382–398.

Smith, K., et al. (2017) Adding Complexity to Theories of Paradox, Tensions, and Dualities of Innovation and Change: Introduction to Organization Studies Special Issue on Paradox,

Tensions, and Dualities of Innovation and Change. *Organization Studies* 38(3–4), 303–317, https://doi.org/10.1177/0170840617693560

Szanto, R. (2022) Intuitive Decision-making and Firm Performance. *Journal of Decision Systems*, https://doi.org/10.1080/12460125.2022.2080796

Thanos, I. (2022) The Complementary Effects of Rationality and Intuition on Strategic Decision Quality. *European Management Journal*, https://doi.org/10.1016/j.emj.2022.03.003

Thorson, K.R., Dumitru, O.D., Mendes, W.B., & West, T.V. (2021) Influencing the Physiology and Decisions of Groups: Physiological Linkage during Group Decision-making. *Group Processes & Intergroup Relations* 24(1), 145–159.

Valencia, A.L., & Froese, T. (2020) What Binds Us? Inter-brain Neural Synchronization and Its Implications for Theories of Human Consciousness. *Neuroscience of Consciousness* 1, https://doi.org/10.1093/nc/niaa010s

Vedel, A., & Thomsen, D.K. (2017) The Dark Triad across Academic Majors. *Personality and Individual Differences* 116, 86–91, https://doi.org/10.1016/j.paid.2017.04.030

Vincent, V. (2018) Intuition in Employee Selection: Examining the Conditions for Accurate Intuitive Hiring Decisions. Doctor of Business Administration Dissertations, p. 43, https://digitalcommons.kennesaw.edu/dba_etd/43

Vincent, V., Guidice, R., & Mero, N. (2021) Should You Follow Your Gut? The Impact of Expertise on Intuitive Hiring Decisions for Complex Jobs. *Journal of Management & Organization,* 1–21, https://doi.org/10.1017/jmo.2021.9

Wikström, V., et al. (2022) Inter-brain Synchronization Occurs without Physical Co-presence during Cooperative Online Gaming. *Neuropsychologia* 174, 108316, ISSN 0028-3932, https://doi.org/10.1016/j.neuropsychologia.2022.108316

Wrosch, C., Miller, G.E., Scheier, M.F., & De Pontet, S.B. (2007) Giving up on Unattainable Goals: Benefits for Health? *Personality and Social Psychology Bulletin* 33(2), 251–265, https://doi.org/10.1177/0146167206294905

When Onboarding Fails (Aug 16, 2022) HR News Editorial team, accessed 29.3.2023, https://hrnews.co.uk/when-onboarding-fails/

Chapter 7

Barabasz, M. (2007) Efficacy of Hypnotherapy in the Treatment of Eating Disorders. *International Journal of Clinical and Experimental Hypnosis* 55(3), 318–335, https://doi.org/10.1080/00207140701338688

Boly, M., Massimini, M., Tsuchiya, N., Postle, B.R., Koch, C., & Tononi, G. (2017) Are the Neural Correlates of Consciousness in the Front or in the Back of the Cerebral Cortex? Clinical and Neuroimaging Evidence. *Journal of Neuroscience* 4.37(40), 9603–9613, https://doi.org/10.1523/JNEUROSCI.3218-16.2017

Chamine, I., Atchley, R., & Oken, B.S. (2018) Hypnosis Intervention Effects on Sleep Outcomes: A Systematic Review. *Journal of Clinical Sleep Medicine* 14(2), 271–283.

Conover, C. (2021) A Proposed Quantum Compass for Songbirds Just Got More Plausible. *Science News*, https://www.sciencenews.org/article/quantum-mechanics-compass-songbird-physics

Cyranoski, D. (2012) Neuroscience: The Mind Reader. *Nature* 486, 178–180, https://doi.org/10.1038/486178a

Dehaene, S. (2014) *Consciousness and the Brain: Deciphering How the Brain Codes Our Thoughts.* New York: Viking Adult.

Dijksterhuis, A., & Strick, M.A. (2016) A Case for Thinking without Consciousness. *Perspectives on Psychological Science* 11, 117–132, https://doi.org/10.1177/1745691615615317

Ecker, S., et al. (2019) Overcoming Noise in Entanglement Distribution. *Physical Review X,* 2019, https://doi.org/10.1103/PhysRevX.9.041042

Ellwood, S., et al., The Incubation Effect: Hatching a Solution. *Creativity Research Journal* 21(1), 6–14, https://doi.org/10.1080/10400410802633368

Fink, J.S., The Placebo Effect in Clinical Trials in Parkinson's Disease, accessed 18.07.2021, https://www.apdaparkinson.org/article/the-placebo-effect-in-clinical-trials-in-parkinsons -disease/

Gerck, E. (2018) Consciousness: The 5th Dimension, https://www.researchgate.net/publication /328262681_Consciousness_The_5th_Dimension

Gilbert, A. (2018) https://www.oxfordstudent.com/2018/02/16/really-thin-line-love-hate -scientists-explore-age-old-question/

Hameroff, S., & Penrose, R. (2014) Consciousness in the Universe: A Review of the "Orch OR" Theory. *Physics of Life Reviews* 11(1), 39–78, https://doi.org/10.1016/j.plrev.2013.08.002

Jang, S.H., & Kwon, Y.H. (2020) The Relationship between Consciousness and the Ascending Reticular Activating System in Patients with Traumatic Brain Injury. *BMC Neurology* 20, 375, https://doi.org/10.1186/s12883-020-01942-7

Kang, D.H., et al. (2013) The Effect of Meditation on Brain Structure: Cortical Thickness Mapping and Diffusion Tensor Imaging. *Social Cognitive and Affective Neuroscience* 8, 27–33.

Koch, C. (2018) What is Consciousness. *Scientific American,* https://www.scientificamerican .com/article/what-is-consciousness/

Koch, C., Massimini, M., Boly, M., & Tononi, G. (2016) Neural Correlates of Consciousness: Progress and Problems. *Nature Reviews Neuroscience* 17, 307–321, https://doi.org/10.1038/ nrn.2016.22

Lohrey, A., & Boreham, B. (2020) The Nonlocal Universe. *Communicative & Integrative Biology* 13(1), 147–159, https://doi.org/10.1080/19420889.2020.1822583

Marshall, M. (2009) String Theory: A Beginner's Guide. *New Scientist,* https://www.newscientist .com/article/dn16950-string-theory-a-beginners-guide/

Maycock, G.A. (1988) Improving Intuitive Abilities for a More Wholistic Approach to Education. *ERIC,* accessed 14.01.2023, https://eric.ed.gov/?id=ED304452

McGlashan, T.H., Evans, F.J., & Orne, M.T. (1969) The Nature of Hypnotic Analgesia and Placebo Response to Experimental Pain. *Psychosomatic Medicine* 31(3), 227–246, https://doi. org/10.1097/00006842-196905000-00003

Moreau, P.-A. (2019) Imaging Bell-Type Nonlocal Behavior. *Science Advances* 5(7), https://www. science.org/doi/full/10.1126/sciadv.aaw2563?testing=

Nani, A., et al. (2019) The Neural Correlates of Consciousness and Attention: Two Sister Processes of the Brain. *Frontiers in Neuroscience* 31(13), 1169, https://doi.org/10.3389/fnins .2019.01169

Nosal, C.S. (2021) On the Relationship between Intuition, Consciousness and Cognition: In Search of a Unified Concept of Mind. *Annals of Psychology/Rocznicki Psycholgiczne* XXIV(3– 4), 345–360, https://doi.org/10.18290/rpsych21242-1s

Owen, A.M., et al. (2006) Detecting Awareness in the Vegetative State. *Science,* https://doi.org /10.1126/science.1130197

Pearsall, P., Schwartz, G.E.R., & Russek, L.G.S. (2002) Changes in Heart Transplant Recipients That Parallel the Personalities of Their Donors. *Journal of Near-Death Studies* 20, 191–206, https://doi.org/10.1023/A:1013009425905

Raccah, O, Block, N., & Fox, K.C.R. (2021) Does the Prefrontal Cortex Play an Essential Role in Consciousness? Insights from Intracranial Electrical Stimulation of the Human Brain. *Journal of Neuroscience* 41(10), 2076–2087, https://doi.org/10.1523/JNEUROSCI.1141-20.2020

Raffone, A., & Srinivasan, N. (2010) The Exploration of Meditation in the Neuroscience of Attention and Consciousness. *Cognitive Processing* 11, 1–7, https://doi.org/10.1007/s10339-009-0354-z

Rezaei, S., Mirzaei, M., & Zali, M.R. (2014) Nonlocal Intuition: Replication and Paired-Subjects Enhancement Effects. *Global Advances in Health and Medicine* 3(2), 5–15, https://doi.org/10.7453/gahmj.2014.012

Robson, D. (2021) Can Lucid Dreaming Help Us Understand Consciousness. *The Guardian*, https://www.theguardian.com/science/2021/nov/14/can-lucid-dreaming-help-us-understand-consciousness

Schafer, S.M., Colloca, L., & Wager, T.D. (2015) Conditioned Placebo Analgesia Persists When Subjects Know They Are Receiving a Placebo. *Journal of Pain*, https://doi.org/10.1016/j.jpain.2014.12.008

Seth, A. (2021) *Being You: A New Science of Consciousness*. Faber.

Seth, A.K. (2018) Consciousness: The Last 50 Years (and the Next). *Brain and Neuroscience Advances* 2, 1–6.

Simard, S. (2021) *Finding the Mother Tree: Discovering the Wisdom and Intelligence of the Forest*. Penguin.

Sohn, E. (2019) Decoding the Neuroscience of Consciousness. *Nature*, https://www.nature.com/articles/d41586-019-02207-1

Strick, M., & Dijksterhuis, A. (2011) Intuition and Unconscious Thought. In *Handbook of Intuition Research*, pp. 28–36. Edward Elgar Publishing.

Tong, Z., et al. (2019) Consciousness: New Concepts and Neural Networks. *Frontiers in Cellular Neuroscience* 13, https://doi.org/10.3389/fncel.2019.00302

Van Campen (2019) *Exploring Drug-Induced Synesthesia*. MIT Press, https://thereader.mitpress.mit.edu/exploring-drug-induced-synesthesia/Van

van Lommel, P. (2011) *Consciousness Beyond Life: The Science of Near Death*. HarperCollins.

van Lommel, P., van Wees, R., Meyers, V., & Elfferich, I. (2001) Near-Death Experience in Survivors of Cardiac Arrest: A Prospective Study in the Netherlands. *Lancet* 358, 2039–2045.

Voss, U., Holzmann, R., Tuin, I., & Hobson, A. (2009) Lucid Dreaming: A State of Consciousness with Features of Both Waking and Non-lucid dreaming. *SLEEP* 32(9), 1191–1200.

Wahbeh, H., Radin, D., Cannard, C., & Delorme, A. (2022) What if Consciousness Is Not an Emergent Property of the Brain? Observational and Empirical Challenges to Materialistic Models. *Frontiers in* Psychology, https://doi.org/10.3389/fpsyg.2022.955594

Yang, C.C., Barrós-Loscertales, A., Li, M., et al. (2019) Alterations in Brain Structure and Amplitude of Low-Frequency after 8 Weeks of Mindfulness Meditation Training in Meditation-Naïve Subjects. *Scientific Reports* 9, 10977, https://doi.org/10.1038/s41598-019-47470-4

Toolkit

Agor, W.H. (1986) The Logic of Intuition: How Top Executives Make Important Decisions. *Organizational Dynamics* 14(3), https://doi.org/10.1016/0090-2616(86)90028-8

Aldunate, N., & González-Ibáñez, R. (2017) An Integrated Review of Emoticons in Computer-Mediated Communication. *Frontiers in Psychology* 7(2061), https://doi.org/10.3389/fpsyg.2016.02061

Barsade, S.G. (2002) The Ripple Effect: Emotional Contagion and its Influence on Group Behavior. *Administrative Science Quarterly* 47, 644–675, https://doi.org/10.2307/309491

Bratman, G.N., et al. (2018) Nature Experience Reduces Rumination and Subgenual Prefrontal Cortex Activation. *PNAS* 112(28), https://doi.org/10.1073/pnas.1510459112

Coutinho, M.V.C., et al. (2021) Dunning-Kruger Effect: Intuitive Errors Predict Overconfidence on the Cognitive Reflection Test. *Frontiers in Psychology* 12, https://www.frontiersin.org/article/10.3389/fpsyg.2021.603225

Hatfield, E., & Rapson, R.L. (2010) Emotional Contagion. In I.B. Weiner & W.E. Craighead (eds.), *Encyclopedia of Psychology*, 4th edn. Hoboken: John Wiley and Sons.

Herrando, C., & Constantinides, E. (2021) Emotional Contagion: A Brief Overview and Future Directions. *Frontiers in Psychology*, https://doi.org/10.3389/fpsyg.2021.712606

Hogarth, R.M. (2001) *Educating Intuition*. University of Chicago Press.

Kahneman, D., & Lovallo, D. (1993) Timid Choice and Bold Forecasts: A Cognitive Perspective on Risk Taking. *Management Science* 39(1), 1703.

Knight, R. (2019) How to Manage Your Perfectionism. *Harvard Business Review*, https://hbr.org/2019/04/how-to-manage-your-perfectionism

López Pérez, R.P. (2023) Understanding Factors Impacting Intuitive Misses: An Exploratory Approach. *SSRN*, http://dx.doi.org/10.2139/ssrn.4321808

Pinilla, A., et al. (2020) How Do Induced Affective States Bias Emotional Contagion to Faces? A Three-Dimensional Model. *Frontiers in Psychology* 11(97), https://doi.org/10.3389/fpsyg.2020.0009

Raoelison, M., Keime, M., & de Neys, W. (2021) Think Slow, Then Fast: Does Repeated Deliberation Boost Correct Intuitive Responding? *Memory and Cognition*, ff10.3758/s13421-021-01140-xff. ffhal-03169096f

Stephens, G.J., et al. (2010) Speaker-Listener Neural Coupling Underlies Successful Communication. *PNAS* 107(32), 14425–14430, https://doi.org/10.1073/pnas.1008662107

Sun, H., Tan, Q., Fan, G., et al. (2014) Different Effects of Rumination on Depression: Key Role of Hope. *International Journal of Mental Health Systems* 8, 53, https://doi.org/10.1186/1752-4458-8-53

Thomas, L. (1983) *The Youngest Science: Notes of a Medicine-Watcher*. Penguin.

Wergin, V.V., Zimanyi, Z., Mesagno, C., & Beckmann, J. (2018) When Suddenly Nothing Works Anymore within a Team – Causes of Collective Sport Team Collapse. *Frontiers in Psychology* 9, 2115, https://doi.org/10.3389/fpsyg.2018.02115

Woiceshyn, J. (2009) Lessons from "Good Minds": How CEOs Use Intuition, Analysis and Guiding Principles to Make Strategic Decisions. *Long Range Planning* 42(3), 298–319.

Index

INDEX

www.ingramcontent.com/pod-product-compliance
Lightning Source LLC
Chambersburg PA
CBHW061024220326
41597CB00019BB/3323